Principles
in Practice

The Principles in Practice imprint offers teachers concrete illustrations of effective classroom practices based in NCTE research briefs and policy statements. Each book discusses the research on a specific topic, links the research to an NCTE brief or policy statement, and then demonstrates how those principles come alive in practice: by showcasing actual classroom practices that demonstrate the policies in action; by talking about research in practical, teacher-friendly language; and by offering teachers possibilities for rethinking their own practices in light of the ideas presented in the books. Books within the imprint are grouped in strands, each strand focused on a significant topic of interest.

Adolescent Literacy Strand

Adolescent Literacy at Risk? The Impact of Standards (2009) Rebecca Bowers Sipe

Adolescents and Digital Literacies: Learning Alongside Our Students (2010) Sara Kajder

Adolescent Literacy and the Teaching of Reading: Lessons for Teachers of Literature (2010) Deborah Appleman

Writing in Today's Classrooms Strand

Writing in the Dialogical Classroom: Students and Teachers Responding to the Texts of Their Lives (2011) Bob Fecho

Becoming Writers in the Elementary Classroom: Visions and Decisions (2011) Katie Van Sluys

Writing Instruction in the Culturally Relevant Classroom (2011) Maisha T. Winn and Latrise P. Johnson

Literacy Assessment Strand

Our Better Judgment: Teacher Leadership for Writing Assessment (2012) Chris W. Gallagher and Eric D. Turley

Beyond Standardized Truth: Improving Teaching and Learning through Inquiry-Based Reading Assessment (2012) Scott Filkins

Reading Assessment: Artful Teachers, Successful Students (2013) Diane Stephens, editor

Literacies of the Disciplines Strand

Entering the Conversations: Practicing Literacy in the Disciplines (2014) Patricia Lambert Stock, Trace Schillinger, and Andrew Stock

Real-World Literacies: Disciplinary Teaching in the High School Classroom (2014) Heather Lattimer

Doing and Making Authentic Literacies (2014) Linda Denstaedt, Laura Jane Roop, and Stephen Best

Teaching Reading with YA Literature

Complex Texts, Complex Lives

Jennifer Buehler
Saint Louis University

National Council of Teachers of English
1111 W. Kenyon Road, Urbana, Illinois 61801-1096

Staff Editor: Bonny Graham
Series Editor: Cathy Fleischer
Interior Design: Victoria Pohlmann
Cover Design: Pat Mayer
Cover Image: Jennifer Buehler

NCTE Stock Number: 57268; eStock Number: 57275
ISBN 978-0-8141-5726-8; eISBN 978-0-8141-5727-5

Library of Congress Cataloging-in-Publication Data

Names: Buehler, Jennifer, author.
Title: Teaching reading with YA literature : complex texts, complex lives / by Jennifer Buehler, Saint Louis University.
Other titles: Teaching reading with young adult literature
Description: Urbana, IL : National Council of Teachers of English, 2016 | Includes bibliographical references and index.
Identifiers: LCCN 2016011761 (print) | LCCN 2016023428 (ebook) | ISBN 9780814157268 (pbk.) | ISBN 9780814157275 ()
Subjects: LCSH: Young adult literature—Study and teaching. | Reading (Secondary) | English language—Study and teaching (Secondary)
Classification: LCC PN1008.8 .B84 2016 (print) | LCC PN1008.8 (ebook) | DDC 809/.892820712—dc23
LC record available at https://lccn.loc.gov/2016011761

For Dudley and Sharon,
who believed in these books, and in me

Contents

Acknowledgments

Many of us who write or teach writing have come across the well-known quote by E. L. Doctorow: "It's like driving a car at night. You never see any further than your headlights, but you can make the whole trip that way." Writing this book has given me new understanding of Doctorow's metaphor. The journey has been long and seeing the way forward was often hard. How grateful I am for the many people who stood by my side as I struggled to reach my destination.

First among those is my extraordinary editor, Cathy Fleischer, who believed I had something to say about young adult literature and helped me figure out how to say it. The time, care, and thought Cathy gave to this project transformed it from a story about what has been in the teaching of YA literature to the story of what can be. She was my thought partner through every page, and I will never be able to repay her for her investment in me.

I owe a similar debt to Kurt Austin and Bonny Graham at NCTE, who waited patiently until I was able to deliver a version of this book that I could feel proud of. Thank you, Kurt and Bonny, for saying that you still wanted the book and that you wanted it to be written by me.

Scott Filkins has been a champion of my work in young adult literature from the very beginning of our collaboration on the ReadWriteThink Text Messages podcast. His careful and enthusiastic reading of the first complete draft of this book helped me more than he will ever know. I wish every author could be blessed with a first reader who is as insightful, generous, and affirming as Scott was with me.

Twenty years ago at Canton High School, Sharon Strean took a risk when she hired an early career teacher who wanted to try new things with high school students and YA lit. Sharon valued what I was doing when I was still figuring out what that was. Without her, this book would not have been possible.

Dudley Barlow, my mentor teacher, took an interest in my work when I was new and then stayed with me through all the years that followed. His willingness even in retirement to read YA lit and imagine new possibilities for English teaching gave me another reason to believe in the ideas I've shared here.

Brenda Holloway, my first National Writing Project role model, introduced me to *In the Middle* and *Seeking Diversity* when I was surfacing from my first year in the classroom. Without ever knowing it, she planted the seed that shaped my career.

I will be forever grateful to the teachers who opened their doors and welcomed me into their classrooms before I knew what I was looking for. Carrie Melnychenko, Daria Plumb, and Jennifer Walsh, your teaching has enriched my thinking and anchored this project. Thank you for trusting me to take what you gave me and use it in service of a larger goal, which is to further the call for teaching YA literature in English class. I hope I have done you and your students—especially Gemma, Alex, Jalen, and John—justice. Thank you as well to Ricki Ginsberg, Kellee Moye, Renee Stites, Beth Scanlon, and April Fulstone, whose contributions added important layers to the classroom accounts provided here. And thank you to the anonymous reviewers, whose comments both praised the manuscript and challenged me to make it better.

My thank-you list would not be complete without mentioning Betty Gibson, whose transcription assistance and thoughts on text complexity were early sources of support; Alex Cuenca, who was friend and witness during the drafting of this book over a summer and several years; Deborah Wiles, whose kind words and wise perspective provided balm when I sorely needed it; my sister, Adrienne Perry, who gave me quiet space to write and told me I could finish; and Sarah Andrew-Vaughan, who was there in the final stages, cheering me on.

Finally, Mark and Ethan, thank you for bearing with me through long days in my office and long weekends at the library when I could have been home with you. The two of you have been reading and loving YA lit almost as long as I've been teaching it. Thank you, boys, for sharing in this reading life with me.

Reading Instruction for *All* Students

An NCTE Policy Research Brief

Reading instruction has always been stressed for elementary school students, but today it takes on increased importance for *all* grades. Reports like *Time to Act* and *Reading at Risk* raise concern about a lack of depth in the literacy education of adolescent students and lament a general decline in reading among young adults. The Common Core State Standards (CCSS) for reading state that "all students must be able to comprehend texts of steadily increasing complexity as they progress through school," and studies of literacy point to the rising expectations for reading in both schooling and the workplace.[1] Documents like these indicate that teachers need to help all students become readers, regardless of whether they are in elementary or secondary school, so they can succeed in the information age.

Two terms are circulating in current discussions of reading instruction: textual complexity and close reading. Textual complexity is defined in the CCSS as a three-part entity. It includes *quantitative dimensions* such as word length or frequency, sentence length, and cohesion, all of which can be measured by computer software; *qualitative dimensions* such as levels of meaning, clarity of language, and knowledge demands, all of which require human readers; and *reader-text variables* such as reader motivation, knowledge, and experience, qualities best assessed by teachers who know students and texts.[2] Both the qualitative dimensions and the reader-text variables depend upon the professional judgment of teachers, especially the reader-text variables, because only teachers know students well enough to help them find the best text for the purpose at hand, something "leveling" systems cannot do. Research on student readers and the texts they read confirms the need for teachers to play a key role in matching individual students with specific books at appropriate levels of textual complexity:

What we know about our students as readers:

- Students come to reading tasks with varied prior reading experiences, or prior knowledge, which can support their reading of complex texts.
- Students who are engaged and motivated readers read more often and read more diverse texts than students who are unmotivated by the reading task.
- Students who develop expertise with a particular kind of reading—science fiction or online games, for example—outside of school may not think this kind of reading will be valued by their teachers.[3]

What we know about the texts students read:

- In and out of school, the texts students read vary significantly, from linear text-only books to multimodal textbooks to online hypertexts, each of which places different demands on readers and requires different strategies and approaches to reading.
- Students read texts from a variety of disciplines, so content area literacy is important.

Reading Instruction for *All* Students

- The level of difficulty or complexity in a text is not the only factor students consider in choosing texts; interest and motivation also matter.
- Readability or lexile levels can vary significantly within a single text, so it is important to consider other dimensions of textual complexity.[4]

Close reading has been proposed as the way to help students become effective readers of complex texts, and it can be useful, especially when used alongside other approaches. The difficulty is that close reading can be defined in multiple terms. It can mean searching for hidden meanings, positioning the text as the only reality to be considered, and focusing on formal features. Close reading is also a highly contested term among college English instructors. Critics condemn it for conceptualizing the text as a closed world, for limiting student access, and for emphasizing form over content.[5]

Furthermore, research shows that reading comprehension depends on a more complex approach. Specifically, reading comprehension results from the integration of two models, text-based and situation-based. The text-based model focuses on the way words are organized into sentences, paragraphs, and whole texts. The situation model refers to the meaning that results from integration of the text-based approach with the reader's prior knowledge and goals. Close reading is aligned with the text-based approach, and it encourages students to see meaning as one right answer to be extracted from the text. Close reading is often conflated with providing textual evidence for making a claim about a text, but any approach to reading can insist on warrants for interpretations of texts. By itself, then, close reading cannot ensure that students will develop deep understandings of what they read.[6]

Implications for Instructional Policy

Research-based understandings about students, texts, and reading underlie instructional approaches that support students' learning to read complex texts across grade levels and disciplines. Policymakers need to affirm the value of multiple approaches and support teachers' efforts to adopt instructional practices that call upon a variety of effective strategies, including the following.

- Recognize the role that motivation plays in students' reading by modeling for students how to engage with complex texts that do and do not interest them.
- Engage students in performative reading responses such as gesture, mime, vocal intonation, characterization, and dramatization to enable active construction of meaning and construct a collaborative environment that builds on the strengths of individual students.
- Have students read multiple texts focused on the same topic to improve comprehension through text-to-text connections.
- Foster students' engagement with complex texts by teaching students how different textual purposes, genres, and modes require different strategies for reading.
- Encourage students to choose texts, including non-fiction, for themselves, in addition to assigned ones, to help them see themselves as capable readers who can independently use reading capabilities they learn in class.

- Demonstrate, especially at the secondary level, how digital and visual texts including multimodal and multigenre texts require different approaches to reading.
- Connect students' reading of complex texts with their writing about reading and with writing that uses complex texts as models so they will recognize and be able to negotiate many different types of complex texts.
- Develop students' ability to engage in meaningful discussion of the complex texts they read in whole-class, small group, and partner conversations so they can learn to negotiate and comprehend complex texts independently.[7]

When teachers can choose from a range of research-based and theoretically grounded instructional approaches, their students learn how to choose from, apply, and reflect on diverse strategies as they take up the varied purposes, subjects, and genres that present complex challenges for readers. Publishers, as well as policymakers and administrators, play an important role in assuring that teachers have appropriate texts and materials to support effective instruction.

Implications for Policies on Formative Assessment

Research shows that formative assessment enables teachers to draw on their knowledge of the students in their classes in order to adjust instruction over time. Accordingly, educational policy needs to affirm the importance of high-quality formative assessment in reading instruction.[8] Formative assessment of reading can take many forms, as the examples below show:

- Teachers can help students develop awareness of their diverse experiences and knowledge—all of which affect the ways they engage with texts. These include reading experiences in previous grades and in out-of-school spaces. Once students have identified their experiences and knowledge, teachers can help students build on them in approaching complex texts—including when their background experiences and knowledge enhance and/or interfere with their ability to read complex texts.
- Asking students to think aloud as they read complex texts can help teachers identify which instructional supports and interventions will best support readers as they face new reading challenges.
- When teachers have identified students who struggle to remain engaged as they read complex texts, they can assess students' interests in order to provide texts that are more likely to foster student engagement.
- Teachers can assess students' ability to think about their reading and about how different kinds of texts impact their reading. This increased awareness can improve students' ability to read complex texts for various purposes.[9]

Implications for Policies on Professional Learning for Teachers

Reading research shows that educational policy needs to include professional development opportunities that enable teachers to match instructional approaches to diverse

Reading Instruction for *All* Students

student needs. In order to support teachers' ability to draw on a complex set of instructional approaches in service of diverse learner reading outcomes, teachers need frequent and sustained opportunities to learn with one another about the range of instructional supports, interventions, and formative assessments as they emerge from the latest reading research and practice. Opportunities to deepen understanding of topics like those listed below will prepare teachers to help students meet the challenges of textual complexity:

- Broaden the repertoire of approaches to reading instruction, drawing on recent and authenticated research.

- Deepen understanding of which combinations of reading strategies are most effective for achieving a particular instructional goal or addressing the needs of a particular student.

- Learn about how disciplinary distinctions open opportunities and challenges for teaching students to read for varied purposes.

- Develop insight into which reading strategies are effective in all disciplines and which are uniquely suited to specific fields.[10]

Preparing students to read complex texts effectively is one of the most important and most challenging responsibilities of schools. With research-based support from policymakers and administration, teachers can enable students at all grade levels to comprehend, draw evidence from, and compare across a wide variety of complex texts.

Endnotes

1. Carnegie Council on Advancing Adolescent Literacy. (2010). *Time to act: An agenda for advancing adolescent literacy for college and career success.* New York, NY: Carnegie Corporation of New York.

National Endowment for the Arts. (2004). *Reading at risk: A survey of literary reading in America.* Washington, DC: Research Division, National Endowment for the Arts.

Common Core State Standards for English Language Arts & Literacy in History/Social Studies, Science, and Technical Subjects, p. 4. http://www.corestandards.org/assets/CCSSI_ELA%20Standards.pdf.

2. Common Core State Standards for English Language Arts & Literacy in History/Social Studies, Science, and Technical Subjects. Appendix A: Research supporting key elements of the standards. Glossary of key terms. http://www.corestandards.org/assets/Appendix_A.pdf.

3. McNamara, D. S., Kintsch, E., Songer, N. B., & Kintsch, W. (1996). Are good texts always better? Text coherence, background knowledge, and levels of understanding in learning from text. *Cognition and Instruction, 14*, 1–43.

Venable, G. P. (2003). Confronting complex text: Readability lessons from students with language learning disabilities. *Topics in Language Disorders, 23*(3), 225–240.

Brozo, W. G., Shiel, G., & Topping, K. (2007). Engagement in reading: Lessons learned from three PISA countries. *Journal of Adolescent & Adult Literacy, 51*(4), 304–315.

Kajder, S. (2010). *Adolescents and digital literacies: Learning alongside our students.* Urbana, IL: National Council of Teachers of English.

4. Hayles, N. K. (2010). How we read: Close, hyper, machine. *ADE Bulletin, 22*(150), 62–79.

Foorman, B. R., Francis, D. J., Davidson, K. C., Harm, M. W., & Griffin, J. (2009). Variability in text features in six grade 1 basal reading programs. *Scientific Studies of Reading 8* (2), 167–197.

Pitcher, B., & Fang, Z. (2007). Can we trust leveled texts? An examination of their reliability and quality from a linguistic perspective. *Literacy, 41*, 43–51.

5. Student Achievement Partners. Guidelines for developing text-dependent questions for close analytical reading. http:// www.achievethecore.org/steal-these-tools/text-dependent-questions.

Bialostosky, D. (2006). Should college English be close reading? *College English, 69*(2), 111–116.

Murray, H. (1991). Close reading, closed writing. *College English 53*(2), 195–208.

Rabinowitz, P. J. (1992). Against close reading. *Pedagogy Is Politics.* Ed. Maria-Regina Kecht. Chicago: University of Illinois Press.

6. Kintsch, W. (1988). The role of knowledge in discourse comprehension: A construction-integration model. *Psychological Review, 95*, 163–182.

7. Adomat, D. S. (2010). Dramatic interpretations: Performative responses of young children to picture book read-alouds. *Children's Literature in Education, 41*(3), 207–221.

Brozo et al. (2007).

Coiro, J. (2011). Talking about reading as thinking: Modeling the hidden complexities of online reading comprehension. *Theory into Practice 50*(2), 107.

Hayles (2010).

Hiebert, E. H. (2011). The Common Core's staircase of text complexity: Getting the size of the first step right. *Reading Today, 29*(3), 26–27.

Heisey, N., & Kucan, L. (2010). Introducing science concepts to primary students through read-alouds: Interactions and multiple texts make the difference. *The Reading Teacher, 63*(8), 666–676.

Juzwik, M. M., Nystrand, M., Kelly, S., & Sherry, M. B. (2008). Oral narrative genres as dialogic resources for classroom literature study: A contextualized case study of conversational narrative discussion. *American Educational Research Journal, 45*(4), 1111–1154.

Palincsar, A. S., & Schutz, K. M. (2011): Reconnecting strategy instruction with its theoretical roots, *Theory into Practice, 50*(2), 85–92.

Pike, M. M., Barnes, M. A., & Barron, R. W. (2010). The role of illustrations in children's inferential comprehension. *Journal of Experimental Child Psychology, 105*(3).

Quirk, M., Schwanenflugel, P. J., & Webb, M. Y. (2009). A short-term longitudinal study of the relationship between motivation to read and reading fluency skill in second grade. *Journal of Literacy Research, 41*(2).

Tunks, K. W. (2011). Exploring journals as a genre for making reading–writing connections. *Childhood Education, 87*(3), 169.

8. NCTE. (2010). Fostering high-quality formative assessment: A policy brief produced by the National Council of Teachers of English. *The Council Chronicle, 20*(1), 12–15.

Reading Instruction for *All* Students

9. Brown, C. L. (2007). Supporting English language learners in content-reading. *Reading Improvement, 44*(1).

Caldwell, J., & Leslie, L. (2010). Thinking aloud in expository text: Processes and outcomes. *Journal of Literacy Research, 42*(3), 308–340.

Collins, P., Land, R. E., Pearson, M., et al. (2012). Enhancing the interpretive reading and analytical writing of mainstreamed English learners in secondary school: Results from a randomized field trial using a cognitive strategies approach. *American Educational Research Journal, 49*(2), 323–355.

Horning, A. S. (2011). Where to put the manicules: A theory of expert reading. *Across the Disciplines, 8*(2). http://wac.colostate. edu/atd/articles/horning2011/index.cfm.

Little, C. A., & Hines, A. H. (2006). Time to read: Advancing reading achievement after school. *Journal of Advanced Academics, 18*(1), 8–33.

McNamara et al. (1996).

Ramsay, C. M., & Sperling, R. A. (2010). Designating reader perspective to increase comprehension and interest. *Contemporary Educational Psychology, 35*(3), 215–227.

Venable (2003).

10. Herman, J., Hanson, T. L., Boscardin, C. K., et al. (2011). Integrating literacy and science in biology: Teaching and learning impacts of reading apprenticeship professional development. *American Educational Research Journal 48*(3).

Liang, L. A. (2011). Scaffolding middle school students' comprehension and response to short stories. *Research in Middle Level Education Online, 34*(8), 1–16. http://www.nmsa.org/Publications/RMLEOnline/Articles/Vol34No8/tabid/2405/Default.aspx.

This policy brief was produced by NCTE's James R. Squire Office of Policy Research, directed by Anne Ruggles Gere, with assistance from Anne Beatty Martinez, Elizabeth Homan, Danielle Lillge, Justine Neiderhiser, Chris Parsons, Ruth Anna Spooner, Sarah Swofford, and Chinyere Uzogara.

Chapter One

Reading with Passion and Purpose

For almost as long as I've been alive, I've been a reader. After falling in love with children's books like *Sylvester and the Magic Pebble*; *The Lion, the Witch, and the Wardrobe*; and *Bridge to Terabithia* in elementary school, I moved on to read lots of young adult literature when I was a teen. Prompted by the shelves at my local library and offerings at school book fairs, I read every Madeleine L'Engle book I could get my hands on. Every Judy Blume. Assorted titles by S. E. Hinton, Richard Peck, and Robert Cormier. The complete Paula Danziger. Mildred Taylor, and Paul Zindel. Isabelle Holland, Ellen Conford, Norma Fox Mazer, and Norma Klein.

Looking at the list today, it reads like a who's who of authors from the early YA canon. In young adult novels, I found literature that was both well written and personally relevant. These were books that piqued my interest and stretched my mind. At the same time, they introduced me to topics that weren't easy to talk about. Sex, for starters: there was a lot I wanted and needed to learn, and Judy Blume helped me. Meanwhile, Madeleine L'Engle was teaching me about religion, classical music, and science. Mildred Taylor was showing me the lasting effects of racism on the lives of African American families. S. E. Hinton was challenging me to empathize with gang members. Robert Cormier was forcing me to see abuse of power and the dark side of human nature. While I didn't love every YA book I read as a teen, I recognized that young adult authors were drawing me out of my own life and into the larger world. They were helping me think about who I was and who I wanted—and didn't want—to become.

Of course, I read plenty of other things during my teen years. Working from a list provided by my eighth-grade English teacher, I sampled the classics: *The Catcher in the Rye* because it was banned. *Crime and Punishment* because the librarian said it was too hard for me. *Jane Eyre* because it was a romance. *Of Mice and Men* because the title was intriguing. At the same time, I read popular culture titles: *The Official Preppy Handbook* because it dictated fashion at my middle school. *Flowers in the Attic* because it was racy and my friends were passing it around. Lots of Stephen King because he was my mom's favorite author. Rosalynn Carter's memoir, *First Lady from Plains*, because I was interested in politics. *All Creatures Great and Small* because I worked part-time in a dog kennel. *The Moosewood Cookbook* because I decided to become a vegetarian. *Writing Down the Bones* because I longed to be a writer.

There was a reason for every book I read, but my choices zigzagged, pulling me in different and competing directions. Looking back, however, I can see how each choice was purposeful. I read to find myself in books, take on the perspectives of others, explore new topics, appreciate beautiful language, develop critical perspectives on the world around me, and connect with fellow readers. My reading was idiosyncratic. It was also personal and deeply meaningful.

Years later, professional literature taught me to name and value these different ways of reading. What I learned from Atwell (1987), Rief (1991), Carlsen (1980), Carlsen and Sherrill (1988), Wilhelm (1997), Beers (2003), Lesesne (2003), Appleman (2009), Morrell (2005), Miller (2014), and Kittle (2013) made me a better teacher. It also made me a stronger reader. Hearing how and why others read helped me to see the range of purposes that reading served in my own life.

School Reading

I had a different reading life at school. In English classes, I dutifully slogged through almost all of the novels assigned to me—from *Great Expectations* in ninth grade to *Madame Bovary* in Advanced Placement English—but I read far more widely on my own. Even though I loved my teachers, school reading was dry. Our work with books took the form of pop quizzes, study questions, notecards, multiple-choice tests, and essays. We read chapter by chapter, at a pace set by the teacher, guided by purposes that felt frustratingly narrow: finding symbols, exploring themes, and studying literary history. (See Applebee [1993] for a discussion of the dominance of these methods in high school English classes.) I was willing to go along with this kind of reading, probably because I was good at it. Sometimes it felt important, and even fun, as when we worked together as a class to make sense of *As I Lay Dying*. But mostly it was an exercise, and it represented only one small piece of who I was and what I sought from books. Still, I was lucky. I had access to other titles at home, and I had friends who were readers. Nothing I was asked to do at school harmed my reading life.

Unfortunately for many other teens, school reading *is* harmful. Or, if *harmful* sounds like too strong a word, let's say it's *neglectful*. When students are assigned books they can't understand, and when they sit in classrooms where they listen to others talk about literature instead of reading it themselves, they are shut out from the opportunity to be readers. Their reading lives stagnate. Or they never get started. Any of us who have taught middle or high school English have encountered students who walk through our doors at the beginning of the year having never finished a book. And yet these same students are expected to join their reading peers and take up the study of literature as an academic pursuit. It's no surprise that they languish in our classes. The playing field isn't level. When we feed them a strict diet of the classics, occasionally garnished with complementary materials from the literature textbook, these students—reluctant readers, struggling readers, and nonreaders alike—are cut off from the larger world of literacy. Students who are engaged and motivated aren't served much better, since only a piece of their reading life is seen and supported in the classroom.

To learn, grow, and thrive, what all of these students need is what I had in my life outside of school: a wide landscape for reading. They need a variety of materials to explore, literate space to move around in, and time to make discoveries. They need what Daniels and Zemelman (2014) call "a balanced reading diet" (p. 63). They need classroom conditions that allow them to become what Miller (2014) calls "wild readers," or people who read in school the way lifelong readers do. They need to hear the message that their reading is useful and good, even if the books they choose for themselves aren't the ones we would choose for them. They need to have their interests validated through the titles we offer in the classroom. Most of all, they need the chance to experience books that both affirm and challenge them—books that they *can* read and *want* to read. Books that help them see what a literate life, in all its dimensions, has to offer.

Today's young adult literature has a central role to play in this reading landscape. Even more than the titles I read in the 1980s, today's YA lit gives teens the opportunity to read broadly and deeply. Contemporary young adult novels present unreliable narrators, multiple points of view, magical realism, satire, ambiguous endings, poetic dialogue, literary allusions, and multigenre formats. They explore disability, art, and injustice, along with more familiar topics such as sports, school cliques, and first love. At the same time, young adult nonfiction titles introduce teens to the power of stories based on oral history interviews, archival research, and scientific fieldwork. As much as any other literary genre, young adult literature can dazzle students with an artful sentence, draw them into moral and ethical debates, and stir them to greater critical consciousness. Young adult literature won't give students everything they need as readers, but it does offer exciting and important learning opportunities for all of us who teach in secondary English classrooms. What matters is what we *do* with these books. We need a vision for YA reading and a pedagogy that can help every student succeed.

Guided by the NCTE Policy Research Brief *Reading Instruction for All Students*, this book invites you to imagine possibilities for the rigorous and relevant use of young adult literature in middle and high school English classes. It brings you into the classrooms of teachers who use young adult literature in different settings and in different ways. If you're familiar with YA literature, this book will give you traction and support for the work you're already doing. If you're new to YA lit, this book will help you build knowledge of the field and make the case for using these books in your own classroom. As English teachers, we have the opportunity and the responsibility to foster the development of students' full literacy lives. Young adult literature gives us a way to begin.

Opposing Camps

Even as we explore the richness of today's young adult literature, we must acknowledge that we live in an educational world dominated by standardized tests and ever-tightening state and national standards. Given these pressures, it can be hard to stand up for YA literature. It isn't easy to speak bravely and confidently about the worth of these books in the face of reading lists that continue to favor the classics and school curricula that place the study of the canon ahead of student engagement. We learn to anticipate attacks on YA lit—sometimes from parents, sometimes from colleagues, sometimes in the media—even as we strive to build our own understandings of what these books have to offer.

Despite the fact that young adult literature is the fastest-growing segment of today's book market, and despite the fact that adults and teens alike eagerly read these books and pass them on to their friends, YA titles are routinely written off as not appropriate or viable for classroom use. Some argue that the books are not complex enough to prepare students for the demands of high-stakes tests or the challenges of the Common Core State Standards (CCSS). Others claim that a curriculum rooted in young adult literature lacks the rigor to support sophisticated work with literary texts and the development of skills students will need for college.

Still others say that YA titles shouldn't be taught in school because of their mature subject matter.

What's worse, too often the very act of promoting young adult literature as valuable and worthy sets us in opposition to our colleagues. Debates over the literature we assign and the teaching methods we employ sometimes drive us into opposing camps. We allow our thinking to be subsumed by pedagogical binaries in which reading workshop goes head-to-head with traditional literature study, and reading for enjoyment is seen as undermining the goal of reading for rigor. Young adult literature may foster a love of reading, the binary suggests, but only classics can teach students how to struggle with hard texts. These dividing lines prevent us from seeing the overriding goal we share, which is to equip students with the skill and the desire to find meaning in the world of books, not just while they sit in our classrooms, but for the rest of their lives.

Students are the losers in these professional wars. When we root our curriculum in core texts that students have been reading since the 1970s, when we keep decontextualized literature study at the center of our curriculum and fail to acknowledge the broader ways that readers engage with books, we keep the status quo in place, and we close off learning opportunities for too many young people. Those who find success in English class will be the ones who have been readers all along: students who know how to balance reading for their own purposes with reading in the way school demands.

We can do better for all of our students. We can offer them a menu of varied texts, and we can invite them to read for varied purposes. We can provide an array of reading experiences: some books read as a whole class, some read in small groups, and some read independently. By offering YA classics as well as contemporary YA titles, we can invest in the long history of young adult literature as a field. YA doesn't have to be the *only* literature students read in English class, but it ought to play a significant part in students' school reading. We can use YA literature to support our students as readers of increasingly complex texts even as we put texts in front of them that speak to their interests and questions. We can make the case that students *will grow* when they read books written expressly for them, just as they will grow through their experiences with other texts. What YA offers is the likelihood of meeting students where they are now—not just as readers, but as teens who are still figuring out their place in the world. YA lit honors that process of self-discovery.

How Research Helps Us Make the Case for YA Lit

Those of us who already read and teach YA literature know there are plenty of testimonials about the quality and worth of these books. People such as Hipple

(1997), Gallo (1992), Crowe (1999), Kaywell (2007), and Salvner (2000) have been offering these testimonials for years. But testimonials will only take us so far if we want to be effective and respected teachers of YA lit. If we choose to include young adult literature in the curriculum, we must provide compelling reasons for teaching it. Our strongest claims about the value of YA lit will be ones that are grounded in research-based understandings about students, texts, and reading. When we can speak knowledgeably about teens as readers—about their developmental needs, the ways they interact with texts, and the conditions that will best engage them—we can make a more powerful case for teaching YA literature.

The NCTE Policy Research Brief *Reading Instruction for* All *Students*, reprinted in the front matter of this book, begins by arguing that to support students' continuing literacy development at the secondary level, we must help all students become readers. There's a call to action here, and a moral imperative. If we want to make rich reading lives possible for *all* of our students, we cannot teach in the ways we've always taught. We must diversify our texts and our methods. We must respond to the needs of the individual students in our classrooms.

This call to help students *become readers* compels us to focus our work, at least in part, on helping students form positive reading identities. Becoming a reader involves more than acquiring skills for decoding and analyzing texts or filling in lines on a nightly reading log. Students must go further and claim the act of reading as part of who they are, and they must make reading a part of what they do in their everyday lives, both inside and outside of school. Their willingness to do these things will increase when they feel a sense of belonging in the world of books. We can open the door to that world by showing them there are texts out there worth reading and that reading those texts can be both beneficial and enjoyable. We can involve them in an ongoing conversation about what reading is *for* and what different kinds of texts can do for them.

If helping students become readers is partly about helping them form reading identities, it's also about patience and progress over time. In the research brief's use of the word *become*, we are reminded that it's never too late. The students in our classrooms might not have been readers in the past, but they can become readers now—if we create conditions that support their individual development (see, for example, Mueller, 2001). Those conditions begin with the texts we provide. We need to introduce students to the great range of books that are available, and we must ensure that students don't feel outmatched by the books we put before them. Because YA titles are designed to be teen-friendly, they signal to students that reading is something they can do. With books like these, reading is accessible, worthwhile, and relevant to their lives in the present moment. Those messages are important for all teens to hear, regardless of their reading ability.

The research brief goes on to call for an approach to reading instruction that is rooted in knowledge of students and texts, as well as strategies that can bring them together. In terms of students, the brief tells us to pay attention to individuals and their reading histories. It reminds us that "students come to reading tasks with varied prior reading experiences, or prior knowledge, which can support their reading of complex texts" (xi; all page numbers for the policy research brief map to the version printed at the front of this book). In addition, some students may have developed "expertise with a particular kind of reading—science fiction or online games, for example—outside of school" (xi). If we know that these other dimensions of students' reading lives exist, we should draw on them as we introduce students to new kinds of texts and the new ways of reading they may demand (see, for example, Smith & Wilhelm, 2002).

In terms of texts, the brief tells us that "in and out of school, the texts students read vary significantly" (xi). We also know that different texts "place different demands on readers and require different strategies and approaches to reading" (xi). Therefore, as we plan our approach to reading in the classroom, we need to notice and value the range of texts students are already reading, and we need to talk about reading as an activity that is shaped by purpose and context. That means foregrounding questions about *why* we are reading any given text, *what* different texts have to offer, and *how* our purposes will guide what we attend to as we read.

Amidst these understandings about students and texts, the research brief centers on the role of motivation in reading growth, instruction, and achievement. Motivation has always been a core element in arguments about the value of young adult literature (see, for example, Herz & Gallo, 2005; Lesesne, 2010). As the brief states, "Engaged and motivated readers read more often and read more diverse texts than students who are unmotivated by the reading task" (xi). Motivation shapes the amount of time students spend reading as well as the number and kinds of texts they attempt to read in a given period. Motivated readers are more ambitious in their approach to texts and more invested in the act of reading.

The research brief makes a second important point about motivation, which is that "the level of difficulty or complexity in a text is not the only factor students consider in choosing texts; interest and motivation also matter" (xii). Too often we assume that students will not read texts that are long or texts they find to be difficult. Research tells us this is a false assumption. Motivation mediates the element of difficulty. Motivated readers *will* choose more challenging texts if they have a personal investment in reading them. Being motivated enriches what students look for, what they find, and what they are able to comprehend.

The takeaway here is that motivation is the foundation for effective reading instruction. Motivation will lead students to greater purposefulness and independence in reading. It will help them improve as readers of complex texts, and it will broaden the range of texts they are willing to try. Because young adult literature is rooted in students' identities as adolescents, and because it is so vast a field, YA lit is uniquely suited to the goal of helping students develop identities as readers, along with the willingness to read widely and critically.

Implications for Instruction: Constructing YA Pedagogy

But we have to do more than put YA titles in front of students. We must employ research-based instructional approaches in our teaching of YA literature. The research brief points the way forward, not just for the use of YA lit in English class, but also for the development of a YA pedagogy—one that places student motivation at the center of our teaching while upholding the goals of rigor and complexity. This is a pedagogy that can push past the binaries that divide English departments. Developing it is less about inventing new lessons and assignments and more about the larger context we create for reading. If we want to teach reading in the ways the brief calls for, we must think deeply about how teaching YA literature effectively is tied to (1) the community we create in our classrooms, (2) the roles we take as teachers, and (3) the quality and relevance of the tasks we devise for students. Together, these three elements define YA pedagogy, and they open up new possibilities for our work with YA lit (see Figure 1.1).

Note that these elements are not in themselves new or unique in English teaching. What *is* unique is the act of blending them and placing YA lit at the core. While the following chapters immerse you in illustrations of these elements in real classrooms, I offer here a short discussion of each one, tracing its roots to principles outlined in the research brief.

1. *A classroom that cultivates reading community*

Our classrooms must be designed to cultivate social interactions and a sense of shared community around books. According to the research brief, we should "develop students' ability to engage in meaningful discussion of the complex texts they read . . . so they can learn to negotiate and comprehend complex texts independently" (xiii). We should also design reading responses that "enable active construction of meaning," and we should "construct a collaborative environment that builds on the strengths of individual students" (xii).

This emphasis on discussion and collaboration means we should give students the chance to do in school what they can't necessarily do elsewhere, which is count on the companionship of others as they read. We need to capitalize on the ways our thinking about books is enriched by discussions that expand our perspectives and cause us to come away with new insights. At school, those discussions can involve the whole class, or they can occur in small groups or between partners. We

---

Figure 1.1. Summary version of a conceptual framework for YA pedagogy.

A Conceptual Framework for YA Pedagogy

Definition of *YA pedagogy*: An approach to teaching YA lit that promotes love of reading, improving skills in reading, and connecting reading to real-world contexts. Designed to provide reading experiences with YA lit that are personally, socially, and academically relevant to teens of all kinds. Foregrounds valuing adolescence and cultivating complex experiences with YA texts.

Three core elements are necessary to put this pedagogy into practice: (1) a classroom that cultivates reading community; (2) a teacher who serves as book matchmaker and guide; (3) tasks that foster complexity, agency, and autonomy.

Why these three elements? And why must they work in tandem?

1. Through social interactions in the classroom, students and teachers create more complex and meaningful readings of YA literature. Reading YA titles together allows students to develop shared understandings about the field, markers of quality literature, and purposes that motivate readers over time.

2. To make the most of what YA lit has to offer, teens need adults to guide them to titles that are suited to their needs and that reward close and careful reading. To benefit from reading YA lit in school, teens need teachers who select books strategically and who frame work with those books in ways that satisfy the demands of the curriculum and the latest standards movement and/or testing regime.

3. The tasks we use to guide students' reading of YA lit should help them develop the same reading and writing skills they would acquire in any other English class. But tasks in YA pedagogy are designed to take students further: to support them in connecting their reading to real-world contexts and to equip them with tools they can use to continue reading closely, actively, and critically on their own.

---

engage students in shared meaning making as a step toward helping them develop the skill to comprehend complex texts independently.

For classroom discussion to be meaningful, however, it must simultaneously connect to students' interests and be grounded in close work with texts. We can call students to blend personal response with analysis of a text in a social environment that fosters complexity. Doing so will deepen students' understanding of how texts work and why they respond as they do to texts of different kinds. We lay the groundwork for this dynamic classroom community by taking teens—and their literature—seriously.

2. *Teachers as expert matchmakers who bring books and students together*

In the past, many of us understood our role as English teacher to be that of expert on the canon. The research brief urges us to envision a new role that reflects expertise based in knowing books, knowing students, and knowing how to bring books and students together. This vision arises directly from what we as teachers know about the needs of students and how to address those needs. The brief calls on teachers "to play a key role in matching individual students with specific books at appropriate levels of complexity" (xi). Teacher expertise is essential here because "only teachers know students well enough to help them find the best book for the purpose at hand, something 'leveling' systems cannot do" (xi).

However, as important as this individual matchmaking work is, we must go further. We must engage in a parallel form of matchmaking that takes into account the demands of the curriculum and the larger contexts of our teaching. As we choose books in response to the interests and needs of particular students, we must also make strategic book selections for small-group and whole-class reading. Our matchmaking work in these areas must be guided by the skills we want to teach and the themes we want to explore as we read YA lit with our students. We need to make careful decisions that are shaped by a vision of different yet complementary reading experiences with YA literature over time.

All of this means we must invest in learning about the books that are available for teen readers so that we can continually envision new possibilities and new opportunities for our students. Rather than read and teach the same books year after year, we can rely on colleagues—and students—to introduce us to new titles written and published expressly for teens. We can find ideas and inspiration by connecting with the larger community of YA lit readers. When we read YA lit with others, we continually expand our knowledge of books, authors, and the conversation about teens and reading. What could be more energizing?

Despite the pressures we may feel from the standards movement and high-stakes tests, it's crucial for us to recognize the power we have to influence the lives of teen readers. Who else but an English teacher can respond in the moment to the intellectual and emotional needs of students by offering them good books? And who else can create shared reading experiences with powerful stories that change the ways students think about the world around them? As teachers we are ideally positioned to make strategic matches between teens and texts that will take our students to new places.

3. *Reading tasks that foster complexity, agency, and autonomy*

In addition to handing students good books, we must give students engaging and meaningful things to *do* with books. We know that our purposes as readers shape what we look for in texts, and we know that what we bring to a text contributes to what we find in it. In the real world, readers are always blending their personal response to a book with their analytic understanding of the text. Readers also instinctively search for connections between books and real-world contexts. Having the freedom to do these things is what allows us to become agents of our own reading lives.

As teachers of YA lit, we can foster complex reading experiences and promote reading autonomy if we devise classroom tasks that invite students to engage in these forms of blending and connecting. We don't have to create new tasks to achieve this goal. Instead, we can recast and reinvent what we already do.

The process of cultivating complexity, agency, and autonomy through reading tasks begins with offering students reading choice. The research brief tells us that effective reading instruction invites students "to choose texts, including nonfiction, for themselves, in addition to assigned ones" (xii). Having the opportunity to choose books helps students to "see themselves as capable readers who can independently use reading capabilities they learn in class" (xii). We know that reading choice has long been a staple of classrooms that include YA literature, but we also know that choice alone does not always help students become stronger readers. We must establish contexts for reading that challenge students to be purposeful and intentional in their choices.

One way to do this is to foreground meta-level questions about why we read. When we invite students to read for the same reasons that real readers do—to pursue topical interests, explore critical questions, take on new perspectives, and gain deeper understanding of their own lived experience—they become more capable and more committed to reading. Students can develop agency and autonomy as readers only if we give them room to shape the course of their reading.

But reading is not solely an individual exercise. It is also collaborative and social. In the real world, readers read with one another. They make meaning of texts through discussion and debate. They ground their reading in larger contexts in which work with books is guided by personal, professional, and sometimes organizational goals. We can apprentice students to these social ways of reading by shifting our approach to familiar classroom tasks.

For example, the research brief offers a number of ideas for social and purpose-driven reading such as assigning "multiple texts focused on the same topic," which helps students "improve comprehension through text-to-text connections" (xii). We can approach this theme-based reading in the familiar way by inviting students to examine how different authors explore coming of age and finding one's place within family, school, or community. But we can take students' reading to the next level by linking it to the world of YA writing and publishing. How are today's authors both imitating and innovating as they produce new titles in relation to current bestsellers? Which authors are creating art and which are churning out copycat books designed to capitalize on a commercial trend? This too is an approach to reading that teaches students to make comparisons and connections across texts, but it's one that is relevant in the world outside the classroom.

Another instructional approach is to cultivate students' skills through writing about reading. The research brief suggests that we "connect students' reading of complex texts with writing that uses complex texts as models so they will recognize and be able to negotiate many different types of complex texts" (xiii). What students are being asked to do here is read less for content and more for knowledge of the ways texts are put together. As students become more conscious of how texts are written, they become more insightful as readers. We can make this work more meaningful by linking the study of texts to writing being done by today's YA authors. What can we learn from interviews in which authors discuss their personal writing process? How can we use what we learn from authors to improve our own writing process? Students become more independent as readers *and* writers when we ground their learning in real-world contexts.

Finally, the research brief urges us to anchor our teaching of reading in conversations about how we approach texts. We must teach students "how different textual purposes, genres, and modes require different strategies for reading," and we must demonstrate "how digital and visual texts including multimodal and multigenre texts require different approaches to reading" (xiii). With these points, the brief reminds us that the reading process is related to the purpose for reading and the nature of the text at hand. We can engage students in meta conversations about what we do as readers of YA books, and we can involve them in evaluating their reading processes. But once more, we can heighten the relevance of that work by embedding it in a real-world context. We might ask questions such as: How do our reading strategies change when we're preparing to write a professional review of a YA book, serve on a YA literature award committee, or analyze how publishers are marketing YA titles to specific target audiences? Meta conversations become relevant when we have a reason to reflect on our reading process and adjust it based on the nature of the reading task.

In each of these ways, with only a slight shift in our approach to instruction, we can foster complexity, agency, and autonomy in students' reading lives. If we want students to grow as readers, we must design tasks that call them to complexity. But we must also give them authentic reasons to read. We can equip them with tools to use in their work with different texts, but if we want them to use those tools of their own

accord, they must develop a personal understanding of what reading is
good for. The result will be a sense of autonomy in reading that they can
carry with them once their time in our classroom is over.

Why Do We Need YA Pedagogy?

The Binary Paradigm

This vision of teaching YA lit with YA pedagogy is something I've come to after
years of teaching in what I call a binary paradigm. If you're a teacher, you know
what the binary looks like. You've probably seen it in your own school. All you
have to do is walk down the hall and glance in the doors of different English
classrooms. Look at the books students are reading and how those books are being
taught, and you'll witness the binary in action.

Here's the first part of the binary paradigm. In some classrooms, students sit
at their desks with a classic novel in front of them. Maybe it's *The Great Gatsby* or
maybe it's *The Adventures of Huckleberry Finn*. The teacher stands at the front of
the room, and students listen to the teacher talk about the text. During class they
turn to pages the teacher has flagged for close reading, and they follow along as
the teacher explains what's going on in key passages or scenes. For homework they
read the next few chapters, sometimes answering study questions designed to serve
as a reading guide. Periodically they take quizzes and write essays. The primary
mode of instruction is class discussion. On some days, the discussion is spirited and
memorable: the teacher's love for the book shines through, and students catch onto
that passion. More often than not, however, what happens isn't discussion. It's
recitation. Students sit back and wait to be told what the book means.

This is the traditional English classroom: a place where the study of literature
is rooted in a teacher-centered approach that we've probably all experienced at
some point in our schooling. If you've taught in this way, you know that this approach fails to engage a lot of our students, and yet it's still our primary model for
reading instruction, especially in high school. We use the space of English class to
expose students to books they probably wouldn't read otherwise, and we set up discussions that we hope will lead students to get what we got from important works
of literature. We tell ourselves that this way of doing English has merit because it
teaches students how to struggle with hard texts and how to read those texts more
critically.

But the truth is, if students aren't reading—if instead they're picking up what
they need to know from listening to class discussion, skimming CliffsNotes, or
watching the movie version of an assigned book—then English class isn't helping
them become better readers. All it's doing is helping them learn how to fake read
(Kittle, 2013) and parrot back others' ideas. What's worse, for students who find

reading to be difficult or who have never experienced pleasure and personal enjoyment in reading, struggling with hard texts is basically an impossible task. We can
blind ourselves to this reality, or we can acknowledge that despite our good intentions, when we teach with these books and these methods we aren't making books
complex as much as searching for ways to make their complexity manageable for
struggling and disengaged readers.

Out of a desire to disrupt these patterns and reach more students, many of
us have turned to young adult literature as part of a student-centered approach
to teaching English. Here is the opposite side of the binary: classrooms where
students lounge on couches and beanbag chairs, reading books they've chosen for
themselves based on their personal tastes and interests. Students read silently or
browse for new books from the classroom library shelves. The teacher may read
with them, or she may move through the room, conferring with individual students
and recording their progress on a clipboard. Alternately, students may meet in
literature circle discussion groups (Daniels, 1994), stand up to give book talks, or
work on writing. Instead of taking quizzes, they keep lists of books they've com-
pleted, and they compose personal responses in reading notebooks. The primary
mode of instruction is one-on-one conferencing, complemented by whole-class
mini-lessons that equip students with knowledge of genres, text features, and reading strategies (see, for example, Atwell, 2014; Miller & Moss, 2013).

This is the workshop version of English class: an environment designed to
meet the needs of individual students through reading choice and age-appropriate
literature. There's more energy here, and body language indicates there's more
real reading going on. But if we stop to take a closer look, there's still cause for
concern. A lot of these students blow through books without thinking very deeply
about the story or the text. Reading quantity happens at the expense of reading
quality. In notebook entries and class discussion, students focus more on their
personal lives than on the ideas in the books or the nuances of the writing. They
find books to love, but they don't read outside their comfort zones, dig deeply into
themes, or participate in larger conversations about the impact of specific books
on our culture. If we're honest, we must acknowledge that reading YA lit in the
space of the workshop may draw more students to books, but without a pedagogy
 designed to ask more of them, it doesn't necessarily push students to improve as
readers of complex texts.

The Binary in My Own Teaching

During my years in the high school classroom, I found myself at various times on
either side of this binary. In my first job at an urban high school in New Jersey
in the early 1990s, I taught in the same traditional ways my former teachers had

taught me. I followed the district's genre-based curriculum and worked my way through the list of required ninth-grade texts, but I struggled to articulate a larger purpose for our work. When we read short stories from the textbook, it seemed that the point of reading was to build knowledge of literary terms, but I didn't know how to make the study of those terms more than a vocabulary exercise. When we read Robert Cormier's *The Chocolate War*, we had the opportunity to explore how authors develop themes in novels, but I didn't have a clear vision for how to structure that exploration, so students spent most of their time taking quizzes and rehashing the plot. In our reading of *Romeo and Juliet*, we focused again on literary terms, but most of the unit was dedicated to the long slog through the text, with the movie as our reward at the end. When we got to Greek mythology, I didn't know what to focus on, so I quizzed students on the names of gods and goddesses, and we made mythology board games.

I cringe when I look back on this time in my career, but my plot-heavy, quiz-oriented approach was more or less the same as what my colleagues were doing. No matter how interesting, important, and well-written these texts were, students weren't invested in them, and neither was I. With this combination of books and methods, I failed to create engaged readers. I also failed to foster complex reading experiences.

On the advice of one of my former teachers who had become active in the National Writing Project, I read Linda Rief's *Seeking Diversity* (1991), followed by Nancie Atwell's *In the Middle* (1987), during the summer after my first year of teaching. I fell in love with those books. I stayed up late at night reading them. The workshop model captivated me: I wanted to create the kind of inspiring classroom environment I was reading about—one where students could find their own books to love. Feeling bold and determined, I built a small classroom library out of the YA novels I had collected when I was a teenager and an assortment of raggedy paperbacks I bought from the used bookstore in my hometown.

When I returned to New Jersey for my second year, my teaching was still incoherent, but I saw more students reading with investment. Their reading was all over the place, as was mine: Stephen King, paperback romances, adult thrillers, occasional nonfiction. Sometimes they—and I—read young adult literature. Like Atwell, I required students to write letters to me in their reading response notebooks. I wrote back. I forged personal connections with students through books, but I couldn't say with any certainty what they were learning as readers other than the idea that reading could be fun. Meanwhile, when I took breaks from reading workshop to cover the core grade-level texts, I defaulted back to quizzes and study questions. I couldn't figure out how to synthesize our reading in the workshop with our reading of core texts. I had fallen into a binary in my own teaching. Moreover, neither side of the binary was getting us to the goal of reading complexity.

At the end of the second year, I quit my job in New Jersey, moved to Michigan, and got hired as a book clerk at Borders Books and Music in Ann Arbor. Based on my enjoyment of young adult literature as a teenager, I began making regular visits to the YA shelves. I studied the titles we stocked. Soon I was reading newly published YA lit, and I was reading it voraciously. The more new titles I discovered—works by authors such as Francesca Lia Block, Chris Crutcher, John Marsden, and Jacqueline Woodson—the more I wanted to return to teaching, mainly so I could share these books with students.

After just one year at Borders, I was lucky to find a job teaching English in a suburban district near Ann Arbor. At Canton High School, I was able to pick up where I left off with the ninth-grade reading workshop. I had my department administrator's blessing, and I had more book knowledge under my belt. Again, however, I was faced with engineering a fit between the workshop portion of the ninth-grade course, which focused on YA literature, and units dedicated to our required grade-level texts, which were classics.

Meanwhile I was also charged with teaching tenth-grade American Lit, a course that seemed to have clearer goals: students were meant to study a body of literature while developing their skills as readers and writers. For some of my colleagues, literature study was chronological; for others, it was thematic. I tried both approaches, but neither centered enough on students to satisfy me. I tried weaving in other methods I was learning. I paired books with movies, as my mentor teacher did. I offered some reading choice through literature circles. I got better at leading discussions, and I discovered how books could engage us in important conversations. We read *Walden* and talked about living simply. We read *Native Son* and talked about racism. I appreciated the sense of connectedness we found through our shared experience of these texts, and I enjoyed watching students construct meaning. When I asked them to write about significant quotes, they had interesting things to say. When I asked them to pose questions about the text, their questions were thoughtful. In certain moments, the work felt fulfilling, but I knew I wasn't reaching everyone. Still, this approach seemed to get us closer to the goal of complexity.

I knew what was missing in American Lit: students needed more opportunity for choice and more texts that were relevant to them. Only as I got better at teaching American Lit could I start to see what was missing in my teaching of YA lit. I wanted to strengthen my ninth-grade class by borrowing from what I saw my most creative colleagues doing in American Lit, but I couldn't figure out how to integrate our different approaches. The more we talked, the more I realized that my like-minded colleagues faced the same struggle. They told me they wanted to inspire readers the way I did with YA lit, but they felt they didn't know enough about the books, and they couldn't figure out how to manage reading choice. I wanted to

engage ninth graders in discussions organized around big ideas, but I didn't know
how to do that through my workshop approach to YA lit.

Consequently, my colleagues and I remained stuck on opposite sides of the
binary, despite our mutual appreciation of what the other side had to offer. Across
the department, we acknowledged that as individuals we had committed ourselves
to these different ways of teaching, but collectively we didn't do anything to bridge
the binary paradigm. We just expected students to adapt in each context.

Eventually I quit teaching to go to grad school. When I became a professor
and started teaching YA literature in college, my students and I studied YA lit as a
literary field; at the same time, we studied our lives as readers. At last I saw glim-
mers of a synthesis. Rigorous reading of texts, reading for personal enjoyment,
social experiences with books: the different dimensions of reading, and the teaching of reading, were starting to become visible.

Then, in the midst of writing this book, I was hired for a literacy consulting
job in a local school district where I encountered the binary all over again. Middle
school teachers ran reading workshops centered on YA literature. Then students
went on to a high school English curriculum steeped in the classics. Teachers
at the middle school took pride in the love their students developed for reading
through choice in the workshop. Echoing Atwell (2007), they expressed frustration
at how students lost that choice at the high school. "I just think it's really different," an eighth-grade teacher told me. "And I'm not sure if that's good for kids. Or
working for kids as readers." She added that she didn't get the sense that the high
school teachers valued YA lit. "But clearly if you look from the outside, the high
school looks more rigorous. They read so many books. No one's questioning that."

A teacher at the high school countered this critique by describing students
who arrived in ninth grade with a lack of reading stamina brought on by having had too much choice in middle school. She went on to complicate the goal of
getting kids to love reading: "I think we need to define 'loving reading' as not just
reading books I feel comfortable with and books that make me feel good," she said.
"Personally I love reading that challenges my thinking, whether it's the way I think
about the world or how it stretches my intellectual ability." However, in conversations with her middle school colleagues, she felt like she had to defend this goal.
"I'm not taking children who you taught to love reading and ruining that by asking them to read a hard text. We all want kids to love reading. But saying 'loving
reading' feels very—[I'm not sure that's the best way to describe reading for high
school. Loving is not my priority. I think you can love reading and never challenge
yourself. And that's a concern that I have."]

As I reflected on these conversations, I saw more clearly than ever before
how students were caught in the middle of the binary, forced to adapt to different
texts, methods, and goals while adults in different buildings remained wedded to

their different approaches. Teachers on both sides believed in the rightness of the work they were doing. Those at the high school made an important point when they argued that students should be expected to read in more sophisticated ways as they grow older. At the same time, the goal of teaching the canon led them to keep assigning texts like *The Odyssey* even when it was clear that students weren't reading them. Still, an administrator defended this practice: "As a literate individual, it helps to have knowledge of that story, as opposed to some obscure YA novel no one's heard about," he told me. "I think there are plenty of kids who didn't read *The Odyssey*, but they *know* about it. Am I bummed they didn't read it? Yeah. But they still wrote about it and thought about it."

Gallo (2001) argued years ago that feeding students a strict diet of the classics only serves to create an aliterate society. He wrote, "We are a nation that teaches its children how to read in the early grades, then forces them in their teenage years to read literary works that most of them dislike so much that they have no desire whatsoever to continue those experiences into adulthood" (p. 36). Unfortunately, despite our best intentions, this dynamic is still present in many English classes. Gallo said that helping our students love reading should be our primary goal as English teachers, and he advocated for YA texts as literature that gives us our best shot at getting there. Again, though, when we position YA books as literature that's mainly good for enjoyment, we preserve the binary, and we shut down other possibilities for these books and our students as readers.

Consequences of the Binary

Only now can I see what we lose by allowing the binary to remain in place. Only now can I see the damaging messages we send to kids about books, reading, and readers through the binary paradigm. Here's what our stance toward books, and our corresponding methods, communicate:

- There are *fun* books and there are *required* books. Required books aren't fun; fun books aren't required.

- The only books worth struggling with are classics. Popular titles, including books written for teens, are meant to be enjoyed, not studied or analyzed.

- Some books are hard and important, other books are entertaining and enjoyable, but few books are both.

- There is pleasure reading, which you do when you read YA lit, and there is analytical reading, which you do when you study the classics, but these modes of reading do not overlap.

- There is reading you do for yourself, which is satisfying and worthwhile, and there is reading you do for English class, which is disconnected from the things you care about.

- Some people read for fun; other people read for an intellectual challenge. If you're going to keep reading, you're going to have to choose one mode over the other. Nobody does both.

These damaging messages don't emanate from the books themselves. Rather, they arise from a narrow vision of texts and teaching. Because of the binary evolution of our methods—traditional literature study for the classics and workshop teaching for YA lit—we've come to view certain texts and methods as locked together. Even if the division of books and methods isn't as rigid as I've described, the *perception* of difference remains. As a result, classrooms where we read the classics and classrooms where we read YA books seem to exist in different universes, driven by different value systems and set up to deliver different outcomes. This locking together of books and methods teaches students to view reading as a series of hierarchies: good books vs. books you look down on; serious reading vs. superficial reading; smart, skillful readers vs. those who settle for entertainment. As a result of our acquiescence to the binary, the potential of both YA literature and the classics is diminished.

It doesn't have to be this way. We can make room for YA lit in classrooms of all kinds, and we can teach these works using a blended approach that marries the goals of rigor and pleasure, skill and enjoyment, stamina and passion. In this way, we can engage and motivate students while helping them become more capable and committed readers of complex texts. Instead of labeling books as good or bad, we can investigate what readers are *doing* with them.

Personalizing YA Pedagogy

YA pedagogy offers a way to imagine new possibilities for our teaching of YA lit, but there's still a lot to figure out when it comes to implementing this approach, including big questions to consider, such as:

- What does everyday work with YA lit look like if we go beyond the reading workshop model?
- How do we teach students to blend personal and analytic work with YA texts as they engage in social reading experiences with their peers?
- How do we introduce YA titles, and frame the purpose of our work with them, if we teach in a context in which YA literature is viewed as "less than"?
- How do we connect our teaching of YA lit to what students have done, and will do, as readers in other English classes?

There is no one right answer to any of these questions. Each of us who teaches YA lit must develop an approach that is right for our context. We must also be patient and accept that our work with YA texts will grow and change over time. As we become more knowledgeable about the books, we will become more sophisticated in our methods of teaching them.

The teachers you'll meet in this book have personalized their use of YA pedagogy in order to engage readers of all kinds—from tweens at the start of middle school to seniors who are about to graduate from high school; from students who are college-bound to those in alternative ed. These teachers are experts now, but none of them started out that way. Each one has a story to tell about discovering YA lit and making the decision to bring it into the classroom. Like all of us who teach YA literature, they built their knowledge of the books gradually, guided by recommendations from fellow readers, their personal tastes and preferences, and sensitivity to the needs of students. Discovering one good YA book whet their appetite for more. Seeing students' responses convinced them that investing in young adult literature was worth it.

While each of these teachers takes a personalized approach to teaching YA lit, what they share is a common stance toward books, students, and reading. When it comes to *books,* they encourage students to enjoy YA lit, but they also challenge students to read YA texts closely and deeply. As for *students,* they communicate that regardless of skill level or prior history, everyone is capable of reading. They use book recommendations to show students that they see them as individuals. While they value students' tastes and interests, they also challenge them to take risks and try new things. With regard to *reading in school,* they establish purposes that go beyond logging pages, completing projects, and taking tests. Instead they create opportunities for students to engage with YA lit in a social environment designed to make reading relevant and meaningful. They show students there is something to get from these books, and they guide them in the getting.

In the chapters to come, I invite you to develop your own version of YA pedagogy by introducing you to teachers and students around the country whose lives have been changed by this literature and this way of teaching it.

Chapter 2 presents an introduction to YA lit as a field and a new way of thinking about the concept of text complexity. I share examples of what com-

---

Stance toward Books, Students, and Reading in YA Pedagogy

- *Books.* We encourage students to enjoy YA lit, but we also challenge them to read YA texts closely and deeply.

- *Students.* We communicate to students that regardless of skill level or prior history, everyone is capable of reading. We use YA book recommendations to show students that we see them as individuals. We value their tastes and interests. We also challenge them to take risks and try new things.

- *Reading.* We establish purposes for reading that go beyond logging pages read, completing projects, and taking tests. Instead we create opportunities for students to engage with YA lit in a social environment designed to make reading relevant and meaningful.

plexity looks like in specific YA titles, and I offer a vision for finding and making complexity through YA pedagogy.

Chapters 3–5 focus on the three elements that constitute YA pedagogy. Chapter 3 explores *classroom reading community* and illustrates what it looks like across three different settings. I show the common stance that connects YA classrooms, and I share a framework to guide you in constructing a reading community that will support YA pedagogy in your own classroom. Chapter 4 defines the role of *teacher as matchmaker* and shows what matchmaking looks like when it takes into account both the needs of individual students and the larger contexts for students' reading. I offer resources to help you build knowledge of YA lit as you search for books that will be right for your setting. Chapter 5 introduces a vision for *tasks that foster complexity, agency, and autonomy* by linking students' work with YA literature to real-world contexts. I take six familiar ELA tasks and show what they look like when we recast them through YA pedagogy. I share examples of how individual teachers have reinvented these tasks in response to demands and possibilities in their local contexts.

Chapter 6 connects YA pedagogy to assessment. I introduce a vision of assessment that values personal *and* analytical work with YA lit. I share three ideas for creative assessments that depart from traditional unit tests and analytic essays, and I discuss what a group of high school students did when they were given the freedom to develop projects that put their knowledge of YA lit to work in their school and community.

Chapter 7 makes the case for outreach as something that goes with the territory when we teach young adult literature. I offer a variety of ideas for outreach that help us get the word out about YA lit and this way of teaching it.

If we want to meet the needs of *all* students, we have to imagine new kinds of reading experiences with new kinds of texts. We can show parents, administrators, and colleagues that YA literature has unique potential to engage our students as readers—young people who come to school with wildly different levels of interest, ability, and investment in reading but who all deserve the chance to love books.

In the face of those who would say otherwise, we should argue that YA lit can provide reading experiences that are both academically challenging and personally meaningful for the diverse teens we teach. We should advocate for a pedagogical approach that sees this blend of intellectual and emotional engagement as essential for student learning. We should have the courage to challenge old orthodoxies and advocate for the young people before us whose questions, passions, and life experiences can be affirmed and extended through literature if we give them literature that is relevant to their needs and questions.

This book is designed to help you foster your own vision for teaching YA lit in the secondary classroom. Those of you who are already immersed in YA lit will find validation for the teaching you currently do. Perhaps the ideas you discover in these pages will help you to refine the vision you already have. Perhaps they will point you in new directions.

Those of you who are new to young adult literature will find ideas—and, I hope, inspiration—in the stories of colleagues who made the commitment to teach YA books in spite of the obstacles they faced. From this foundation, you can build your own version of YA pedagogy that will bring these books—and your students' reading lives—to life. You have the power to teach YA literature. All you have to do is make the decision to begin.

Young Adult Literature and Text Complexity

As we build the case for young adult literature in the secondary classroom, we face a number of challenges. Unfortunately, we know it's inevitable that some of our colleagues will look down on these books. Given that we live in a culture that denigrates and degrades teenagers, negativity toward their literature shouldn't come as a surprise. Author Sherman Alexie commented on this phenomenon shortly after he won the National Book Award for Young People's Literature for his YA novel, *The Absolutely True Diary of a Part-Time Indian*. In an essay about YA lit published in the *New York Times Book Review*, Alexie noted that some acquaintances thought he was dumbing down by writing for teenagers. Others asked if he wouldn't have preferred to win the same award for an adult, serious work. "I thought I'd been condescended to as an Indian," he said. "That was nothing compared to the condescension for writing YA" (Rabb, 2008).

What's frustrating about people's criticisms of YA lit is how rarely they reflect actual knowledge of the books. And yet if we're lucky, at some point we'll encounter a colleague who isn't a YA lit reader but who takes an interest in what we're doing. When that happens, we can be poised with quality books to recommend. We might start with Alexie's novel, and then we might suggest other strong titles such as *The Golden Compass* by Philip Pullman, or *I'll Give You the Sun* by Jandy Nelson, or *Challenger Deep* by Neal Shusterman, or *All American Boys* by Jason Reynolds and Brendan Kiely, or *Bone Gap* by Laura Ruby, or *Most Dangerous* by Steve Sheinkin. Any one of these books would probably surprise a newcomer to the world of YA lit. "This stuff is really good," they might say. "It's sophisticated. It's literary. It's amazing! But why is it considered YA lit? What *is* YA lit, anyway?"

These are great questions, in part because they get to the complexity of young adult literature as a field. They encourage us to take into account the larger social, cultural, and economic contexts that surround YA lit. They point to the broad constellation of people who are reading, writing, and marketing this literature, and they allude to its many genres, subsets, and variations. In YA lit we find the problem novel, the series novel, the commercial novel, and the crossover novel. We also find short story collections, nonfiction texts, poetry, graphic novels, and multigenre novels. Given all of this variation in what YA lit can be, how do we come up with a satisfactory answer when people ask us what it is?

Questions about how we define YA lit are actually a perfect setup for conversations about YA pedagogy. If we can complicate the way our colleagues think about the books, we set the stage for showing them the complexity that's in the books. Once we engage other adults in exploring what this literature has to offer, we can start talking about its potential to challenge, stretch, and change teen readers.

What *Is* YA Lit, Anyway?

To define what YA lit is and isn't, we first have to consider the different kinds of people who might answer the question. If you ask an ordinary literate citizen—that is, your average reader who's heard of YA lit but hasn't spent much time reading it—he or she might say that a young adult novel is any book with a teen character in it. This is both true and not true. Many of our most well-known classic novels feature children or young teens as protagonists. Think of books such as *To Kill a Mockingbird*, *The Adventures of Huckleberry Finn*, and *Lord of the Flies*. While these novels are read by teens, they weren't written for teens, nor do they reflect a teen sensibility. Instead they offer portraits of adult society filtered through the eyes of a child. They may be about a young person's experience, but they aren't YA lit.

Following a parallel line of thought, others will say that YA lit is any book that a teen will read. But if we take into account the wildly eclectic interests that lead teens to books—and to titles as varied as Calvin and Hobbes comic strip collections, the Guinness books of world records, and the Kurt Cobain biography *Heavier Than Heaven*—we have to concede that this definition is too loose to help us.

If you ask a critic—someone who approaches questions about YA lit from a literary standpoint and whose thinking reflects years of reading in the field—you'll get a more substantive answer. In a seminal essay, "Middle Muddle" (2000), YA librarian and critic Patty Campbell wrote:

> The central theme of most YA fiction is becoming an adult, finding the answer to the internal and eternal question, "Who am I and what am I going to do about it?" No matter what events are going on in the book, accomplishing that task is really what the book is about, and in the climactic moment the resolution of the external conflict is linked to a realization for the protagonist that moves toward shaping an adult identity. (pp. 485–86)

In a companion piece, "Our Side of the Fence" (2004), Campbell elaborated on her ideas by focusing on patterns in YA novels along the literary lines of form, voice, and structure:

- The central theme of YA fiction is becoming an adult. No matter what events are going on in the book, accomplishing that task is really what the book is about. . . . [T]he narration moves swiftly to a point where the protagonist has an epiphany that matures him or her in some vital way and, as a manifestation of that inner change, solves a problem that has been central to the plot. Very occasionally the protagonist may reject the epiphany, which leads to an ending that is ironic or unhappy. . . . There is no requirement for hope, or even cheerfulness, in the YA novel.

- The central action in YA fiction is essentially internal, in the turbulent psyche of the adolescent. . . . However, this internal action must not be contemplative monologue but embedded in straightforward external action.

- Voice is all-important here and is the quality that most clearly distinguishes YA from adult fiction. . . . Whether it is told in first or third (or even second) person, to be a YA novel a book must have a teen protagonist speaking from an adolescent point of view, with all the limitations of understanding this implies.

- To be a YA novel, then, a book must have a climactic epiphany of new maturity as the subtext and be told in the YA voice from a limited adolescent viewpoint. In addition, it must be relevant to the lives of young readers in some way. (pp. 360–61)

Of course, the question of what is relevant to the lives of young readers is another topic for debate. In a speech about *The Astonishing Life of Octavian Nothing, Traitor to the Nation*, one of the most brilliant and ambitious YA novels ever written, YA author M. T. Anderson (2009) spoke about our collective tendency to underestimate teens, their passions, and their intellect:

> They are *incredibly* eccentric, deeply impassioned about their interests, fantastically— even exhaustingly—knowledgeable on the subject of topics like, say, drum and bugle corps, or horse-riding, or the United Nations, or submarine warfare. Their commitment to complexity of thought is, if anything, fiercer than an adult's—because they have to fight so fiercely to defend it.

Anderson reminds us that to see the intelligence in teen literature, we first have to believe in the intelligence of teens.

We also need to believe in the importance of teens' everyday lives. One danger of emphasizing epiphanies, the journey toward adulthood, and the development of greater maturity in YA protagonists is that we may fail to pay sufficient respect to the complexity of teens' concerns in the present moment. It would be a mistake for our definition of YA lit to reinforce the cultural belief that the only worthy thing a young person can do is work to *stop* being a teen. Therefore, writing that explores what it's like to be a teenager—and that does so from a teen's perspective, with thoughtfulness and nuance—is always something to look for and value in YA lit.

But what if we shift the discussion and ask for input from those whose work centers on publishing, selling, and cataloging YA literature? This is a necessary move to make as we build our definition since the way we think about a book is not solely a measure of its content. A book's identity is also shaped by how it is categorized. In conversations with people such as agents, editors, and school and library marketing directors, we find that defining YA lit is less about literary elements and more about sales decisions. In a 2008 essay published in the *New York Times*, Margo Rabb, whose first novel, *Cures for Heartbreak*, was sold as YA, wrote about the surprise of finding the YA label attached to her book:

> My literary novel about death and grief, which I'd worked on for eight years, was a young adult book? Apparently, I had unintentionally slipped across an increasingly porous border, one patrolled by an unlikely guard. "The line between Y.A. and adult has become almost transparent," said Michael Cart, a former president of the Young Adult Library Services Association and a columnist for Booklist. "These days, what makes a book Y.A. is not so much what makes it as who makes it—and the 'who' is the marketing department."

Here the takeaway message is that YA lit is a commercial category. Calling a book YA determines how it will be packaged and positioned in the marketplace. It gives booksellers a way to link a new title to others of its kind. For those of us who read YA lit, this is helpful in that it gives us a place to browse in the bookstore and a way to understand what we're seeing on the shelves. And yet this method of defining YA has its own limitations. What happens when publishers get the label wrong? Stephen Chbosky's *The Perks of Being a Wallflower*, for instance, was initially marketed as adult. So was Judy Blume's *Forever*. (Incidentally, so was *The Catcher in the Rye*, arguably the most truly teen-centered book in the American literary canon but one that was published before YA was a field or a commercial concept.) Just because a publisher says a book is YA doesn't mean it actually is.

If we keep going with these questions about defining YA literature—if we ask a librarian, a teacher, a parent, or a teen—we'll probably get a different answer from each person we talk to. People's answers reveal their positionality (that is, their stake in the books and the nature of their work with them) and their underlying ideological beliefs (on literature, reading, and teens). Consequently, when we come across articles written about YA lit for popular audiences, we often wade through layers of misinformation and bias without ever getting any new or useful information (see, for example, the widely read derogatory essays about YA lit published by Meghan Cox Gurdon in the *Wall Street Journal*, "Darkness Too Visible," June 4, 2011, and Ruth Graham in *Slate*, "Against YA," June 5, 2014). Lacking a more informed perspective, people end up believing what they want to believe about young adult literature.

What I love about YA literature is how it's many things at once. It's both a literary form and a sales category. It's literature about teenagers in which adults often play integral roles. It's written in an engaging and accessible way, but it also features books that are lengthy and difficult. It's a marketing division, but it's one in which some titles are cross-listed on the adult shelves. It's written for teens, but it attracts a large adult readership (see, for example, Roger Sutton's blog post "Why Do We Even Call It YA Anymore?" June 8, 2014).

To me, the best YA novels are those that defy categorization. My favorite YA titles are the ones that surprise me. They take risks and blur genres. In the process, they do important work. They ask questions about identity and formative influences on identity. They expose social inequality. They explore philosophical ideas. They place teens' everyday experiences in a larger context. They depict the complexity of human beings. They offer new knowledge gleaned from original research. They are race-conscious. They are critical. They are literary and metaphorical. They do all these things while filtering the meaning-making process through the minds and hearts of teens. The borders of the field are porous, and what we find within the field is continually changing. This is information we can use to challenge people's thinking about YA lit.

Finding and Making Complexity in YA Lit

The complexity involved in defining YA literature challenges us to take an equally complex approach to teaching YA lit. YA pedagogy is designed to attend to the complexities of teens' lives while also bringing out the complexity inherent in the literature itself. When we commit to this literature and this way of teaching, we do so knowing that many well-meaning people will criticize our decision. If our colleagues believe that young adult literature isn't complex, it stands to reason they won't be able to imagine there's anything in it worth teaching.

Those of us who read YA texts know that neither of these ideas is true, and yet they present a real obstacle for our work in the classroom. Adults aren't the only ones who internalize this message. Students are likely to arrive in English class with their own assumptions about YA lit that we'll need to disrupt. If teens themselves believe that YA books are too simplistic to be worth their time, we have to be prepared with tools and frameworks designed to show them otherwise.

All of this means that while part of our work as teachers involves changing the conversation about YA lit, another equally important part involves changing the conversation about complexity. No one will deny that teens can and should be reading complex texts. What we need to be asking, though, is how people define text complexity. As is the case with young adult literature itself, the conversation is ideologically loaded. Sometimes calls for increasingly complex texts are really code for keeping classic literature at the center of the curriculum. The classics are important, and they're great for some readers, but there are many other books out there worth sharing with our teens. Students and teachers alike need opportunities to read new books alongside familiar titles from the canon.

Other times people define text complexity by talking about Lexile levels, which are quantitative measures of text elements. Lexile levels are assigned to books using software that analyzes word frequency and sentence length. Books with higher Lexile levels are assumed to be more challenging and therefore more complex. But Lexiles don't take into account a book's content, nor do they attend to age appropriateness or writing quality. That means books with mature themes or sophisticated storytelling techniques may rate low in terms of Lexile when they're actually very complex overall. Numerical ratings can never capture the deeper dimensions of complexity, which are found in what books ask of readers and what they have to offer.

I want to argue for a different approach to the topic of text complexity, and that is to place the reader at the center. Rather than labeling books using arbitrary and external measures of complexity, or sorting them according to their perceived literary and cultural prestige, let's focus on what readers can do with texts. Reading is a dynamic process, and that means text complexity isn't a static trait. A text

can be more or less complex based on what a reader brings to it or what a reader
discovers or sees. In other words, complexity can be *found* within a text, but it can
also be *made* based on how we teach the text in our classrooms.

That's not to say that every book is equally complex. Some books contain
more layers and display more ambition than others. But if we think about text
complexity as something that gets created in the interaction between a reader and a
text, then we broaden our vision of what a complex text can be.

By saying that complexity can be found and made, I want to suggest that
there are two key dimensions of text complexity, and we need to attend to both
in our teaching. Complexity can be found *in* the text—in the overall quality of an
author's writing and thinking. But complexity can also be found in what readers
do with texts—in the meanings they create based on their purpose, context, and
motivation for reading. This means that as we evaluate texts for their inherent
measures of complexity, we also need to explore how and why texts *become* complex
for individual readers.

Finding complexity in a text is likely to be a familiar concept to all of us who
are English teachers. We find complexity every time we engage in the act of close
reading. Close reading gives us a way to notice text features and see more clearly
how texts are put together. It allows us to savor beautiful language and delve more
deeply into metaphorical meanings. Close reading is sometimes viewed as an act
of tearing a text apart, but a different way to understand it is as an act of love (see
Lehman & Roberts, 2014). We can share that love with our students by showing
them how to find complexity in young adult literature.

Making complexity, on the other hand, may be a more difficult concept to
explain. It helps to start by thinking about how we make complexity in our own
reading lives. If you think back to the books you've read that have stayed with you,
books that challenged you or changed you in some way, they're bound to be ones
that actively engaged you as a reader. What you brought to the text, sought from
it, or discovered in it allowed you to construct a complex reading experience. You
made complexity by reading the text closely and connecting it to some larger context that was relevant to you. Whatever complexity was in the text already became
stronger and deeper because of the meanings you created as you interacted with it.
Not unlike Rosenblatt's (1995) reader-response theory, the heart of making complexity is in the transaction between the reader and the text.

If you think about what the process of making complexity entails and the
conditions that allow it to happen, you'll probably agree that we readers make
complexity in lots of different ways, some that are personal, others that are social,
and still others that are analytical. For example, making complexity is personal
when we bring our current interests, questions, and circumstances to a book and
use those to shape and guide our reading. It's social when we listen to the ideas of

other readers, notice what they notice, and allow their ways of thinking to change the way we think about a text. It's analytical when we go back into a text to look more carefully at its individual elements and then use that analysis to understand its meanings more deeply. To read in these varied and complex ways, we need to experience agency and autonomy as readers. We also need to be immersed in a social environment that takes our reading interests seriously, supports us in our reading development, and challenges us to read better.

This way of thinking about text complexity opens the door for bringing young adult literature into the classroom. Because YA lit can speak honestly and directly to teenagers, and because the issues the books explore lend themselves to discussion and debate, it's easy to see why YA lit is ideally suited to the task of teaching teens how to find and make complexity. First, since all YA lit circles back to the question, "Who am I, and what am I going to do about it?" (Campbell, 2000), it is literature that's tailor-made for engaging students in personal forms of complex reading. Second, because teens enjoy sharing these books with one another, YA lit invites them to seek out and cultivate the social dimensions of complexity. And finally, when we make room in our teaching for occasional whole-class reading of these books, we have the opportunity to show students how working closely with a text can help them gain more from it. We all know that literary analysis has more meaning when the texts we're analyzing matter to us (Lehman & Roberts, 2014). The stories teens encounter in YA lit give them reasons to read both closely and personally.

What this means is that we can teach in ways that bring out the complexity already in YA texts, and we can teach students to make additional complexity for themselves if we set up a classroom environment that's designed to guide students in blending personal, social, and analytical ways of reading. This act of blending is the essence of YA pedagogy. We teach students to make complexity when we welcome the personal agendas they bring to their reading of a book and then go on to show them what it looks like to shift the lens and read the book in other ways. We set the stage for making complexity when we embrace the complementary nature of personal, social, and analytical dimensions of reading.

But we can't forget that we will be working to develop this pedagogy within what YA author A. S. King (2015) calls "a teen-bashing culture." This low regard for adolescence may be the biggest obstacle of all when it comes to bringing YA lit into the classroom and teaching with a YA pedagogy. Mainstream messages that circulate in schools and our larger society tell us that teenagers are hormonal and impulsive, that they are unthinking and unwilling to work hard, and that their concerns are shallow and superficial. But these messages reflect a concept of adolescence that is a social construction, not a developmental reality (Finders,

1998). They lead us to construct deficit views of teenagers that position youth passively, present their life circumstances as demeaning, and fail to take into account the varied experiences of real adolescents. Instead of recognizing these ideas about adolescence as "a social construct, or a package of ideas and descriptors determined by time and place rather than natural or inevitable characteristics" (Sarigianides, Lewis, & Petrone, 2015, p. 15), we tend to accept these messages uncritically. We allow stereotypes about teenagers to lower our expectations for teens and their literature.

As we gain experience in our work with teens, we learn to push back on stereotypes and see the individuality in our students. To become more skillful and sophisticated in our teaching of YA literature, we also need to push back on the ways social constructions of adolescence have set us up to think about YA lit. When we bring these books into the classroom primarily because we believe students will "relate" to them, we're still operating out of culturally constructed ideas about teenagers (Sarigianides et al., 2015). Even as we offer students books that we hope will have "teen appeal," we need to unpack all the different things that *appeal* can mean. Different works of YA lit will have greater or lesser appeal to different teens. The same book may appeal to different teens for different reasons. Readers' experiences with YA lit are far more varied and complex than social constructions of adolescence would lead us to believe.

As teachers of teens and teen lit, we may need to rethink assumptions about YA lit that we haven't previously thought to question. To give students the reading experiences they deserve—experiences that engage them emotionally while challenging them intellectually—we must move beyond thinking that the main reason to teach young adult literature is because of its assumed teen appeal. That's not to say that teen appeal isn't important. It is. But our students will be better served if we develop a more complex vision of how and why YA lit might matter in the classroom and what it has to offer *as literature*. Once we discover for ourselves how YA lit explores serious issues, gets at emotional truths, and gives readers windows into the humanity of other people, we can start to imagine new and better reasons for teaching it.

Just putting books in students' hands isn't enough. To mine the richness of YA literature, we need to call students to the work of making complexity. As author John Green put it in a podcast interview I conducted with him, if teens "can be in a place where they feel safe, they feel like they can have fun, but at the same time they're being called to thoughtfulness, and they're being convinced that intellectualism, thinking with some depth, has quality to it, then it's magical what can happen" (Buehler, 2009). Green is right. Magical things can happen when we take teens seriously, and the environment we create has everything to do with whether teens will engage thoughtfully as readers of YA lit. Our stance toward these books, and the approach we take toward reading them in school, will determine how students respond.

Stance and approach are both crucial elements when it comes to teaching young adult literature effectively. Making complexity is about finding the sweet spot in reading and in teaching by blending personal, social, and analytical experiences with texts. By teaching students to make complexity in their reading of YA lit, we set them up to do more and get more as readers of this literature.

Pushing Back on the Lexile Approach to Complexity

Before I move on to offer a framework for finding the complexity that's inherent in our best YA texts, I want to first say a bit more about the dominant way of talking about text complexity in education today—complexity as a Lexile score.

In recent years, the conversation about reading has been dominated by talk of Lexiles. Given that in secondary classrooms we typically encounter students whose reading levels vary widely, it may seem logical to have a system for sorting texts and readers. It's true that some books contain longer sentences and harder words than others. As a general rule, if we want to promote reading growth, it makes sense to avoid giving students books that are too easy or too difficult. With the help of Lexile measures, the conversation goes, we can match readers with texts at just the right level of complexity.

The Lexile framework has proved to be attractive to schools as well as publishers. Sales of leveled reading programs are strong, especially in districts serving large numbers of students who are reading below grade level. In fact, many reading intervention classes are organized around Lexile levels; so are many state and national reading assessments. With the widespread use of programs such as Accelerated Reader 360 and Read 180, the quantitative approach to evaluating text complexity has taken a firm hold on our profession.

When I first began hearing about Lexile levels, I didn't know what they were. What I did know was that the topic of Lexiles was a lightning rod in the conversation about reading. While curriculum coordinators in some districts were embracing this approach to selecting reading materials and assessing readers, the literacy leaders I knew were rejecting it (see, for example, Lesesne's posts about Lexiles on her blog, *The Goddess of YA Literature*, e.g., "What the 'L,' Part 2" (July 16, 2015), and Miller's posts on *The Book Whisperer*, e.g., "Guess My Lexile" (July 5, 2012). Their critiques of the Lexile framework were so scathing I didn't give the topic further thought. And yet it kept coming up—even in out-of-school settings and even in my own community.

I realized I needed to start paying more attention to Lexiles a couple of years ago, when, in the morning carpool, my son and his friends were talking about the books they liked to read. I heard them list genres that middle school boys often love: sports books, funny books, adventure books, nonfiction books. Then, in passing, our neighbor JR mentioned his Lexile level. I wondered, does JR think this number is meaningful? Does he use it to choose the books he reads at school? Does his teacher? Does his Lexile score tell him something about who he is as a reader? Does it limit the range of books he's given access to?

The topic of Lexiles came up again a few weeks later when I was looking up books online. In my everyday reading life, the electronic catalog on my local library's website is one of my go-to YA resources. Whenever I hear about an interesting new YA title in a review journal or on social media, I look it up at the library. If the book is in the collection or on order, I put in a reserve request. This system allows me to get copies of new titles as soon as they come out, and it ensures that I always have an appealing stack of books in my to-be-read pile. In the course of exploring the catalog, I noticed there was a new listing at the bottom of each children's and YA book page. After the typical copyright information, someone had added a category for the book's Lexile measure. Why, I wondered, did the library staff decide that Lexile information was important to include in the catalog? And who, among thousands of library patrons, was using it? Maybe it's intended for teachers, I thought, or parents in search of books that fit what the school has told them about their child's reading level. If the school provides a child's Lexile score, parents may feel a responsibility to select reading materials in the appropriate Lexile range.

I knew the Lexile approach was flawed, but I'd never taken the time to find out why. Here was this numerical label that kept popping up in my reading life, and I had no idea where it came from or how it was determined. Through a little online research, I learned that the Lexile concept was first introduced in the late 1990s by analysts working at MetaMetrics, a private education measurement company located in Durham, North Carolina. Programmers developed computer software to measure word frequency and sentence length in 125-word chunks of text. Books are broken apart into those 125-word chunks, a Lexile measurement is calculated for each one, and then all the measurements are averaged to produce a Lexile level for the text as a whole. No wonder so many educators reject Lexiles, I thought. Sure, numbers measure *something* in a text, but what good are numbers when they're detached from meaning?

As an experiment, I began looking up random titles in the library catalog. I was curious to see how different books rated, both in terms of their specific Lexile measure and in relation to one another across the broader Lexile scale, which extends from Beginning Reader levels below 100L upwards to 2000L and beyond.

I started by looking up a handful of classic YA titles. As expected, I found books at a range of Lexile levels, from Laurie Halse Anderson's *Speak* at 690L to M. T. Anderson's *The Astonishing Life of Octavian Nothing* at 1090L. Most knowledgeable readers of YA lit would agree that in terms of difficulty, these measures reflect commonsense assessments of text complexity. Both novels are heralded as master works of young adult literature, but because the prose style of *Octavian Nothing* reflects eighteenth-century literary conventions, readers have to put forth extra effort to make sense of its challenging syntax and archaic vocabulary. While these Lexile measures are reductive, and while they fail to do justice to either book's power and importance, I could concede that at least they are logical, given the way these two books are written.

I continued my search for other well-known YA titles, noting that most fell somewhere in the 600L to 1000L range. In the 600s, I found Sherman Alexie's *The Absolutely True Diary of a Part-Time Indian* (600L), Walter Dean Myers's *Monster* (670L), and Paolo Bacigalupi's *Ship Breaker* (690L). Ascending the scale, I found Markus Zusak's *The Book Thief* at 730L, Suzanne Collins's *The Hunger Games* at 810L, John Green's *The Fault in Our Stars* at 850L, and Andrew Smith's *Grasshopper Jungle* at 910L. Again, based on what I know about each of these books, I could accept the general logic of their Lexile measures. I didn't necessarily like it, but I could accept it.

However, when I looked on the Lexile.com website and discovered a chart that lists Lexile text ranges "to guide reading for college and career readiness" (http://cdn.lexile.com/m/cms_page_media/123/Lexile%20Map_8.5x11_FINAL_ Updated_May_2013_Grayscale.pdf), I learned that books in the 740L to 1010L range are designated for readers in the fourth and fifth grades. Even though a note beside this chart states that a book's Lexile measure "should not be the only factor in a student's book selection process" and other factors such as "age-appropriateness, interest, and prior knowledge" should also play a part in matching books with readers, I was alarmed. Faced with the pressure to choose books viewed as appropriately complex to prepare students for college, many high school teachers will write off books that fall within this Lexile range, even though that is where we find some of our best YA literature.

Things became even more complicated when I started looking up literary classics. Working from a mental list of books that serve as staples of the middle and high school literature curriculum, I began plugging in titles. I wasn't surprised to discover that the classics also spanned a range of Lexile levels. What did surprise me was how close in Lexile level these classics are to the YA titles I'd just examined. I found *Of Mice and Men* down at 630L, followed by *The Odyssey* and *The Catcher in the Rye* at 700L and 790L, respectively. Next was *To Kill a Mockingbird* at 870L, and up at the top, *The Adventures of Huckleberry Finn* at 990L.

How are we to make sense of these Lexile levels? How do we understand that these venerable titles—books we revere for their cultural importance, books we hold up as important to teach in school precisely because of the challenge we say they provide our students as readers—measure the same as young adult literature when it comes to Lexile level? If we buy into this quantitative paradigm in the debate about what makes a complex text, we find that YA lit holds its own. Within the Lexile framework, you can show me a classic, and I can show you a work of young adult literature that provides an equally complex reading experience. But imagine walking into any teacher's lounge in the United States and making that argument to a group of English teachers. They would find the notion laughable. Sure, a classic and a work of young adult literature might measure the same in terms of Lexile level, they would say, but there's a lot more at stake when it comes to complexity. So how helpful, really, are Lexile levels?

What I take from my brief study of Lexiles and quantitative measures of texts in general is that they don't get us very far in the conversation about text complexity. On the one hand, it may be helpful for YA lit advocates to know that in terms of word frequency and sentence length, many of our most popular and respected YA titles are equally positioned with the classics. This is a useful point to be able to make in defending the use of YA lit in the secondary classroom. But the more digging I did in the library catalog, the more arbitrary the Lexile framework became. A title that is truly appropriate for fourth and fifth graders, such as Jeff Kinney's *Diary of a Wimpy Kid* (1000L), falls in the same Lexile range as *Lord of the Flies* (770L), a book we commonly teach in high school. This is silly. We need more complex ways of thinking about complexity.

Finding It: Complexity That's Inherent in the Text

If we want to be able to offer students and colleagues a different approach to finding the complexity inherent in YA texts, it helps if we can offer them something concrete. Part of the popularity of the Lexile framework is its simplicity. The Lexile program focuses on just two text elements—word frequency and sentence length. It counts these things and then it cranks out a score.

Those of us who appreciate books for their artistry and themes will never advocate for a scoring system approach to complexity. But we can counter the Lexile framework with a framework of our own—one that takes the form of questions designed to highlight the various and complementary dimensions of a literary text. To take into account the different parts of a text and the ways they work together, these questions need to explore both how the text is written and the content it contains. To put it another way, they must focus on *style* as well as *substance*. Through these questions, we guide readers to notice all there is in a text to discover, and we empower them with a framework for reading and evaluating literature they can take with them once their time in our class is over.

These questions about finding complexity focus on what I have learned to look for and appreciate in books as a result of all the years I have spent as a reader. They invite readers to examine, first, the style of the writing, including language elements such as word choice, sentence structure, and voice; the structure of the narrative, in terms of its organizational devices and form; and other elements that give the text shape, such as epigraphs, footnotes, visual images, and graphic design. The questions go on to explore the substance of the storytelling, including the struggles and inner life of the main character; the world the author has constructed and the details that allow us to enter into that world; the use of literary devices such as metaphor, allusion, repetition, dialogue, and internal monologue; and, finally, the book's themes and the interconnectedness of its textual layers. I wrote these questions to give readers an approach to complexity that's grounded in language, story, and meaning—not in numbers generated by a computer program.

Here are both elements, and questions about those elements, that we might use to help our students find the complexity inherent in the style and the substance of YA texts:

Complexity of Style

- *Language:* Can we find examples of elegance in language use? Are the sentences artfully constructed? Can we hear a rhythm in them? Are the words carefully chosen? Does the author incorporate figurative language or poetic expression? Can we hear voice in this writing?

- *Structure:* What is the architecture of this book? How is it built in terms of form and structure? What organizational devices do we see? How do chapters and sections give shape to the work? How do other elements such as titles and subtitles, vignettes and interludes, shifts between past and present, or multiple points of view work together in service of the whole?

- *Other stylistic elements:* Are there other distinctive elements in the text such as epigraphs or footnotes? What about interesting use of punctuation or italics? What do these elements add to the text? How does graphic design, in terms of visual images or font, expand or enhance content? How do these various stylistic elements work together?

Complexity of Substance

- *Character:* How does the author construct an inner life for the main character? What is there to explore in terms of the character's thoughts and feelings, conflicts and contradictions, struggles, growth, and change?

- *Setting:* How does the author bring us into the world of the story? What details help us to see, smell, hear, and imagine this place? How do these and other details evoke historical or social context? What did the author have to know or find out in order to construct this world and bring us inside it?

- *Literary devices:* How does the author use literary or cultural allusions, intertextual references, dialogue, internal monologue, metaphor and symbolism, magical realism, or repetition to build meaning?

- *Topics and themes:* What questions does the book ask? What ideas does it explore? What arguments does it make? What new lenses does it provide for seeing the world and making sense of our own lives? Where are the epiphanies and what significance do they hold? What is at stake for teen readers in this book?

- *How the book is put together:* How effective is the interplay between plot layers and thematic layers? What thinking is involved in assembling these layers? How do bigger concepts and ideas serve as context for a character's questions and growth? How does the author achieve unity and coherence by connecting stylistic elements and thematic ideas throughout the text?

> **Elements That Help Us Find Complexity in YA Texts**
>
> *Complexity of Style*
>
> - Language
> - Structure
> - Other stylistic elements
>
> *Complexity of Substance*
>
> - Character
> - Setting
> - Literary devices
> - Topics and themes
> - How the book is put together

Putting the Questions to Work

To illustrate what it might look like to take this approach to text complexity, and to provide evidence of the complexity we can find in young adult literature, I offer an analysis of complexity in two ambitious, accomplished, well-loved YA novels: *We Were Here* by Matt de la Peña and *Ask the Passengers* by A. S. King.

Although these books are written in different styles and set in different places, each explores that central question of young adult literature: "Who am I, and what am I going to do about it?" Beyond the power and emotional honesty of their storytelling, both books stand out as exceptional works of YA lit because they place a teen's process of self-definition and self-discovery in a larger social context, and they do so in artful, sophisticated ways.

These are books that appeal to teens as well as teachers, librarians, and critics. (As a side note and a disclaimer, I teach both titles in my college young adult literature class. Based on the positive response from students and the critical conversations they inspire, I bring them back year after year.) YA award committees have celebrated these books with numerous honors. YALSA, the YA library services division of the American Library Association, selected *We Were Here* for its annual list of Best Fiction for Young Adults as well as its list of Quick Picks for Reluctant Young Adult Readers. *Ask the Passengers* was also selected for the BFYA list. It went on to win the *Los Angeles Times* Book Prize, and it was chosen as a finalist for the Amelia Elizabeth Walden Award, which is given annually by the Assembly on

Literature for Adolescents of NCTE (ALAN) to a book that demonstrates literary merit, widespread teen appeal, and a positive approach to life.

To highlight the different forms of complexity these books present, I return to the list of questions and use them to walk you through a close reading of each text. For those of you who are unfamiliar with the books, I begin with brief plot summaries to set the stage for the discussion that follows. Ideally my story overview and subsequent analysis will inspire you to find these books and read them yourself. For those of you who have already read one or both titles, I hope my analysis will remind you of the richness of their writing and the significance of their themes. While these two novels are certainly not the only ones I could have chosen to feature, I include them here because they are personal favorites—books that illustrate the intelligence as well as the heart of young adult literature.

Close Reading to Find Complexity

On the level of text, both *We Were Here* and *Ask the Passengers* offer pitch-perfect dialogue, well-developed settings, figurative language, and allusions to classic literature within an unconventional narrative structure. On the level of story, both books present characters who are struggling to figure out who they are and who they can be given the labels they are burdened with. In *We Were Here*, the context for the story is the juvenile justice system. What does it mean to be a group home kid, and how can you ever escape that label? In *Ask the Passengers*, the context is small-town America. What does it mean to be a teen who is questioning her sexuality, and how can you ever be more than the category others put you in? In both novels, the main character is thinking about his or her life in relation to ideas found in books, what society has told them, and the things they are learning from their relationships with others.

Finding Complexity in *We Were Here*

To explore complexity more closely, let's look first at *We Were Here*.

Summary. When the story begins, main character Miguel has just been sentenced to spend a year in a group home as punishment for an unnamed crime. As part of his sentence, the judge has assigned him to write in a journal so that a counselor can see how he thinks. Miguel doesn't plan on breaking out and running away. That idea comes from Mong, another group home resident. If they can travel down the California coast and get to Mexico, Mong reasons, they can start new lives.

At first Miguel wants no part of this plan. Mong is crazy. He's violent and psychotic. What's worse, Miguel's roommate, Rondell, wants to join them, and he can't even read. But when Miguel looks around the group home and considers his future, he figures he has nothing left to lose. On the night they escape, Miguel grabs the petty cash envelope and their official files. He also packs some of the books he's discovered at the group home: classics such as *The Color Purple*, *Of Mice and Men*, and *The Catcher in the Rye*. On a surface level, we read to find out if the three of them will make it to Mexico. But on a deeper level, we read to find out how they will come to terms with who they are and what they've done.

Complexity of style. Stylistic complexity in *We Were Here* can be found, first of all, in the novel's language. This is a book that's all about voice and the distinctive worldview that voice can reveal. We come to understand Miguel in part through his internal struggles and his interactions with other people. But it's through language—his words and expressions—that we are able to grow close to him as a character. De la Peña writes in a first-person voice that's authentic to who Miguel is and where he comes from. Sometimes that involves street slang and sometimes it includes strategic use of profanity. For example, just after Miguel arrives in the group home, he writes a note in his journal titled "A Serious Question for Whatever Counselor's Reading This":

> Yo, you really think a punk-ass place like this could make a kid *better*? How's that make any sense, man?
>
> Lemme ask you something: If you send a normal kid to a group home with a bunch of dummies for nine months what's more likely to happen? The normal kid ignores all the shady shit around him and gets his life straight, or he just turns into a damn dummy his own self?
>
> For real, think about it. (p. 14)

Miguel is right: identities do get formed in places like this. The power of what he's saying can't be separated from the way he says it. Language helps us to understand how Miguel thinks and feels. Through voice we get an immediate impression of Miguel's bitter attitude and streetwise cynicism. Language develops and reveals his character.

Another form of language complexity in a passage just a couple of pages later shows us a different side of Miguel. After Jaden, the group home counselor, shows Miguel the room where he'll be staying, Miguel sits on his bed and stares at the initials carved into the headboard. In his journal, he writes that in that moment, something clicked in his mind:

> I realized how alone I was. Just another random kid in their system. A half-Mexican ghost from Stockton who messed up his family. I'd spend this year with a bunch of other ghosts from other nowhere places until they said I could leave, and then I'd have to go haunt some other spot. And I was trying to think if I could ever go back home. Maybe when my moms dropped me off she was dropping off my ass for good.

My whole family would probably turn their backs on me. And I'd have to roll solo like this forever.

Anyways, staring at all those initials, the shit hit me hard. I didn't have nobody that cared about me anymore.

Not even my own self. (pp. 16–17)

Here de la Peña's language choices create complexity in Miguel, the scene, and the larger story. Through figurative language, he shows the contrast between Miguel's tough exterior and his inner pain. When Miguel describes himself as "a half-Mexican ghost from Stockton who messed up his family," we get a glimpse of his torment and despair. Tough words take on greater significance when they're paired with metaphors that expose Miguel's hidden vulnerability. By describing group home kids as ghosts who serve their time and then "go haunt some other spot," de la Peña helps us understand why Miguel, and other kids like him, might start wondering what they have to live for. Figurative language captures that mindset in a more complex way than a literal explanation ever could.

If stylistic complexity in *We Were Here* takes shape through language, it's also developed through the book's narrative structure. De la Peña's decision to use journal entries to tell Miguel's story does several complex things at once. Because the entries are written in the present but include flashbacks to the past, we're able to learn about Miguel's life before the group home. Seeing how his life used to be makes his new reality even more sobering and sad. The narrative technique of switching between past and present allows us to piece together what happened in Stockton. Because the flashbacks are often traumatic for Miguel, they invite readers to try to figure out not just what he did but what kind of person he is now that he carries the burden of wrongdoing. Journal entries allow Miguel to admit to himself what he can't and won't admit to other people, which is the intensity of his self-hatred. There's complexity in the way de la Peña uses narrative structure to reveal these aspects of Miguel slowly to the reader. The narrative approach mimics Miguel's slow and painful process of dealing with guilt.

A few other text elements contribute to stylistic complexity in *We Were Here*. A poem by Denis Johnson, "From a Berkeley Notebook," serves as the book's epigraph. With lines about encounters with strangers and changes that occur from moment to moment, the poem introduces key themes in the book. Occasional landscape photos, some beautiful, some desolate, appear at turning points in the novel, marking the different phases of Miguel's journey. Finally, at certain moments—most notably when the boys write their names as graffiti on a rock—the book's standard font shifts to one that looks like handwriting. This visual device helps further communicate the idea that Mong, Miguel, and Rondell are human beings. Through words they write themselves into the world, and they show how important it is for every human being to feel seen.

Complexity of substance. On the level of substance, complexity in *We Were Here* arises from the struggle Miguel endures as a character and the way de la Peña connects the different layers of the story to develop larger themes. Identity work is at the heart of the book as Miguel tries to figure out who he is and who he can be in light of the crime he's committed. Part of that work involves wrestling with complex moral questions about the line that separates good from bad and right from wrong. When Miguel thinks about how his own life changed in an instant, he realizes that what happened to him could happen to anyone:

> People always think there's this huge hundred-foot-high barrier that separates do-ing good from doing bad. But there's not. There's nothing. There's not even a little anthill. You just take one baby step in any direction and you're already there. You've done something awful. And your life is changed forever.
>
> And here's the thing: it's not even that your life changes because of what you *did*, I don't even think. . . . People change because they discover that this supposed line between being a good person and being a bad person doesn't actually exist. . . .
>
> It reminds me of when you stand right up near the tracks watching a big-ass Amtrak train barreling toward you. And you think, Yo, I could just take one little step forward, onto the tracks, and I'd be dead. And deep down you assume there's some kind of line there you could never cross. A barrier. Something that wouldn't ever let you take that step even if you tried. But guess what? There's no line. You can do anything. (pp. 119–20)

It's an existential moment for Miguel, and it's one that asks us as readers to grapple with complex philosophical ideas. If there is a line and anyone can cross it, then maybe there's really no difference between good people and bad people. If this idea is true, then what does that mean for the rest of us? Could our lives also change in an instant, just as Miguel's did? Could we too be neither wholly good nor wholly bad?

Throughout the book, Miguel struggles to reconcile himself with the guilt, grief, and regret he carries. He struggles to find a reason to keep living. Interest-ingly, and powerfully, the act of reading proves to be central to his healing process, and it proves to be one of the most complex layers of the entire novel. De la Peña incorporates classic literature, official files, and the stories of others in the arc of Miguel's journey. He shows us what Miguel reads, how he reads, and the different purposes that reading serves in Miguel's life at this time.

When Miguel first arrives at the group home, reading is a way for him to escape: "When I'm following what a character does in a book I don't have to think about my own life. Where I am. Why I'm here" (p. 40). He figures he'll do what Jaden, the group home counselor, told him Malcolm X did in prison, which is take advantage of his time to learn as much as he can. But from the first book he pulls off the shelf, Miguel is doing something more than escaping. He's reading his own life in relation to the lives of others. In *The Color Purple*, which he notes is "pretty much the saddest book you could ever read," what he's most drawn to in the story is how the main character, Celie, survives her pain. "It's mad crazy how just writing letters makes the woman feel better about herself" (p. 40).

He reads a number of other books—*Their Eyes Were Watching God, The House on Mango Street, Of Mice and Men*—but books aren't the only things he reads. As mentioned earlier, when Miguel leaves the group home, he steals the petty cash envelope along with his, Mong's, and Rondell's official files. Eventually he decides to read those files. When he does, he is stunned by what he learns. "How's that even fair?" he wonders. "To have so many bad things happen in one life?" (p. 136). Reading the files changes Miguel. The stories they contain give him new insight into Mong and Rondell as people. Given the traumas they've endured, neither of them can exist as a stereotype for him now. He holds their stories up against his own.

As Miguel continues to read, his thoughts move back and forth between his, Mong's, and Rondell's real lives and the lives he finds in literature. In *The Catcher in the Rye*, he likes Holden's voice and his honesty, but he can't help feeling critical of Holden for complaining about his life when Mong and Rondell "never say a *word* about it, they just deal" (p. 143). Miguel doesn't stop reading about Holden, though, and he doesn't stop thinking. By the time he finishes *Catcher*, the book has won him over, mostly because of how much Holden cares about his little sister. "I got a theory that if a big brother looks out for his little sis he's probably a good person, you know? No matter what bad stuff he might get into" (p. 278).

But *Catcher* doesn't just win Miguel over. It transforms him. De la Peña actively builds connections between Miguel's life and Holden's, and he shows us how Miguel uses Holden's life to gain clarity and to heal. In Holden's story, Miguel finds a model for how to redefine his purpose in the world:

> It was meant to be. Almost like Holden Caulfield and the rye fields. Only I'm not try-ing to save random innocent kids who're running around. I'm trying to make a place where so-called bad ones could come when they wanna get away from the world or even themselves. And not just group-home kids like me, Mong and Rondell. But regu-lar ones too, like I used to be. Ones who maybe messed up once or twice, and now that's how people think of them. When they get here they can talk to me and Rondell and each other. Or they can just keep quiet. Maybe they only need a rest. It could be up to each individual kid. And whenever they're ready they can go back home. (p. 279)

If reading helps Miguel reinvent himself, it also helps him realize that what he's been doing all along is writing his own story. Reading the stories of others shows him that his own story is worth telling. Even though the process is painful, Miguel says he's "writing it anyway 'cause I know that's how those authors I've been read-ing would do it, like in *The Color Purple*. They'd just tell the whole story, no matter how hard it was to say, because people need to read it. That's why I'm telling everything too" (p. 350).

Thus complexity in *We Were Here* exists on many levels at once: on the level of language, character, theme, and intertextuality. Teens who read this book will be challenged to think about how lives get defined and how stories get written. They will see how people make sense of themselves in relation to the texts around them. They will see how de la Peña has done this too in developing Miguel's story. He has written a story that talks to other stories. His book is informed by the books he invokes in the text. His character is in dialogue, at least metaphorically, with other characters. The complexity we can find here resides in all the layers, ideas, and references we are able to unpack.

Finding Complexity in *Ask the Passengers*

For a different but parallel take on complexity, let's look at *Ask the Passengers* by A. S. King.

Summary. Astrid never wanted to move to Unity Valley. It was her mother's idea to leave New York City and return to the small town where her grandmother grew up. But fitting in is hard, especially for Astrid. People think she's weird. Normal girls don't build birdhouses or lie on picnic tables and stare at the sky. What's worse, Astrid might be gay. She isn't sure. The question is confusing and there are deeper issues at stake. What do you do with your love when you don't feel safe to express it? Astrid sends hers up to the passengers flying on airplanes overhead. She figures that if she gives her love away, no one can control it. She'll be free.

But it's impossible to be free in a place like Unity Valley. Behind the façade of perfection, people in this town are small-minded and mean. Reading philosophy in humanities class gives Astrid an antidote. Question everything; know thyself: the messages are powerful and Astrid needs them. But how do you find truth? What is truth for Astrid? For anyone? What would it take to feel less alone? *Ask the Passengers* is the story of Astrid's quest to discover her own truth, challenge the status quo, and summon the courage to construct a different reality.

Complexity of style. On the level of style, complexity can be found in the range of literary devices King uses to develop Astrid's voice and reveal her character. There is much to notice and appreciate stylistically in the text, including metaphors, strategic use of italics, repetition, and internal monologue. These writing choices bring Astrid to life by showcasing her intelligence and wit, and they give readers access to her complex inner world.

The metaphors Astrid uses to describe other people and her environment show how she thinks and what she faces in Unity Valley. They give us insight into her social criticism and dry humor but also her vulnerability. For example, when she says her humanities class is "a little like a shield I can put on every morning that will protect me from people like Aimee Hall and her pack of gossiping, tennis racquet-hugging compulsive hair-straighteners" (p. 21), we learn that intellectual ideas fortify Astrid and why such fortification is necessary. We learn that with the exception of humanities class, the school week "is like a holding pattern. It is the invisible man. It is a black hole" (p. 84). Most of the time, Astrid feels like she's at the mercy of classmates who have a knack for "making shit up and spreading it like mulch so the weeds of sanity can't poke through" (p. 86). In certain moments when she's alone, Astrid glimpses her real self in the mirror—"the me who's waiting to come out"—but to cope, "I stuff her back inside my Unity Valley suit" (p. 90).

Through these metaphors, we see Astrid's isolation and her yearning. But that's not King's only stylistic method for showing us the dimensions of Astrid's character. Another distinctive element of the text is the use of italics. King marks many things in the text with italics, but they work most powerfully when she uses them to present foolish or upsetting statements made by other people. These statements are always followed by brief internal monologues that illustrate Astrid's response to what she's just heard. We see this combination for the first time in a passage that introduces readers to Astrid's family and Unity Valley:

> Mom says: *You two have a chance to really fit in here. Your father and I will always stick out because—well, you know—because of our education and our way of thinking. But you two can really be small-town girls.*
>
> Ellis bought this. She's living it. As far as I can tell, it's working for her.
>
> Mom says: *We have so much space here! The supermarket is so big! The roads are safe! The air is clean! The schools are better! No crime! And the people here stop and say hello!*
>
> Sure, Mom.
>
> They stop and say hello, and then once you pass, they talk the back off you like you were nothing. They assess your outfit, your hairstyle, and they garble what you say so it comes out ugly. If I don't hear it firsthand, I hear it secondhand.
>
> About black kids: *I hear that Kyle kid got himself a scholarship. Had to be black to get it. I can't see how that's fair.* Jimmy Kyle got that scholarship to Villanova because he's a straight-A student and wants to go to law school.
>
> About the two Latino freshman girls: *The parents don't even speak English. This is America, isn't it?* Franny Lopez is third-generation American, and her parents don't even speak Spanish. Michelle Marquez's mother has it bad enough without having to learn a second language. Mind your own business.
>
> About my family: *Did you see they have birdhouses all over their yard? I don't know about you, but that's inviting bird shit, and who wants bird shit?*
>
> They say: *It's just not natural that he makes his girl use a hammer.*
>
> Maybe this sort of thing happens in your town, too. (p. 7)

King's stylistic moves here are clever, efficient, and powerful. By placing the things Astrid hears in italics, King marks those statements as outside of Astrid and different from her own ways of thinking. By introducing each statement with a colon and writing the taglines in present tense ("Mom says," "they say"), King shows that such statements are not unique speech events, but rather the kind of thing Astrid hears all the time. Passages like this one show us that Astrid didn't become different when she started thinking she might be gay. She's different because she recognizes hypocrisy, sees through it, and rejects it. King adds one final layer of stylistic complexity by using second-person voice to address readers directly at the end of the scene. It's a meta moment in the text, one that challenges us to pause in our reading and think about the world we live in. When Astrid notes that "maybe this sort of thing happens in your town, too," she's inviting us to apply her social criticism to our own communities. Stylistic complexity resides in all the things there are to notice about the way text features like these work together to construct meaning.

King uses a similar combination of literary devices to illustrate Astrid's internal struggle over whether she is gay. Here the statements in italics depict the recurring sound track of Astrid's thoughts, and the internal monologue reveals the extent of her self-questioning. That questioning is particularly acute after Astrid has seen Dee Roberts, her coworker at their weekend catering job. Whenever Astrid's feelings are jumbled and her mind is confused, she seeks solace by going outside and sending messages to the passengers flying in planes overhead:

> My brain people say: *Astrid, baby, it's because you're not gay.*
>
> They say: *You're not strong enough to be gay.*
>
> They say: *Mom would never forgive you if you're gay.*
>
> I try to stop thinking about it . . . but now all I can think about is Dee and how this all started. How she told me how gorgeous I was. How flattered I felt. How exhilarating it was to be *wanted*. This is why I doubt. It's the loophole. It's the question no one ever wants to ask.
>
> Am I doing this out of desperation? Is it some weird phase I'm going through? And why, if any of the answers are *yes*, does it feel so right?
>
> There is a 747 high, leaving a crisp white line through the cloudless autumn sky. I ask the passengers: *Am I really gay?*
>
> But they don't answer me. They are reading their in-flight magazines and sipping ginger ale. I send them love—as much as I can gather. I ask them: *What do I do now?* (pp. 38–39)

In scenes like this one, stylistic complexity helps to convey Astrid's unsettled frame of mind. By using the tagline, "My brain people say," King personifies Astrid's thoughts and shows how they seem to live physically inside her. Her brain people have taken up residence; they are visitors she can't get rid of. By using italics to present both the things Astrid's brain people say and the questions she sends up to the passengers, King shows how Astrid tries to manage her confusion. It's another meta element in the text, one that illustrates how Astrid thinks about *what* she thinks and how she tries to figure out what to do next.

The other major way King builds stylistic complexity into the text is through her approach to narrative structure. Each chapter is written as a collection of short scenes that allow us to follow Astrid through the different contexts she must navigate, from the family dinner table to the hallways at school. Then, in a parallel narrative layer, many chapters also include a vignette that features the story of an actual passenger on an airplane. Designed to look something like a flight report, these vignettes are set off from the rest of the text. They are printed in a different font and marked by the icon of an airplane, which is followed by a heading that includes a passenger number, the passenger's name and seat number, the flight number, and the arrival and departure cities.

The timing of the scenes and vignettes is such that we read a moment in Astrid's life and then the vignette shows us what's happening in that same moment in the life of a passenger. The featured passenger has no direct link to Astrid. Rather, King juxtaposes their stories and then leaves it up to the reader to figure out how they connect. This is an example of how the stylistic complexity of the writing contributes to the thematic complexity of the novel. Through this textured and layered narrative structure, King offers readers a complex reading experience. The novel's themes about love and truth become more significant and universal when we read Astrid's story in relation to the stories of others.

Complexity of substance. Readers who don't know better may be tempted to label *Ask the Passenger*s as a simple coming-out story—if there is such a thing. While Astrid's process of questioning is certainly at the heart of the novel, two other story layers add complexity to the book's themes and extend its purpose. They also extend those meta aspects of the text I mentioned earlier. One is intertextuality and the other is magical realism.

King introduces the element of intertextuality with a set of three epigraphs that frame the story. Although normally I would mention epigraphs in a discussion of stylistic complexity, the content of the epigraphs in *Ask the Passengers* guides readers to anticipate complexity of substance. By quoting Euripedes ("Question everything"), Socrates ("The only true wisdom is in knowing you know nothing"), and an ancient Greek aphorism ("Know thyself"), King signals that Astrid's identity work will be rooted in a larger intellectual tradition. This intertextual move, and several others that follow, connect Astrid's quest for self-knowledge to key texts and thinkers in the history of Western philosophy. King shows how reading about the ancient Greeks gives Astrid new lenses for thinking about her own reality.

When Astrid discovers the figure of Socrates in humanities class, his life becomes a touchstone for her own. As she learns how Socrates lived, Astrid gains the courage to live her own life differently. Given the pressure to conform, both in

Unity Valley and in her own family, it helps Astrid to know that "his favorite thing to do was to prove to people that what they thought was truth might not be true" (p. 43). It also helps her to know that Socrates's life was unconventional:

> He didn't have a job. He was poor. He didn't even write down his own amazing ideas. All he cared about was truth and living a good life—while trying to define what *a good life* meant.
>
> So if we go by Mom's standards, Socrates was the biggest loser of all time. (p. 44)

There's complexity here not just in the intertextual reference but in the way King shows Astrid using what she's learning to push back against her mother's expectations.

Later, when Astrid reads Plato's *Republic* and learns about the Allegory of the Cave, she develops a deeper critical framework for thinking about Unity Valley. King shows the relevance and the irony of this text in Astrid's life through the scene in which Astrid and her classmates first encounter and react to its ideas:

> We start our unit on the Allegory of the Cave. It's a part in Plato's *Republic* where he wrote a dialogue between his brother Glaucon and his teacher, Socrates. The short version: People chained in a cave are only able to see a wall. The wall has shadows cast from a fire they can't see. They guess at what the shadows are. Their entire reality becomes these shadows.
>
> Clay has read it before. Of course. Knows *all about* the Allegory of the Cave. "The only life these prisoners know is the sounds and shadows of the cave. Imagine living like that!" he says. "Or maybe we are living like that, right?"
>
> Ms. Steck stops him before he can spoil the rest. Apparently there is more excitement to come for the prisoners in the cave. For now, all we have to worry about is a three-hundred-word essay from the point of view of one of these prisoners exploring the realm of belief versus the realm of knowledge.
>
> Which, if you think about it, is a really funny subject to explore around Unity Valley. (p. 111)

Not only do scenes like this one show how philosophical texts work inside *Ask the Passengers* to support its themes about questioning and rewriting reality, but on a meta level, they also show how the Western canon can still be important in the lives of teenagers. Astrid's experience in humanities class illustrates why people read the classics, and it introduces teens to a more complex understanding of the purpose of literature. Her reading of Plato's *Republic* reminds us that people turn to ancient texts as a way of joining a larger conversation about what it means to be human. Great Books courses exist because readers want firsthand experience with the ideas those books contain. In *Ask the Passengers*, humanities class provides Astrid with that experience. King's use of intertextuality situates Astrid's story in the larger world of thinkers and the longer arc of intellectual and cultural history.

Philosophical texts are the gateway into Astrid's process of grappling with life's great questions. Even more important, when teens see Astrid read in this way, they are exposed to a model of what it might look like to do that kind of reading themselves.

The last major aspect of complexity in *Ask the Passengers* is King's use of magical realism. Soon after Astrid begins reading about Socrates, she decides that she wants him to have a more familiar name—"something laid back and modern, so I can relate to him better." She stares at the picture in her textbook, and by the end of study hall, she names him Frank. Frank Socrates. "Makes him more huggable," she says (p. 53).

We could laugh at this move and write it off as silly, but soon Astrid is calling on Frank (she calls him Frank S.) for emotional and moral support. At key moments, she conjures his presence, willing him to appear. For example, when she goes to a gay bar with her friends for the first time, Frank S. shows up as a natural part of the scene, "edging in like he's about to order a drink." Astrid explains that he's smiling, too, "because it's my brain that put him there." She tells us that he puts her at ease, "which is better than how I felt up until now as a robot" (p. 72).

As readers we wonder what to make of Frank S. Is he really there? Is he a hallucination? Or is this some kind of magic in the story? The beauty of magical realism is the complexity it adds to the text, because the answers to all of these questions are elusive. All we know is that Astrid sees Frank S. in these moments. She experiences his company and his presence is a comfort to her. As the story continues, Frank's contributions become more strategic. When Astrid is doing well, he just smiles and gives her a thumbs-up (p. 151). When her troubles deepen, he speaks. At one point, he shows up on a bench by the back door of her house. Astrid waves to him, but he isn't smiling. "Shame you had to lie," he says. "I just didn't think it was the right time," Astrid replies. He nods and asks, "Is there ever a right time?" (p. 170). Later, when Astrid is at her lowest, she asks herself, "*Just how many things do I have to invent in my head to survive this?*" She makes Frank S. appear, and he gives her his answer. "As many as it takes," he says (p. 188).

In this way, Frank S. becomes Astrid's conscience, her moral compass, and her spirit guide. He is a figure who challenges her to discover and reveal her own truth, no matter how painful. Readers, however, must make their own sense of his role in the story. This requires a different kind of work with the text: a different form of questioning and a different degree of meta-level thinking.

In the end, the complexity of *Ask the Passengers* resides in all that King has given us to work with. Through literary devices, she invites readers to understand Astrid's mind and empathize with her feelings. Through intertextuality, she shows us how Astrid's search for self-knowledge is situated within a larger philosophical tradition of questioning reality and looking for truth. Astrid's story points the way for readers to try out their own readings of philosophy, ask their own questions, and look more critically at their own communities. Finally, by building a novel in which vignettes and magical realism are woven into a central coming-of-age story line, King challenges readers to figure out how different narrative elements work together. The complexity of the text invites us to construct a more complex reading experience.

Owning Our Own Version of Text Complexity

As teachers we need to insist on an artful and nuanced approach to the topic of text complexity. We need to develop arguments that empower us to talk back to quantitative evaluations of texts, and we need to offer an alternative way of framing the conversation. With a systematic method for noticing and naming the complexity in young adult literature, we can demonstrate that the same things we value in the literary canon are present in books for teens. It's true that not every YA novel is equally complex. But books with elegant language, sophisticated narrative structure, artful use of literary devices, well-developed characters, and universal themes are indeed available—and plentiful—in the field of YA lit. When we can demonstrate how YA titles are in dialogue with other classic and contemporary literary texts, we can further advocate for their relevance and worth.

Our arguments will take on greater authority and weight when they showcase both the power of a book's writing and the significance of its themes. The questions I've offered in this chapter can serve as a guide to help readers identify what individual texts have to offer along these parallel lines of complexity. By attending to style as well as substance—that is, by looking closely at a book's individual elements and then stepping back to consider how those elements work together to convey meaning—we can build a solid case for finding text complexity in young adult literature. Not every YA title will pass the test, but a great many will.

When we teach students to make nuanced judgments about complexity, we help them to better understand what different books can give them. By providing them with a framework for thinking about complexity, we empower them as readers. We equip them with tools that will serve them in their reading lives for the long run. We help them become more aware of how texts are put together and more discerning about what books can be good for. With a common vocabulary for talking about text complexity, teens can notice and name an author's distinctive stylistic markers and unique contributions. They can also learn to view every text as one that reflects a series of intentional writing decisions, which sets us up to talk about a book's writing craft as well as its story lines.

These last few pages have made the case for *finding complexity* in young adult literature, revealing the complexity that already exists in these texts if we know how to look for it. We further the case for the complexity of YA lit through the next step: showing how students can *make complexity* in the ways they read YA lit. Teaching through YA pedagogy, which I talk about in the next few chapters, can set them up to do just that.

In school and in life, we should be offering students books that will both stretch and satisfy them. We need books that are carefully crafted and books containing content that will engage students deeply as thinkers. Ideally, students will go on to look for more books like these after they leave us—books that will continue to provide them with meaningful reading experiences. We want them to have the skills to read these books independently and the motivation to keep reading them once their time with us has ended. With young adult literature—and a pedagogy designed to teach it—we invite them to cultivate both.

YA Pedagogy Element 1: Classroom Community

There's a moment in M. T. Anderson's historical YA epic, *The Astonishing Life of Octavian Nothing, Traitor to the Nation*, when main character Octavian pauses to wonder about his circumstances. He puzzles over where and how he's being raised. He begins to reflect on the oddness of his daily life, and he wonders what the scholars at the Novanglian College of Lucidity want from him. "In episodes such as these," Octavian writes, "I began to ponder the mystery of who I was, and what that might mean" (p. 24).

Whenever I try to explain the essence of YA lit to people who don't read it, I come back to this line. Here Anderson captures something essential—both about teen literature and, more broadly, the experience of being human. At some point, we all wonder who we are and what that might mean. We engage in this wondering throughout our lives, but the wondering is most acute in adolescence.

I believe that conversations about who we are and what that might mean should sit at the center of what we do in English class. Fortunately, in many classrooms around the country, where thoughtful teachers cross paths with capable and willing students, they do. But students need to want and be able to read the books at hand for such conversations to take place. Because YA lit is accessible and because it puts so much value on existential wondering and the identity development that stirs, it serves as uniquely powerful material for drawing students into these conversations. Whether the character is a young slave in the American Revolution, like Octavian Nothing, or a youth in juvenile detention, like Miguel in *We Were Here*, the best YA lit takes teens seriously by showing how and why such wondering matters.

Students should expect their English class to be a place where they'll have the chance to hear what their friends think about important issues books raise. They should also expect their thinking about the books to be deeper because of the interactions they have with their teacher and their peers. They should expect that reading will allow them to reflect on their own lives, and they should expect the process of reading books in the company of others to enable them to discover more than they would on their own. Reading YA lit in English class makes all these things possible.

But bringing YA lit into the classroom in and of itself won't make those conversations happen. For our work with YA texts to have quality and complexity, it needs to take place in a rich and vibrant classroom reading community. If we want our students' reading of YA lit to be more than entertainment, we have to create a classroom community that calls students to complex work with these books. And this is where the first core element of YA pedagogy fits in. Our students will make complexity as readers of YA lit if they read in a classroom community that values them, their literature, and the meanings that get created among readers through the texts they share.

Why Is Classroom Community Important for YA Pedagogy?

If we want students to enjoy a feeling of playfulness and fun as YA readers, balanced by moments of seriousness and rigor, we should create classroom reading communities that cultivate rigorous and relevant work with these books. When we offer students the chance to read YA lit in school, we should call them to anchor their experience of discovery and surprise in stories in increasing knowledge of how stories work. We can create conditions that will allow students to feel comfortable together but also challenged and stretched as learners. To thrive as readers of YA literature, they need to feel both.

Classroom community is an essential component of YA pedagogy because it shapes the way students approach the books and make sense of what their reading is for. Classroom community is what determines whether our teaching of YA lit is complex or superficial, memorable or forgettable. Therefore, it's important for us to think carefully about the classroom communities we create—and what they will signal to students about our common purpose in reading young adult literature.

So What Are the Qualities That Distinguish Classroom Community in YA Pedagogy?

What classroom community looks like and feels like is going to differ from place to place. Still, the patterned ways of thinking, believing, and interacting that we see in classrooms guided by YA pedagogy reflect shared principles. Classroom communities become visible in patterns of classroom practice and in shared ways of thinking and believing. If this is true of classroom community in general, what are the distinctive markers of classroom community in YA pedagogy?

To answer this question, we need to look to the stance that teachers and students take toward the books and their collective work with YA lit. Even as teachers adapt their approach to meet the needs of particular students in specific contexts, there are four qualities we can expect to find in common across these classrooms: (1) belief that the work is important; (2) discussions that blend personal response and literary analysis; (3) a sense among students that they are known and valued; and (4) collective investment in a shared experience.

Here's a bit more about each of these ideas.

> *Belief that the work is important.* When teachers approach YA literature with the same seriousness they devote to the classics, and when class discussions focus on connections between books and students' lives, students come to believe that the work matters. Conversations about YA lit feel authentic and real because there's a sense that something important is at stake. Students are being called to clarify their thinking about issues that are relevant to them as teenagers. The books take them seriously. So does their teacher. The work they're being asked to do isn't merely preparation for some future task; it's important right now.

> *Discussions that blend personal response and literary analysis.* Although classroom discussions usually begin with students' personal response to reading, students come to expect that analysis of the text will always be part of their collective work. However, analysis is not merely an exercise. It is done in context and it happens in unscripted moments. As the teacher listens to what students are saying, he decides when to zoom in on plot and stylistic elements of the text and when to zoom out on issues the text raises. By bringing up literary concepts in the course of discussion, he helps students deepen their knowledge of how texts work.

Analysis, blended with personal meaning making, allows students to find and make greater complexity as YA readers.

A sense of being known and valued. Because choice is an element of YA pedagogy, part of the teacher's role is to be a book matchmaker and guide (a concept I introduce in more detail in Chapter 4). As a result of this individual attention, students learn that while the class is about YA lit, it's also about *them*: their preferences, interests, and needs. They have a sense of being known and valued. That feeling deepens during class discussion. Through the books the teacher recommends and the ways she listens to students' ideas, she demonstrates that she sees them as individuals. She will use her knowledge of YA lit to help them get where they want and need to go.

Collective investment in a shared experience. In the YA classroom, students don't read alone. They share their experiences with books and they construct meaning together. Whether they are reading independently, in small groups, or as a whole class, they know they will have opportunities to talk about their reading. They want and need to make sense of books together. They seek out discussion and debate, they listen, and they challenge one another. They know their learning is deepened through the give-and-take of social interaction. Because conversations are about things that matter and because their voices are valued, students become collectively invested in the class. They work together as members of a reading community.

Qualities of Classroom Community in YA Pedagogy

- Belief that the work is important.

- Discussions that blend personal response and literary analysis.

- A sense of being known and valued.

- Collective investment in a shared experience.

I came to these ideas after listening carefully to the ways teachers and students talked and interacted around YA lit in three very different settings. As I reflected on what I saw, heard, and felt in these classrooms, I was struck by the similarities. Whether students were college-bound seniors in a YA elective class, middle schoolers in a reading workshop, or teens whose life paths had led them to an alternative school, they were invested in the books—and in this way of being taught.

This was an epiphany for me, and it was the seed for the ideas I later developed into a framework for YA pedagogy. Only after I spent time in these classrooms did I realize that the mere act of reading YA lit isn't what had turned these students into readers; it was this way of experiencing YA lit in school. Being guided by a knowledgeable and caring book matchmaker, being called to blend personal response to a book with analytical ways of thinking about it, and being immersed in a classroom community where talking about the books was essential to making meaning—this was the pedagogical combination that took students to a deeper place. It was this *pedagogy* that allowed students to thrive as YA readers.

Granted, this is an approach to teaching literature that most of us aspire to enact no matter what texts we teach. My point is that it's an approach that takes on greater power when we anchor it in the teaching of young adult literature. Through the combination of this literature and this pedagogy, students in our classrooms are helped to feel seen and valued—as teens.

I had taught YA lit for many years, but only when I saw it being taught by others did I realize how much pedagogical stance matters. It's one thing to believe in YA lit as a teacher and to know that students connect with this literature. But it's another thing to see what happens when teachers deliberately cultivate a classroom community that takes reading YA lit seriously—and then goes further.

In the next section, I bring you into each of these three classrooms so you can see what teachers and students were doing with YA lit on a particular day when I had the chance to visit. I focus on how teachers' ways of interacting with students and books created classroom communities that fostered enthusiasm for YA lit as well as complex reading of it. After these scenes of classrooms in action, I share some of the things each teacher said to explain her approach to teaching YA lit in response to the needs of her students and the particularities of her school context. Through these portraits, I hope you will begin to imagine new possibilities for the teen readers in your own classroom.

Portraits of Classrooms

Carrie Melnychenko's YA Elective at Huron High School in New Boston, Michigan

The context. Huron High School is an 870-student public high school located in a small town in a suburban area of southeast Michigan. After several years of success teaching YA lit in the context of a literature circle unit in her tenth-grade English class, Carrie designed and launched a YA elective. Students who take her YA literature class are sophomores, juniors, and seniors of all academic ability levels. They spend one trimester in her course, which is co-taught with special education teacher Leslie DesJardins.

The classroom. When I step inside the door of Carrie's classroom, the first thing I notice is the walls. They're covered with images of books. Posters of movies based on YA novels hang throughout the room. So does student work. One bulletin board contains printouts of YA book covers in row after tiny row, like a colorful patchwork quilt. In the back corner, the branches of a leafless tree are strung with handmade paper ornaments, each of which features the title of a YA novel on the front and an accompanying student testimonial on the back.

Just inside the front door, a small wooden bookshelf offers copies of books to check out. I recognize many of the titles on display: *Reality Boy* by A. S. King. *Boot Camp* by Todd Strasser. *The Fault in Our Stars* by John Green. *The Impossible Knife of Memory* by Laurie Halse Anderson. *Tyrell* by Coe Booth. The sign at the bottom reads, "Books That Teens Love." Along a side wall, two wardrobe-size shiny silver cabinets contain all the lit circle titles and whole-class novels Carrie has accumulated over the course of four years teaching this YA elective. Between the books and the environment around the books, this is a room that calls students to be readers.

The lesson. While we wait for students to arrive for fifth hour, Carrie tells me they're nearing the end of their whole-class reading of Dana Reinhardt's *How to*

Build a House, a novel about love, divorce, and family. Discussions over the past few days have triggered heated debates about the causes and consequences of cheating in romantic relationships. Carrie wants to keep the conversation going, but she also wants to ensure that classroom talk stays appropriate.

As students file in, I listen to their chatter. Most are seniors. With just two weeks of school left and prom on Friday, they have a lot to think about: graduation, colleges, jobs, their futures. That's part of Carrie's reason for choosing this book. Her students are on the brink of adulthood, and so is Harper, the book's main character. Their reading of the novel has focused on literary elements, character development, and writing craft, but it's focused just as much on the lives students are building for themselves.

Once the bell rings and students settle into their seats, Carrie begins with a warning. She reminds them that she appreciates their honesty and she values their open discussions, but those discussions need to be mature. "So think about what you say before you say it," she cautions. "I don't want to jeopardize what I have with this class on YA lit. It's too important to me. And I think it's important to a lot of you, too."

Then she shifts into their work for the day by introducing the warm-up question that students are recording in their reading logs. The question is simple: what advice would they give Harper at this point in the book? She's becoming close to Teddy, the boy whose house the group is rebuilding, and she's struggling to sort out her feelings. Can she trust Teddy? Is she ready to be in love again?

As soon as Carrie opens the floor for discussion, students start to volunteer opinions. Most say that Harper should be careful. She was burned in her last relationship, so now she has greater fear of being hurt. She's also going to leave Tennessee at the end of the summer and go home to California. Most students agree that Harper needs to protect herself.

Daniel interjects a different point of view. "You don't *know* she's going to get hurt. She's *afraid* of getting hurt. But I mean, everyone is."

Carrie lights on his comment. "Wow, I like what you just said. Say that last part again."

"Obviously it happened to her once," Daniel says. "She's going to be afraid of it. But, like, everyone is."

Carrie repeats his statement: *Everyone is*. We sit for a minute, letting the words sink in.

> ### *How to Build a House* by Dana Reinhardt (Wendy Lamb Books, 2008)
>
> Main character Harper has chosen to spend the summer in rural Tennessee building a house for a local family who lost their home in a tornado, but what she's really seeking is escape from painful losses she's experienced after her father and step-mother's divorce and a betrayal by her boyfriend. As Harper and her fellow teen volunteers learn the steps involved in building a house (Step One: Select the Perfect Site; Step Two: Lay the Foundation; Step Three: Put up Walls), they also explore what it takes to build lasting relationships with other people. 2009 ALA Best Books for Young Adults.

Debate continues about whether Harper is setting herself up for heartbreak and whether long-distance relationships are possible. Someone says you have to just commit to making it work. John poses a question. "How do you know you can make it work?"

Once again, Carrie interrupts the conversation and draws students' attention to their classmate's exact words. "Man, John asked a really big question right now, and I wish I had an answer. How do you know it's going to work?"

A girl offers the example of her grandparents, who just celebrated their golden wedding anniversary, but Carrie circles back to the question of how do you know. She mentions a few details about her own twenty-year marriage. "I know there are little things you do to make it work," she says. "But I don't think at first you *do* know for sure. It's a risk, isn't it?"

After a few more minutes of conversation, Carrie turns the focus back to the book. She wonders why no one is concerned about Teddy getting hurt. Rosalie thinks it might be because Teddy isn't the main character. Other students chime in with talk about gender roles. Carrie mentions that she's been teaching the book for several years and only today did it dawn on her that she's never challenged students to consider Teddy's feelings.

After a few more minutes of talk about emotional vulnerability and generational differences, Carrie sits down in a brown leather office chair that she's placed at the front of the room. She opens her copy of the novel and reminds students where they left off yesterday. Then she begins to read aloud.

Students follow along in their own copies, and for the next twenty minutes we listen as the rhythm of Carrie's voice draws us into the story. Every so often she pauses to pose a question or make an observation. Discussion still centers on relationships, but it also touches on literary elements such as foil characters and the significance of specific details in the text. From time to time, Carrie poses questions about Reinhardt's choices as an author. "Authors put things in there for a reason," she says. "Why do you think she put that scene in the book? What's the purpose of it?"

When there are just a few minutes left before the end of class, Carrie closes the book and instructs students to finish the chapter on their own for homework. She asks them to keep thinking about the issues they discussed today: relationships, choices, and the complexity of their teenage lives.

Markers of Community in Carrie's Classroom

What's most striking to me about Carrie's classroom is the student buy-in I observe. These are teens who are primed to talk about literature and deeply invested in relating literature to their lives. The four markers of classroom culture in YA pedagogy are apparent in the way students interact with the book, Carrie, and one another.

Belief that the work is important. Whether Carrie poses a question about an ethical issue in the novel or Reinhardt's writing, students are poised and ready to answer. They respond to Carrie, but they also direct their comments to one another. They sometimes disagree. Instead of evaluating their answers as right or wrong, Carrie often responds with a wondering of her own, which signals to students that she is participating alongside them in the process of shared meaning making. In this room, Harper's choices matter. That's because implicit in her choices are deeper questions about how to be in relationships with other people. Everyone in the room has a stake in that.

Discussions that blend personal response and literary analysis. Carrie is open to the personal things students want to share. Her questions often center on students' experiences and the opinions they are forming. But there is no question that this is an English class. Throughout the lesson, Carrie is at the helm, bringing their focus back to the book, asking them to speculate on what's happening in the story, and directing their attention to literary elements in the text. There is no script for what she's doing, but she's clearly guiding students to think about the story through a literary framework.

A sense of being known and valued. Students' desire to talk reveals their trust in Carrie. They can tell she is genuinely listening from the way she leads discussion: highlighting points made by individual students, sharing pieces of her own life as students share theirs, and taking it all seriously. They know she will make room for each person's voice. At the same time, they know she will hold them to a high standard. She tells them this directly when she reminds them of her expectations at the start of class. She also tells them directly that the course matters to her, just as she knows it matters to them.

Collective investment in a shared experience. Students' investment in this book is rooted in the social dimension of Carrie's classroom. They want to hear their classmates' opinions on the issues the book raises because those varied perspectives give them more to think about. Hearing Carrie read the story to them adds to their sense of investment. As they listen to her voice, they experience the book together.

Carrie's Rationale

When I ask Carrie about her reasons for assigning *How to Build a House*, she emphasizes the relevance of its content to students' lives. Because the book focuses on multiple kinds of relationships, including those with parents, siblings, friends, and romantic partners, it gives her the opportunity to get students talking about what constitutes a healthy relationship and what isn't healthy. The book's treatment of divorce is also powerful for students, many of whom have had their own experiences with blended families. "The discussions they have because of this book are amazing," she says. "And they're honest and they're raw. It's almost like they never got to talk about this in four years of school, and all of a sudden they have a chance. They *want* to talk about it."

At the same time, Carrie stresses that students want more than a therapy session from the YA lit class. "Collectively my students want to be able to analyze something. Author's craft. Character analysis. *Something*. They want the chance to chew on it for a while and rethink their thoughts on things." Their ability to do so is directly linked to Carrie's stance as a teacher. She is intentional about listening, questioning, and valuing what her students have to say. She notes that a student once told her the reason so many teens hate reading in high school is because teachers ask questions they already know the answers to. For that very reason she doesn't work from a teacher copy of the novel. "I'm not here to tell them what's in it, as if here I am, the guru of the book. No, I'm going to sit back in my chair and go, what do you think? What would you do? It becomes a big conversation. That's what they like. Those are the things they'll remember."

Daria Plumb's Modern Readings Class at Riverside Academy in Dundee, Michigan

The context. Housed in a former church and located in a residential neighborhood, Riverside Academy is an alternative high school that serves about fifty students in a rural part of southeast Michigan. Most students are referred to Riverside, usually by their principal, because they've fallen behind academically. Some ask to come to the school because they feel they need a new start or a smaller environment. A few are there because they've been expelled from other programs. Almost all manage serious challenges outside of school such as struggles with substance abuse, involvement with the juvenile court system, frequent moves, loss of a parent, or being a teen parent.

Daria teaches YA lit in a yearlong course called Modern Readings that's part of Riverside's four-course English sequence. Since there are no elective offerings and no other English teachers at the school, all students study YA lit with Daria. In addition to the YA course, students also read YA books on a daily basis just before lunch in a time slot designated for school-wide silent reading.

The classroom. Daria teaches YA lit in the basement of Riverside. Downstairs from the large common area on the main floor where students gather for morning meeting, two classrooms are shared by four teachers. The feel of Daria's room is spare: instead of desks, students sit in groups at round or rectangular tables. A world map hangs on one wall and a blank whiteboard hangs on another,

but apart from a clock and wooden letters that spell *Hollywood*, there are few decorations of any kind. That's because the focus of this room is books.

Books are everywhere. One wall holds a series of homemade wooden shelves, the kind made from long strips of lumber that rest on metal brackets. A couple of the boards bow slightly under the weight of books that are double stacked. Rows of titles in the back are hidden behind assorted piles in the front. The sign above them reads "Realistic Fiction." A side alcove contains a line of freestanding wooden shelves that rise chest high. These hold titles grouped into other genre collections: sports fiction, nonfiction, dystopian fiction, humor. Books are in stacks, books are leaning sideways, books are scattered about on tops of flat surfaces. The arrangement is messy but in a lived-in way. This is a room where books are being read, shared, and enjoyed.

The lesson. Upstairs, the morning meeting is underway, but Daria has pulled me aside for a quick chat before class begins. Yesterday students got their first taste of John Green's *The Fault in Our Stars*, which they are considering for their next whole-class novel, but after listening to Daria read aloud the first seventeen pages, they aren't convinced the book is for them.

The Fault in Our Stars by John Green (Dutton Books, 2012)

Here is a book that needs no introduction. A *New York Times* bestseller, a popular movie, and one of the strongest crossover titles since Harry Potter, *The Fault in Our Stars* explores the relationship between Hazel Grace Lancaster and Augustus Waters, teenagers with cancer who fall in love. 2013 ALA Best Fiction for Young Adults.

Soon the students file in and Daria takes roll. She starts class with a recap of their first pass at the novel from yesterday. Then she throws out a question: "How many of you don't like this book so far?" she asks. When she calls for a show of hands, I'm surprised at the number that go up, but Daria is unfazed. "Okay, what's the problem?" she asks.

Students call out complaints: "It sucks!" "It's boring!" "It's depressing!"

Daria laughs at this last one. "It's two kids with cancer!" she says.

They chime in with more complaints: "The female character's not even attractive, so I don't have anything to think about." And then: "It seems too typical." Daria asks, "What do you mean?" "I don't know, the tragic love story," the student replies.

Daria explains what the book is about to the students who were absent. A girl with cancer is going to a cancer support group, which she doesn't like. She's friends with a kid named Isaac who's lost one eye and will soon lose the other. Then she meets Isaac's friend, who she thinks is hot, and they feel an immediate connection.

"My concern is there's too much talking and not enough action," Daria says. "We're going to give it a couple of days and see if we like these characters. If we don't, we're going to bail on it."

She pulls up an electronic version of the text and displays it on the projector screen so that students can follow along as she reads. Augustus Waters is asking if Hazel Grace is a regular at support group, and a few moments later he's telling her she's beautiful.

"Oh my god!" a student calls out.

"Oh my god," Daria repeats. "What's the problem?"

"It's too much talking," the student replies. Other students comment that Hazel is complaining too much. "My grandma had leukemia and she wasn't as bad as that," someone says. "If I was dying, I'd be going out," someone adds.

Daria redirects the flow of conversation. "So let me ask you this," she says. "You know in stories—you know in *good* stories—the main character has to change. So do you think Hazel will change?" Some students say no. Others say she might die, given the oxygen tank she's hauling around. Daria continues to probe. "So what happens—" She interrupts herself. "Who's our narrator?" Hazel, the students reply. "What happens if Hazel dies? Could the book just stop, or do you think they'll pick up a different narrator? Sometimes we see dual narrators," she adds.

"We saw three narrators in *Unwind* and two narrators in *Thirteen Reasons Why*. Let's see who picks up in the next chapter."

Daria reads on into Chapter 2. Students notice how Green capitalizes certain words and phrases, like *Cancer Perk*. Daria explains that he does that on purpose to call our attention to them. She mentions that they watched a video of John Green, and she asks them to tell me what they thought of him. "He's on cocaine," one student says. "He could be on an ADD commercial," another adds. Daria laughs at this. "Do you think *that guy* could write a depressing book?" she asks.

They talk a bit more about living with terminal illness. Daria asks what a person's options are. "You can make fun of it," one student says. "You can find humor in anything," another adds. "Or you can whine and complain," Daria says. "What would you guys rather them do? Remember one of the things John Green says," she continues. "He wants these kids to be real teenagers."

She reads a little further, asks for predictions of what might happen later in the book, and then tells students they've reached a stopping point for today. In the time that remains, she invites them to talk to me about their experiences as readers in her class. They call out titles they've enjoyed: *Hole in My Life* by Jack Gantos. *The Perks of Being a Wallflower* by Stephen Chbosky. *Bang!* by Sharon Flake. *Fat Kid Rules the World* by K. L. Going. *I Will Save You* by Matt de la Peña. They talk about their class discussions, how everyone jumps in. They mention writing assignments, how they help you remember the book better. I ask what changes for them over time with books and reading in this class. "I understand them more," one person says. "I find them more interesting," someone adds.

Markers of Community in Daria's Classroom

All the students Daria teaches have come to her school because they were failing somewhere else. Many had never finished a book before. And yet in her class, they become readers. Through their shared experiences with young adult literature, they create a classroom community where reading is who they are and what they do.

Belief that the work is important. Daria's students may push back on *The Fault in Our Stars*, but they're not pushing back on reading. The choice of book matters to them. Even in their complaints, they reveal what they want and need as readers: characters they can picture and think about; stories that aren't typical. In their willingness to be skeptical about this new book, they demonstrate that they aren't there to please their teacher. They would rather hold out for a story that feels right.

Discussions that blend personal response and literary analysis. As Daria seeks students' feedback and vets their gut-level responses to the book, she uses literary concepts to help them understand what's going on in the text. She asks them to think about features they've seen in other books, such as multiple narrators, and consider whether those same features might apply here. She reminds them that there are certain things they can expect from good books, one of which is a main character who changes. In these unscripted moments, she is reminding them of the things they already know about stories, and she's calling them to be discriminating in their approach to this one. In the context of their banter, she helps them continue to build their textual knowledge, zooming in on stylistic devices, such as the use of capital letters to emphasize certain words, and then zooming out to remind them that what they know about the author can add another layer to their expectations for what a book will give them.

A sense of being known and valued. Students trust Daria enough to be candid with her, and she trusts them enough to take their responses seriously. Later I learn that students in this class decided not to continue with *The Fault in Our Stars*. Instead, they chose to read A. S. King's *Please Ignore Vera Dietz*. Daria listened to their opinions and made a change when they were unhappy. Her willingness to act on students' feedback let them know that it was worthwhile to be involved and safe to be honest. She proved to them that their opinions matter.

Collective investment in a shared experience. When Daria reads aloud to her students, they are engaged with her: responding to the story in the moment and connecting what they know and have experienced—in other books and in their lives—to this whole-class novel. They are sharing their experience of the book, just as they have shared the experience of other books. In the process, they are building shared knowledge of stories.

Daria's Rationale

Daria's primary goal is to create readers but to do so in a way that doesn't feel too schoolish. She knows she teaches students who have been alienated from reading in the past. She knows she can change their mindset by giving them a say in what they read and by teaching them about how stories work. That's why she isn't wedded to particular books as whole-class novels, and it's why she focused mainly on the characters and their likability when she introduced *The Fault in Our Stars*. The story itself mattered less to her than students' investment in the story. "I didn't want to hear them complain," she said. "That's not going to be a good experience."

Through shared work with a text, students build shared knowledge about literature. "We can talk about plot, character, setting, and have a common starting point. I know there's debate about whole-class novels. You're not going to reach every kid. But we can look for connections between stories." Sometimes the connections students come up with surprise Daria. In the year the class read Lois Lowry's *The Giver*, followed by Robert Cormier's *The Rag and Bone Shop* and Terry

Trueman's *Stuck in Neutral*, one student pointed out that across the three books, the setting went from a small community, to one room, to the inside of a kid's head. Daria says it wasn't her intention to put the books together in that way, but the student made his own connections.

Over her years of teaching in an alternative school, Daria has also learned that the practice of reading aloud is crucial to her students' overall experience as readers. "We talked about having movies in your mind and picturing it. A lot of my kids had no idea what I was talking about. They'd never had that happen. I want them to listen and try to imagine what's happening. And then we can stop and I can check for understanding." But something more is at stake here than building reading comprehension skills. "They want *me* to read it," she explains. "They don't want to listen to John Green read it. They want me sharing the story with them. There's something very intimate and personal about it. To me that says something really important about what reading is."

Jennifer Walsh's Reading Workshop at Forsythe Middle School in Ann Arbor, Michigan

The context. Forsythe Middle School is a public middle school located in an affluent college town in southeast Michigan. Serving 650 students, around 35 percent of whom are students of color, Forsythe is more racially diverse than either of the other two schools I visited. Jennifer teaches YA lit in three contexts at Forsythe: seventh-grade Language Arts and eighth-grade Language Arts (both of which are mixed-ability classes that she sometimes co-teaches with a special education teacher) and Read 180, a class that targets struggling readers. Jennifer teaches her seventh- and eighth-grade classes as reading/writing workshops with a heavy emphasis on YA lit. She supplements the Read 180 curriculum with whole-class read-alouds of YA novels.

The classroom. It's a Friday when I visit Jennifer's eighth-grade English class, and the first thing I see when I walk down the hall to her room is a sign on her door. Handwritten in blue marker on large white butcher paper, it reads, "Bring your novel!" She's even drawn a picture of an open book with an arrow pointing down to it. Like many other reading workshop classrooms, Fridays are devoted to independent reading.

Inside the room, it's a riot of books and color. One wall is lined with floor-to-ceiling freestanding bookshelves, five in all, each one densely packed with YA lit. Under the long whiteboard along another wall are a couple of shorter shelves that hold more books. On top of one, a picture book about Zora Neale Hurston is displayed next to a couple of bottles of hand sanitizer. A couple of nonfiction titles— Steve Sheinkin's *Bomb: The Race to Build—and Steal—the World's Most Dangerous*

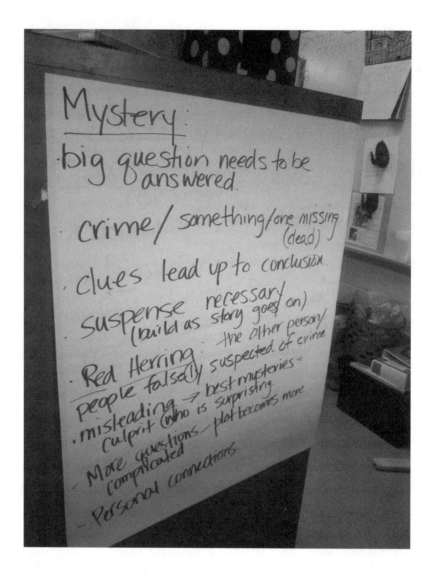

Weapon and Albert Marrin's _Black Gold: The Story of Oil in Our Lives_—are propped on the whiteboard tray. Books in cardboard boxes, books in plastic bins, books on Jennifer's desk: this room is swimming in books.

Other handwritten butcher paper signs hint at structures that guide reading in this class. On the whiteboard, a table of contents reminds students of items that should be in their reading notebooks. On the side of a file cabinet, a butcher paper sign titled "Mystery" features a handwritten list of the elements that readers expect to find in that genre. Next to it, another piece of butcher paper titled "Wall of Questions" offers a snapshot of things students were wondering as they read Laurie Halse Anderson's _Chains_. On a bulletin board in the back corner of the room, cut-out letters in purple and gold ask, "What are you reading?" Beneath the question, construction paper hearts feature students' answers. I study the titles: *Wonder* by R. J. Palacio, *Countdown* by Deborah Wiles, *Matched* by Ally Condie, *Uglies* by Scott Westerfeld, and many more. Just from the visuals, I can tell that reading in this space is dynamic and personal. It's also guided by the kind of literary sensibility we'd expect to find in any language arts classroom.

The lesson. The workshop routine is familiar to me. I take a seat in a tattered upholstered chair in the corner to watch how reading will play out in this setting.

As class begins, Jennifer directs students to update their booklists. It's halfway through the quarter, so they should be halfway to the page number goal they set for independent reading. Students are asking if *Chains* counts and Jennifer assures them it does—all 300 pages.

"Are we going to do a poetry read-aloud?" a student asks. Jennifer says yes. She asks them to pull out their poetry booklets. She projects Langston Hughes's "The Dream Keeper" on the screen at the front of the room and calls a student to come up and read it aloud. Afterward, Billy, her co-teacher, prompts students to respond in writing. "Think of how it relates to *Chains*," he says. "You can relate it to any of the books we're reading," Jennifer adds. "*The Book Thief, To Kill a Mockingbird, Chains*, or even your independent novel." Someone asks the student to read the poem again, and she does.

A minute or two later, they repeat the routine with Emily Dickinson's "Dear March—Come In." "Okay, so this one's a seasons poem," Jennifer says. "Relate it to what March is like for you." Billy adds, "Think about how March is the change of seasons. We start moving into spring. There's always a lot going on—events, holidays, St. Patrick's Day, March Madness if you're into that—a lot of cool stuff happens in March."

When students complete their writing, Jennifer reminds them that their poetry booklets should be inside their reading notebooks, and all of them should be placed up front in the pink milk crate. Then she tells them they have a choice in reading today: they can catch up on *Chains*, they can read for their book group, or they can read their independent book. She offers a listening station for students who prefer to hear *Chains* on audio. Billy tells the students in his group that he's going to check their notes on *Chains*. He expects at least three bullet points about the story each day.

Once students quiet down to read, Jennifer walks around with her clipboard, recording each student's book title and page number on a chart. Then she settles into a director's chair next to her desk and reads along with them. The room is peaceful and calm, and it stays that way until the bell rings.

Since her next class is advisory, Jennifer invites me to stay and ask questions about what I saw. We discuss the book groups—how she designed them to give upper-level readers additional experience with historical fiction. On book group days, Billy works with his students on *Chains* and Jennifer meets with two other groups in the library. I'm interested in how students in those groups made the choice between *To Kill a Mockingbird*, a classic novel, and *The Book Thief*, which is YA. She glances up at a student I recognize from her last class. "Let's ask Grant," she says. "Grant, can you come here for a second? What made you pick *The Book Thief*?"

Grant says it's partly because the story is about World War II, but he was also intrigued to read a book narrated by Death. When I ask how it's going so far, he highlights challenges: how the narrative skips around so it's not all chronological, but how it's a different kind of read for him and he likes it. He also likes the book groups. I ask him what the discussions are like. "We just talk about what's happening and what we think might happen," he says. "Then we go deeper. Not just the story, but what the story is trying to say." He mentions some of the topics they've touched on: Death's interest in colors, how Death is like God, how they don't know Death's gender.

Meanwhile Grant's friend Alex has been listening in. He's another of Jennifer's workshop students, but he's in the same course during a different hour. He

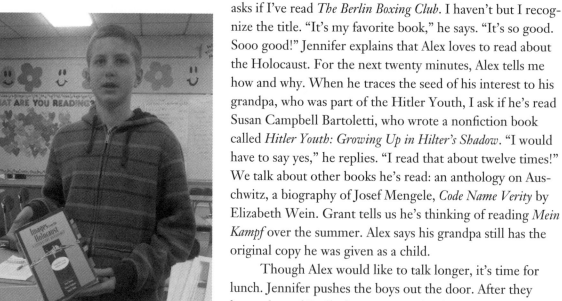

asks if I've read *The Berlin Boxing Club*. I haven't but I recognize the title. "It's my favorite book," he says. "It's so good. Sooo good!" Jennifer explains that Alex loves to read about the Holocaust. For the next twenty minutes, Alex tells me how and why. When he traces the seed of his interest to his grandpa, who was part of the Hitler Youth, I ask if he's read Susan Campbell Bartoletti, who wrote a nonfiction book called *Hitler Youth: Growing Up in Hilter's Shadow*. "I would have to say yes," he replies. "I read that about twelve times!" We talk about other books he's read: an anthology on Auschwitz, a biography of Josef Mengele, *Code Name Verity* by Elizabeth Wein. Grant tells us he's thinking of reading *Mein Kampf* over the summer. Alex says his grandpa still has the original copy he was given as a child.

Though Alex would like to talk longer, it's time for lunch. Jennifer pushes the boys out the door. After they leave, she and I talk about gateway books and the bright energy of these eighth graders.

Markers of Community in Jennifer's Classroom

On the days when students read independently, it takes more digging to identify markers of the reading community they've constructed together. But when I listened to Alex and Grant talk about their experiences as readers in Jennifer's classroom, the same distinctive qualities that I saw in Carrie's and Daria's classrooms became visible to me.

Belief that the work is important. Alex's ability to talk about the connections he made between reading and a topic that he's personally invested in reveals what YA pedagogy makes possible. Students get to explore their interests, develop their knowledge, and improve their skills in a classroom environment where their teacher takes them seriously. Alex's work in this class matters. It's not just about school; it's about his life.

Discussions that blend personal response and literary analysis. Grant's comments about discussion in his book group show that he and his classmates are doing the same kinds of blending that we've seen in whole-class discussions elsewhere. Their discussions about *The Book Thief* begin with their experiences as readers ("what's happening and what we think might happen"). Then they zoom in on specific elements of the text (the character of Death) and its meanings ("not just the story, but what the story is trying to say").

A sense of being known and valued. Even in ordinary questions like the one Jennifer posed to Grant ("What made you pick *The Book Thief?*"), students learn that she is paying attention to them as individuals. She's giving them choice, but she's also developing knowledge about their interests and preferences. That knowledge allows her to guide them to relevant books, track their progress over time, and see them as people with unique interests she can honor and support through reading.

Collective investment in a shared experience. When students come to class on Fridays, they're sharing more than a day of silent reading. They're sharing in practices that give texture and shape to their reading community. Each time they write bullet points in their notebooks, make intertextual connections, or compare their current reading to the goals they set at the start of the quarter, they're creating artifacts of their reading lives. As individual students, they're called to create personal stories about the group experience they've shared.

Jennifer's Rationale

To run this workshop, Jennifer has to read a *lot*. She has to know books and she has to know her students. She has to juggle many moving parts at once: individual reading goals, multiple book groups, and whole-class literature study. It's a daunting amount of work and a big responsibility. But when she tells stories about her students, the payoff is clear. Take the case of Alex.

"Alex could barely read when he got here," she tells me after he goes to lunch. "He could barely read. He wasn't interested in anything. He hated reading. He would tell you he hated reading. He struggled with reading thirty pages a night. He struggled with finding books." Based on the conversation I just had with Alex, I can hardly believe it. Clearly he changed as a reader during the workshop.

We talk about how well Jennifer gets to know her students through their reading. "Of course I have different relationships with these kids than other people do," she says. "I talk to them on a different level. I have to know what their interests are in order to provide books for them. I have to know them differently than teachers who are like, 'okay, here's the textbook.' You know? It's different when you talk about real books."

Developing a Personalized Classroom Community

While the qualities you've just been reading about—belief that the work is important, discussions that blend personal response and literary analysis, a sense of being known and valued, and collective investment in a shared experience—are the hallmarks of classroom community in YA pedagogy, it's important to note that there is no one right classroom community, and there is no one right way of implementing YA pedagogy. Each of us must personalize our work with these books and develop an approach that is right for our context. We have to take into account the needs of the particular teens we're teaching; the demands of the course, the department, and the curriculum; and expectations within the community.

Given that a focus on YA is still not the norm in most English classes, we who teach YA literature have a responsibility to think carefully and strategically about how our teaching will complement, extend, or fill gaps in what students have done in other English classes. We need a vision for teaching YA lit—and we need to figure out what we want our own version of YA pedagogy to look like. The first step is to ask ourselves what our stance toward this literature will be. To clarify our stance, we need to reflect on our beliefs about reading, our goals for students as YA readers, and our expectations for students' social interactions in the classroom. The following questions may help guide this reflection:

- *Beliefs*. What do I believe about YA literature? What are my prejudices about the books? What are my blind spots? How can I complicate my thinking about YA lit so that I will be both open-minded and judicious in my teaching of it?

- *Goals*. What do I want students to "get" from reading YA texts in my class compared to what they would get from reading them on their own and compared to the reading they do in other classes? What do I want students to accomplish through reading YA lit in my class and in this school?

- *Expectations.* Based on my answers to the above questions, what do I want students to come to expect about the ways they will engage with these books in my classroom? What do I want the feel of our room, and our work in this room, to be?

Because our stance toward YA lit as teachers will influence how students think about, talk about, and read these books, stance is the single most important element in classroom community. Once we begin to figure out that stance and shape it, we can work deliberately to construct classroom reading communities that will support our work in YA pedagogy. We can decide in advance the messages we want to send about what kinds of books are worth reading, what reading is for, and why reading matters. Those messages lay the foundation for classroom community and, by extension, YA pedagogy.

Classroom communities don't just happen. We create them from moment to moment through talk and interactions. Our conversations about YA lit and the stance we take in the classroom will create the space students need in order to join with us in *making complexity* as YA readers. When we take YA lit seriously, and when we invite students to invest in shared reading with one another, we take the first steps toward constructing a classroom community that will support meaningful work with these books. Once students experience a vibrant reading community in school, they will continue their reading lives with a richer understanding of what reading YA lit—and reading itself—can give them.

And yet students need more than simply a space in which to read. They need more than the company of their friends as fellow readers. In addition to these things, they need for their reading to be guided by a knowledgeable expert, someone who sees and values them as teenagers and who is prepared to provide direction, both in their individual reading lives and along the larger arc of English class. That's where the second element of YA pedagogy comes into play, which I discuss in the next chapter: teacher as matchmaker.

**Chapter
Four**

YA Pedagogy
Element 2: Teacher
as Matchmaker

Outside the door to Jennifer Walsh's classroom at Forsythe Middle School, an eighth-grade student named Gemma kneels next to a white laundry basket. A fluorescent green sign posted on the wall above it reads, "Free books!" I watch Gemma as she sorts through the offerings. Reading back cover blurbs and flipping through pages, she makes quick decisions about which books to put back and which ones to keep. It doesn't take long before she's got a pile started on the floor. When I notice the book she's placed on top, I feel a sense of connection. It's Gary D. Schmidt's Newbery and Printz Honor novel, *Lizzie Bright and the Buckminster Boy*. I've read this one, plus several others by Schmidt. I'm a big fan of his. I don't know Gemma, but I'd love to start a conversation with her. The first thing I'd ask is what she likes to read and why she added this particular book to her pile.

Later that morning in the teacher's lounge, Jennifer tells me a bit more about Gemma. When she's in school, Gemma is a straight-A student who's ranked at the top of her class. Since last year, however, her attendance has been erratic. She struggles with anxiety. I mention a new YA nonfiction book

I just read on this topic: *Freaking Out: Real-Life Stories about Anxiety*. It's a collection of first-person essays written by teens. I watch as Jennifer opens her laptop and looks up the book on Amazon. Moments later, she's ordered it for Gemma.

Later that week I get a chance to talk with Gemma in the library. As I learn about her reading life, I learn about her as a person. For a while now, Gemma's favorite books have been nonfiction titles related to her struggle with anxiety. "I would go and sit in doctors' offices and hear them talk about all this stuff that I didn't really know about," Gemma says. "So I was like, okay, I'm going to try and learn some of this stuff because it's happening to me. I started reading more nonfiction and memoirs about anxiety and phobias. It makes you really knowledgeable, and I like that. I like to know that I have a good understanding of what's happening to me."

Like all the teens we teach, Gemma is in the midst of figuring out who she is and how to cope with her challenges. What Jennifer understands is that matching students with the right book at the right time (Lesesne, 2003) can make a real difference in that process. Through reading, Gemma has learned more about her own mental health. She's also found reassurance that she's not alone in her struggles. Her reading is personal; it's also purposeful. Jennifer sees the value this individualized reading has for Gemma, and she's willing to spend her own money to support it.

To help Gemma grow as a reader, however, Jennifer needs more than money. She needs knowledge of books—and a commitment to expanding her knowledge each year. That's because for every student like Gemma there's another whose needs are different. If we as teachers truly want to support teens as readers, we must develop broad, deep, personalized book knowledge. As we build that knowledge, it makes sense to invest a good portion of our effort in building knowledge of young adult literature. YA lit might not be the only literature Gemma reads, but in these books she can find information—and characters and stories—that speak to her immediate needs and questions. When we take YA lit seriously, we signal to the students in our classrooms that we take *them* seriously. We can use YA lit to affirm students in the present moment. We can also take them to new places by showing them books they wouldn't otherwise see.

Going Further with Matchmaking

But we can't think only about the needs of individual students when we make book matches. In YA pedagogy, we have to go further and think about the skills we want to teach, the learning tasks we want to design, the conversations we want to have, and the themes we want students to explore through their work with YA texts. That means in addition to students, our matchmaking work needs to consider the curriculum. If we want to stretch teens academically as well as personally through their reading of YA lit, then we need to give careful thought to the books we choose, and we need to make careful decisions about how we will use those books to engage students in different ways over time.

And yet no matter how carefully we plan, we know we face an extra burden when it comes to proving the worth of YA lit. That means our matchmaking work must also take into account the larger contexts of our teaching. We need to consider the classes taught by our colleagues, the expectations for literacy learning in our district, the norms and mores of the local community, and the education policy landscape. We must choose books that we can stand behind as both engaging *and* challenging—titles that are compelling for teens to read but also suitable to the kind of work we expect students to do in middle and high school English classes. We need books that will hold up under scrutiny from officials in the curriculum office, accreditors from the state, and parents who may be nervous to see their teen read texts that depart from the traditional canon. We must be ready with answers when we're asked to explain how reading YA lit will equip students with the knowledge and skills to pass standardized tests, adapt to the latest educational standards, and prepare for college. Our matchmaking work, and our ways of talking about the matches we've made, must be context-specific, politically savvy, and respectful of the teaching that goes on around us.

If this seems like a lot of extra hoops to jump through, or a burden that gets in the way of simply sharing great books with teens, it shouldn't. Approaching matchmaking in this way doesn't have to limit us. On the contrary, it actually gives us a stronger framework for our reading of YA literature and our selection of titles. It helps us become more strategic about choosing titles that meet readers' needs along multiple dimensions, and it prepares us to pitch our work with these books in ways that get various constituent groups on board with what we're doing.

On the other hand, if this approach to matchmaking seems daunting, with too many layers and variables to manage, don't despair. All of us build knowledge of YA lit gradually. It takes time and we don't have to know everything at once. In fact, it's better if we don't. Working slowly and deliberately to develop personal knowledge of YA literature is what will allow us to teach these books effectively in our local context.

Based on who we are as readers and where we teach, we will probably focus more attention on some dimensions of matchmaking than others. Still, by thinking about matchmaking as an interactive process that supports individual students but also takes into account the demands of our individual settings, as well as the current moment in education policy, our book choices and our ways of talking about them will be smarter.

Multiple Dimensions of Matchmaking

So how do we go about reading YA literature and thinking about the work of matchmaking with these multiple contexts in mind? Let's begin with the literature itself. We can start by reading to discover what's available in YA lit—including current, classic, and lesser-known titles. Here are some things for us to keep in mind as we seek to build broad knowledge of YA lit as a field:

- If we commit to using YA titles as foundational texts in our classrooms, we need to build knowledge of the current publishing context. We need to know *today's favorites*, even if they represent a passing fad. If our students are reading these books, then we should pay attention, and we should strive to understand what they offer. Whether it's entertainment, escape, or answers to personally meaningful questions, we can build on these forms of appeal as we bring new books into the classroom.

- We also need to know *YA classics from the past*. As in every other field of literature, certain YA titles stand the test of time. Books like *The Outsiders*, *The Contender*, and *The Chocolate War* are some of our earliest modern YA classics. Each title did something that other books had not done before. It took a risk, offered a new vision, introduced a new voice. Students need to understand that today's authors stand on the shoulders of those who wrote in the past. There is a story to what has happened in this field over the past forty years, and we can draw on that story as we frame the work we ask students to do with YA lit. Their reading of each new title will be more complex—and more informed—if they can connect it to titles written in earlier times.

- Finally, we need to know *YA titles that fly under the radar*. We need to seek out books that teens probably wouldn't find on their own. These are books that don't make the bestseller list and don't get passed around the lunchroom. While they might have more limited audience appeal, they could be transformative for certain readers, and they could serve as gateways to new kinds of literature. Apart from "the big five" publishing houses (i.e., Hachette, HarperCollins, Macmillan, Penguin Random House, and Simon & Schuster), we need to be on the lookout for books from smaller presses: titles that aren't backed by major marketing campaigns and supported by lots of advertising dollars. Annick, Cinco Puntos, Peachtree, and Carolrhoda Lab are all small presses, or special imprints owned by larger publishers, that offer lesser-known but important YA titles.

YA Titles That Fly under the Radar

Some of our strongest and most interesting YA titles are published by small presses. Small publishing houses such as Annick, Cinco Puntos, and Peachtree, and special imprints such as Carolrhoda Lab (a division of Lerner), are often willing to invest in books that explore lesser-known topics and bring us new voices.

For example, in Sharon E. McKay and Daniel Lafrance's *War Brothers: The Graphic Novel*, published by Annick Press, teens can read about child soldiers in Uganda. Through Cinco Puntos Press, teens can read Benjamin Alire Sáenz's historical novel *Sammy and Juliana in Hollywood*, the story of Chicano teens growing up in a New Mexico barrio town during the Vietnam era. Cinco Puntos Press also published the nonfiction graphic novel *Pitch Black*, written by Youme Landowne with artwork from Anthony Horton, which depicts the brief interaction between a white woman and a black man who was living at the time in a tunnel beneath the New York City subway system. Peachtree Publishers brought us Cynthia Levinson's *We've Got a Job: The 1963 Birmingham Children's March*, which tells a previously unpublished history of the Civil Rights Movement, and *Watch Out for Flying Kids! How Two Circuses, Two Countries, and Nine Kids Confront Conflict and Build Community*, the nonfiction account of a youth circus troupe in St. Louis, Missouri, and their sister troupe in Israel. Finally, Carolrhoda Lab published both Sally M. Walker's nonfiction book *Written in Bone: Buried Lives of Jamestown and Colonial Maryland*, a book about forensic anthropology, and Carrie Mesrobian's bold YA novels *Sex and Violence* and *Perfectly Good White Boy*.

Teachers who wish to follow the work of these and other small presses can refer to "Under the Radar," a regular review column published on the ALAN website (http://www.alan-ya.org/publications/under-the-radar-2/).

As we explore YA literature as a field, we must also keep in mind the particular contexts in which our matchmaking work must fit. Here are some principles to consider as we make matches that meet the needs of students, community, curriculum, and policy:

- When we make matches to meet the needs of *individual students*, we can start by looking for "readalikes" that will support and affirm interests students already have. We can also look for offerings that will take students in new directions. It helps to base readalikes in what we know about students' individual reading purposes. If we strive to understand what students want to accomplish as readers, we will be better able to hand them books that will help them fulfill those aims.

- When we do matchmaking that is sensitive to the *local community*, we search for YA titles that respect local cultural mores and that are culturally relevant to local teens. We also look for books that will introduce teens to other cultures and other lived experiences.

- When we make matches to fulfill the demands of the *curriculum*, we seek variety and balance. We strive to introduce students to an array of YA texts that are diverse yet complementary. We select titles that will allow us to achieve different teaching purposes across different phases of the course, and we place books in the curriculum according to the purpose we want them to serve. We think carefully about which titles are best suited for whole-class reading, which would work well in literature circles, and which make sense to offer as independent reads. We think about individual books in relation to the whole: that is, we consider how texts and tasks work together to give students a comprehensive reading experience. We also consider how we can use these books to meet state and national standards and prepare students for standardized tests.

- Finally, when we approach matchmaking in light of the current *policy context*, we rehearse mental pitches for the books as we read them, anticipating how we can highlight their value in response to debates in the realm of education policy, the latest accountability movement, and new developments in literacy teaching. We think strategically about how we will frame what individual YA titles have to offer in relation to current conversations about what students should be learning and what we should be teaching. We listen for buzzwords we can work into our arguments. We make note of calls we can respond to and claims we need to refute as we go about making the case for YA lit. (I'll say more about this in Chapter 7.)

Alongside these literature-based and context-based frameworks for matchmaking, there's one more principle to keep in mind: we must read with an eye toward our blind spots. We need to make the conscious choice to read outside our comfort zones. We must be open to reading YA titles that don't necessarily appeal to us but that might appeal to our students or complement books we already teach. We must keep asking ourselves, what perspectives are missing in the books I've chosen so far? Which other voices do students need to hear? What other kinds of stories do they need to read?

Strategic Matchmaking

It's certainly challenging to think about all these things at once, but we can use lists to

What Is a Readalike?

Readalikes are books that are connected in some way—often through topic, style, or theme—to an earlier title that a reader has enjoyed. Teen services librarians offer readalikes whenever a patron asks for the recommendation of a new book that's similar to the one they just read. During the heyday of Stephenie Meyer's Twilight series and the Harry Potter books, librarians provided bookmarks filled with readalikes for each of these two popular series. Readalikes help readers keep going once they discover individual books that matter to them.

It's important to know that readalikes don't have to follow obvious trails of connection. For example, if a teen wants a list of readalikes for Suzanne Collins's Hunger Games trilogy, an easy response would be to offer a list of other recent dystopian trilogies with a love angle as a subplot, such as the Matched trilogy by Ally Condie, the Legend trilogy by Marie Lu, the Delirium trilogy by Lauren Oliver, or the Divergent trilogy by Veronica Roth. But there are other, less obvious, readalikes for the Hunger Games series. Perhaps a student wants to read about abuse of government power in a contemporary realistic setting rather than an imagined dystopian world. In this case, readalike titles could include Cory Doctorow's *Little Brother* or Anna Perera's *Guantanamo Boy*. Alternatively, if the appeal of the Hunger Games books isn't the political element but instead the strong female narrator, readalike titles could focus on girls who stand up to authority in a variety of genres, including *Beauty Queens* by Libba Bray, *Graceling* by Kristin Cashore, and *The Disreputable History of Frankie Landau-Banks* by E. Lockhart.

The important thing about readalikes is to base suggestions in specific things the reader says about his or her enjoyment of the original book. The goal is to help the reader follow and cultivate a focused thread of connection.

remind us of various factors to keep in mind across the dimensions of our match-making. I offer two such lists in Figures 4.1 and 4.2.

As we read in the field and strive to assemble a collection of books that will expose students to diverse literary offerings, we can use the first list, Figure 4.1, to ensure that we're seeking out titles that vary across genre, format, and point of view. As we read with our curricular context in mind and consider how we might teach the various titles we discover, we can use another list (Figure 4.2), along with a series of accompanying questions, to help us think about the suitability of different books for the different structural components of English class.

Figure 4.1. Reading YA lit for diverse literary offerings.

Genres and Subgenres	Formats	Point of View
Contemporary realistic fiction (e.g., romance, LGBTQ, friendship, bullying, boarding school stories, teens on society's margins, teens overcoming trauma, sports lit, humor)	Novel Graphic novel Verse novel Documentary novel	***Narrative voice*** (e.g., first person, second person, third person, omniscient)
Fantasy (male as well as female protagonists)	Multigenre novel	***Gender*** (female narrator, male narrator, transgender narrator)
Science fiction (e.g., dystopian fiction [political critique], post-apocalyptic fiction [environmental disaster], steampunk [incorporates technology and aesthetic designs inspired by 19th-century industrial steam-powered machinery])	Multiple narrators Story collection Poetry collection Picture book	***Sexual orientation*** (straight narrator, lesbian or gay narrator, questioning narrator) ***Racial/ethnic identity*** (e.g., white narrator, person of color narrator, Native American narrator, immigrant narrator)
Nonfiction genres (e.g., biography; memoir; historical account; scientific study; cultural, political, or environmental criticism; studies of philosophy, social science, and/or the arts)	Photographic, illustrated, or visual text	***Ability*** (able-bodied narrator, narrator with a disability)
Other genres (e.g., mysteries, thrillers, horror, historical fiction, magical realism, literary retellings, satire, short stories, poetry)		

Figure 4.2. Reading YA lit for utility and purpose.

Whole Class	Small Group	Independent Reading
• Books that take up big, universal questions • Books that relate to important issues in the lives of adolescents • Books that connect to current political, cultural, or social issues • Books that provide a critical take on a mainstream issue or idea • Books that contain intertextual references • Books that could be connected with other texts or topics within a text set	• Books that relate to one another by genre, topic, or theme • Books that offer differing perspectives or points of view on the same topic or theme	• Books that are very easy or very hard • Books that target a fairly small audience • Books that appeal to very specific, even narrow, interests • Books that satisfy very specific literary tastes

Each of us will go about matchmaking in ways that respond to the needs and demands of our local context. Still, it can help to see how other teachers have approached the work of matchmaking—choosing some books that serve individual students and others that provide meaningful shared experiences—all while attending to the goals of the curriculum.

Carrie Melnychenko: Leveling the Playing Field

When Carrie Melnychenko and her co-teacher, Leslie DesJardins, decided to design their YA literature elective course at Huron High School, their primary goal was to create lifelong readers. They knew that the arc of students' reading over the course of a twelve-week trimester would include two novels read together as a whole class, two rounds of literature circles, and one book read independently. But deciding which titles to offer in which segments of the course took lots of consultation and thought. Carrie and Leslie had to put aside personal preferences and read with their students in mind. "I'm not reading for me," Carrie says. "I'm reading for them."

Several years earlier, as a reader who was new to YA lit and in search of YA titles to try in a literature circle unit, Carrie relied on colleagues in the Eastern Michigan Writing Project teacher research group for book recommendations. That approach worked for her at the time, but when she decided to create an entire YA lit course, Carrie knew she needed to develop deeper knowledge of the literature.

In partnership with Leslie, she devoted most of a summer to reading YA texts. "And that's hard," Carrie admits. "We probably read fifty books to get the fifteen we use."

Carrie and Leslie knew they had to be deliberate in their book choices, so as they read they designed a chart to help them look at books comparatively. This was partly a practical matter and partly a matter of equity. "In a co-taught class, you get everybody," Carrie says. "You get kids who can barely write paragraphs, and you get kids who are going to go to [elite colleges] next year." She and Leslie used that awareness to guide their book choices. They kept track of things like the gender of the narrator and how difficult, intellectual, or edgy the reading would be. They looked for books that would appeal to students of different maturity levels. "We wanted to be sure that a special ed kid could sit in our class alongside a valedictorian and neither one would gouge my eyes out," Carrie says. "We wanted a balance. Books that would reach out to all kinds of kids."

Part of their process of vetting titles involved deciding which ones would fit best in which segment of the course. "Some [books] you can tell will work for independent reads," Carrie says. "Others are worthy of a literature circle." When it comes to literature circles, one thing Carrie considers is widespread teen appeal. She explains why she offered Laurie Halse Anderson's *The Impossible Knife of Memory* (a book about a teen girl's struggle with her father's alcoholism and post-traumatic stress disorder brought on by his military experiences in the Iraq War) as an independent read instead of a lit circle title. "It has to reach out to more than a few students. I knew there would be a few," she says, "but I didn't think there would be five or six of them."

What surprised Carrie was that after the first few times running the YA lit class, she and Leslie ended up removing almost all of the lower-reading-level books they'd been offering as literature circle options. "Our reads have gotten more sophisticated," Carrie says. "My students don't want simplistic stories. They want to be challenged. And if you don't give them that, they will complain." Students' responses to books have helped Carrie and Leslie evaluate the fit of individual titles for the readers in their particular context. Carrie mentions the example of *No Right Turn* by Terry Trueman. "It's short. It has a male narrator. It's a simple story with a simple conflict and the language is not too complex. They are bored by that book. And I love Terry Trueman!" The same thing happened with *Absolutely Maybe* by Lisa Yee. Carrie loved the book but her students didn't feel the same way. "The kids say there's not enough there, not enough conflict. Nothing shocking. It's too simple of a story. So I moved it to the [literature circle unit in the] tenth-grade class, and tenth grade likes it."

Carrie has found that in addition to wanting more substance, her students become more discerning over time. They become more aware of the level of ambition in a book and what an author does or doesn't try to accomplish. "They realize that some YA writers are just more intellectual people than others. So when they come across a John Green or a Matt de la Peña, they realize that there's a lot of stuff in there. A lot of stuff to figure out. That's what draws them in. I'm talking about authors who aren't just telling a story. They're doing more than that. They're making kids think. They're asking a bigger question."

Carrie mentions the example of de la Peña's *We Were Here* which she offers as a lit circle choice. Students are moved to read about how the three main characters are dealing or not dealing with their lives, but then they come across the literary connections to *The Catcher in the Rye* and *Of Mice and Men*. "And they have read those books," Carrie says. "And so they say, *dang*! Look what this author is doing!" She goes on to talk about students' reactions to John Green's novels, which she also offers for lit circles. "He's asking them to think about their lives in a bigger way. Their place in the world, other people's place in the world. When I think about *Paper Towns*, I think about chasing a dream you didn't even know existed. You're chasing your version of something. And the kids get that, a lot more than adults would ever think they do."

One decision Carrie and Leslie faced was selecting which two novels would serve as whole-class reads. They chose Dana Reinhardt's *How to Build a House* because they wanted to assign a book about relationships told from the point of view of an ordinary girl facing ordinary problems. "They need to hear a girl narrator who's not shooting an arrow through someone's face," Carrie says.

They assign *How to Build a House* near the end of the trimester because they believe it's a book that works best when students have developed a level of classroom community that supports serious and sometimes personal conversations about their own families and relationships. The book that she and Leslie use to launch the course is K. L. Going's *Saint Iggy*. "I picked it because I was blown away by all the literary devices," Carrie says. "I knew I could take [students] to a higher level, and I could do it with a book that was going to interest them." Beyond the literary devices, an equal draw for Carrie was the voice of the main character. Iggy is a genuine, open-hearted boy, but his parents are drug addicts. He lives without a safety net. "You want this kid to do well," she adds. And yet Iggy is destined for tragedy. "I think that's why I chose it."

It may sound as though Carrie came easily to the decision to launch the course with *Saint Iggy*, but that's not true. Because some moments in the book are so sad, Carrie first thought she wouldn't be able to use it. She told Leslie they couldn't teach the book because of the ending. There's no hope, she said. But Leslie argued Carrie out of that position. "It's realistic," Leslie insisted. "It's true to life. It shows that everyone doesn't live the Cinderella story. What happens is a more realistic ending to that boy's life than getting out and living in the suburbs. It gives kids a clear picture of how life really is. How life is going to end up for a lot of people."

Once Leslie encouraged Carrie to risk teaching *Saint Iggy*, Carrie discovered that the book offered a benefit in her classroom she hadn't anticipated. "I'd ask questions that revolve around street smarts, and certain students would get it right away. That takes some guts. Others would say, why do you know all that? So many of our books are heavy on academia. They focus on things like what's the symbolism? In a way, *Saint Iggy* levels the playing field for these kids as readers. You don't have to come in with this huge vocabulary to analyze the book. They feel competent to talk about things."

That notion of leveling the playing field through books is perhaps the biggest takeaway for Carrie as she reflects on her experience teaching YA lit. Because of the books she has chosen and the range of life experiences they represent, kids who haven't previously been strong students find new traction and a new sense of belonging in English class. That happens while they're sitting in the same room with classmates who are taking AP calculus. "I still feel like that's the one thing that I'm probably most excited about whenever I teach YA lit," Carrie says. "Kids who felt like they didn't have a voice—because they didn't have a *literary* voice—come in with a real one. And they use it."

And yet despite all the book knowledge Carrie has gained over five years of teaching YA lit, the work of matchmaking still takes insight and intuition, especially when it comes to supporting students as independent readers. "I think it's different for each kid," Carrie says. "Some kids will tell me, 'I want a love story,' or 'I want some crazy action. I want to feel like I'm on this ride.' Others want to think deeply about life, but they won't tell you that. They'll say, 'I want a book that makes me think about stuff.' I'll say, 'What stuff?' And they'll say, 'I don't know, all kinds of stuff.' Which usually translates as, I'm trying to figure some things out, and I haven't quite done that yet. They want navigation."

As long as Carrie teaches YA lit, her matchmaking work will continue. So will her need to keep building book knowledge and using it to provide students with rich reading options. "We're always changing the books for this class," Carrie says. "It's so hard to keep them happy now! When we first started, it wasn't like that. They were so grateful for the class, it was like I was giving them a gift. Now they still want the gift, but it's like, you've got to give me a really good gift here. . . . When I read *Eleanor and Park*, I knew that was a gift book—if you give it to the right kids. It's all about choice. The right kids are going to embrace that book."

If we look across the story of Carrie's experience as a YA lit matchmaker, we can identify a set of core principles that guided her practice:

- *Developing personalized book knowledge*. Carrie could rely on colleagues for recommendations to get her started as a YA reader, but at some point she needed to take the reins and direct the path of her own reading. She needed to develop enough knowledge of what was out there to make informed choices, and she needed to own the choices she made. Developing personalized book knowledge deepened her authority as a YA teacher.

- *Reading widely.* Carrie and Leslie used a chart to guide their reading. They made a deliberate decision to select books that would serve all the different kinds of readers in their classroom. To be discerning in their offerings, they had to be willing to read more books than they ultimately used. Not every YA book deserves to be in the classroom—or deserves to stay, once kids become more sophisticated and demanding readers.

- *Reading with a partner.* Carrie's co-teacher, Leslie, was an invaluable partner through the process of reading and matchmaking. Reading with a partner gave Carrie someone to talk with as she weighed the merits and limitations of various titles. With Leslie's help, Carrie could explore more books and, ultimately, reach more students. Book knowledge develops faster when two people are reading instead of one. Having Leslie as a fellow reader also gave Carrie a way to think more deeply about the titles she was considering. Leslie helped Carrie develop a stronger sense of the learning that would be possible with a book like *Saint Iggy.* Reading together added energy and vision to their matchmaking process.

- *Listening to students.* Carrie and Leslie's matchmaking work didn't end once they made an initial set of decisions about whole-class reads and literature circle titles. Students' responses to books helped them know which titles were serving their purpose and which were lacking. Listening to students helped them gain a sense of how demanding, how edgy, and how deep students wanted their reading material to be. Carrie and Leslie acted on this knowledge, and their matchmaking work became more skillful as they learned more about students' goals and needs.

- *Making strategic decisions about where to place books.* As Carrie and Leslie read, they weighed the fit of each book in relation to the structural components of the course. They knew that certain books wouldn't have enough substance to hold up as whole-class reads or even lit circle offerings, but that didn't mean they had to throw those books out. Organizing multiple kinds of reading experiences in the course gave them room to incorporate a broader range of titles. To make good use of the books, they had to consider what each one did and didn't try to do. Based on that evaluation, they could place each book where it best fit. Thinking strategically became a crucial aspect of their matchmaking work.

Building Knowledge for Matchmaking

Carrie understands that people who don't know better almost always harbor low expectations for young adult literature. "When they hear 'YA lit,' they think it's all plot driven. A candy read almost. I had a teacher say to me, 'I like those kinds of books, too—the kind where you can kick off your shoes and read by the side of the pool.'" Of course comments like these sting. They underestimate not just the books but also what we as teachers do with them in the classroom. "These kids are reading *I Am the Messenger*," Carrie says. "That is not a flip-flop book." Carrie is right. With its multiple interwoven story lines, mysterious plot, and ambiguous ending, Markus Zusak's novel presents a complex and challenging read for adults and teens alike.

And yet Carrie knows enough about book placement and book access to understand where these impressions come from. "I get it," she says. "If you haven't immersed yourself in YA and you just see what Target sells, which are a lot of vampire stories—if that's all you see, you don't know the complexity of what's out there."

For most of us, finding quality YA books takes effort. Even what we see in an average bookstore represents only a tiny portion of the richness in this literary field. Not only are bookstores inclined to offer bestsellers at the expense of quieter titles, but they are unlikely to carry many backlist titles at all. That means we'll discover some good new books by browsing the shelves—more, of course, if we're browsing in a good independent bookstore—but we aren't likely to find distinguished titles from even a few years ago. Most stores just don't have room to stock them.

Libraries tend to offer broader and deeper YA collections, but the choices there can be overwhelming. We can study the shelves, examine the displays, and even seek guidance from the teen services librarian, but that doesn't change the fact that we will still be faced with a dauntingly large number of books to consider. How do we begin navigating all these offerings?

Fortunately, a number of valuable tools can help readers find their way in the field. I have come to rely on five in particular that I always recommend to teachers who are new to YA lit: (1) YA book awards and booklists; (2) professional review journals; (3) the YALSA-BK listserv; (4) social media resources; and (5) workshops and conferences. Here are some details and tips on each of these resources:

> 1. *Book awards and book lists.* The easiest place to start learning about quality new titles is with annual YA award lists. Award committees are made up of people who know and love YA lit; each one is usually a blend of librarians, critics, teachers, professors, and/or authors. Because awards are given and lists are announced annually, they provide a regular source of strong new titles each year. Not all good books are honored with book awards, but awards call attention to many titles that might not gain attention otherwise.
>
> Since the introduction of the Michael L. Printz Award for Excellence in Young Adult Literature in 2000, the number of YA lit awards has grown dramatically. Because many awards are narrowly focused,

teachers can use them to find books that are distinguished for literary merit, books in different genres, books representing a particular kind of life experience, and books that blend literary quality and teen appeal.

Literary awards. The Printz Award is the biggest YA literary award. It's given by YALSA, the Young Adult Library Services Association, which is a division of the American Library Association (ALA). Literary awards given by other organizations can further expand our options. Additional awards given annually for literary merit in YA lit include the National Book Award for Young People's Literature, the *Los Angeles Times* Book Prize, and the Boston Globe-Horn Book Award. Teachers looking for new voices in YA lit will appreciate the William C. Morris Award, given annually by YALSA to the most outstanding novel by a debut author.

Genre awards. YALSA's Excellence in Nonfiction Award is a great way to expand one's reading beyond novels. In addition to naming a winner and four finalists, the committee publicizes its complete list of nominated titles on the YALSA website. Outside of YALSA, there are awards for historical fiction (the Scott O'Dell Award), mystery (the Edgar Awards), and science fiction and fantasy (the Andre Norton Award). Although the term *graphic novel* refers to book format (e.g., graphic novels come in all genres, from memoir to fairy tale retelling), YALSA's list of Great Graphic Novels for Teens is another useful resource. So are the Eisner Awards, given annually by the comic book industry.

Diversity awards. As readers become more aware of the importance of diversity in YA lit, awards for diversity introduce readers to books representing literary excellence across a range of lived experiences. The ALA provides a number of diversity awards and diversity lists. Some are given on the basis of the author's identity: the Coretta Scott King Awards and the Pura Belpré Awards honor authors of books representing the African American and Latino experience, respectively. The Stonewall Book Awards honor books representing the LGBTQ experience, and the Schneider Family Book Awards do the same for books representing the disability experience. Teachers looking for books that explore feminism and social justice issues can make use of the Amelia Bloomer List and the Jane Addams Children's Book Awards.

Literary merit and teen appeal. For recommendations of books that combine literary merit and teen appeal, teachers can turn to YALSA's list of Best Fiction for Young Adults, which features approximately fifty to eighty novels a year. They can also consult the Cybils Awards, given annually by the book blogging community to books in a range of categories, from fantasy to nonfiction to graphic novels. The Amelia Elizabeth Walden Award is given annually by ALAN (the Assembly on Literature for Adolescents of NCTE) to honor a novel that features literary merit, widespread teen appeal, and a positive approach to life. Another helpful resource is YALSA's list of Popular Paperbacks for Young Adults, which is organized around four new topics, themes, or genres each year. Past lists have focused on humor, unreliable narrators, teens behind bars, and books that won't make you blush.

Reluctant readers. For books that appeal to teens who typically don't like to read, YALSA's annual Quick Picks for Reluctant Young Adult Readers is invaluable. Teachers who wish to identify the best books in terms of literary quality can look for titles that appear on both the Quick Picks and the Best Fiction for Young Adults lists. Usually eight to ten titles each year appear on both lists.

(For more information about using book awards to navigate the field of YA lit, see Buehler, Plumb, & Walsh, 2013.)

2. *Professional review journals.* There are six big review journals that YA authors, publishers, and librarians tend to pay attention to: *Booklist,* the *Bulletin of the Center for Children's Books, Horn Book Magazine, Kirkus Reviews, School Library Journal,* and *Publishers Weekly.* My favorite of these is *Horn Book.* As a subscriber, I receive a new issue by mail every two months, but readers can access some of each month's content online for free. I enjoy *Horn Book*'s succinct, well-written, and discerning reviews. I like knowing that every summer I will be able to read speeches given by the winners of the Newbery, the Caldecott, and the Coretta Scott King Awards. I also love reading occasional articles and essays on trends in YA lit and changes in the field over time.

3. *The YALSA-BK listserv.* Teachers who need specific book recommendations, such as recent titles that would pair well with *To Kill a Mockingbird* or books to suggest as readalikes to students who are hooked on a current bestseller, can ask members of this online listserv for help. For those of you who are unfamiliar with listservs, they are electronic mailing lists that allow you to communicate with a group of people through email. Send an email to the list and it goes out to all the list's members. In the case of YALSA-BK, which is run by teen services librarians, it's free to subscribe, and anyone can participate. For YA readers, the YALSA-BK listserv provides a quick and efficient way to participate in a virtual YA reading community.

YALSA-BK is an amazing resource in general, but it's especially useful when you need help right away. I began subscribing to YALSA-BK in 2001. At that time, there was so much activity on the list that I set up a separate email account just for my daily YALSA-BK messages. Although there is less traffic on the list now due to the rise of blogs and social media, I still occasionally call on the wisdom of what list members refer to as "The Collective Brain" when I need help finding YA titles on a specific topic or theme.

4. *Social media resources.* Instead of watching television, I use social media to relax in the evenings; it's a form of escape that simultaneously adds to my YA book knowledge. I use an e-reader called Feedly to keep up with new blog posts written by YA authors, librarians, and teachers I've chosen to follow. Each night when I go to my Feedly reader, I get a

daily digest of book news. After I read my Feedly updates, I turn to Twitter for additional news. Through Twitter I get links to essays and news stories about YA lit, announcements of local YA events, and highlights from YA sessions at professional conferences. Twitter also serves as a site for regularly scheduled book conversations, which are identified by hashtags such as #titletalk. Perhaps best of all, Twitter gives teachers another way to feel part of a virtual reading community. Having daily access to others who read, teach, and promote YA lit can be a source of energy and comfort, especially for those of us who feel isolated in our daily work.

5. *Workshops and conferences.* If social media makes it possible for teachers to participate in virtual reading communities, workshops and conferences allow us to find reading communities in person. There are dozens of these each year, but one in particular will be of interest to those of us who teach YA lit: the ALAN Workshop, a two-day NCTE Postconvention Workshop held annually on the Monday and Tuesday before Thanksgiving. The workshop brings together some 500 teachers, librarians, professors, and critics in a passionate celebration of all things YA. Each day consists of keynote speeches and panel discussions by leading authors in the field, plus breakout sessions hosted by teachers, librarians, and other teen advocates. As part of the registration fee, each attendee receives a large (and heavy!) box filled with free books. Some teachers come to ALAN even if they can stay only for the first morning because they know they'll be going home with hundreds of dollars' worth of free new books for their classrooms. The single best way to begin building a classroom library is to attend ALAN on a regular basis.

Early career teachers can attend ALAN with the support of a Gallo Grant, funded by Don Gallo, one of the organization's original leaders. Middle school teacher Renee Stites attended ALAN for the first time on a Gallo Grant. Afterward, she reported that not only was she transformed by her experience, but her classroom was transformed as well. "After ALAN, when I went back to my classroom, I felt like that whole joy of reading just exploded," Renee said. "I had seen firsthand what authors do, and I got to see sort of inside the book, and then I could take that back and share that with my students and say here's what he said, and here's what she said, and that's why they wrote it. Think about this great story that's here. And that seemed to fill my room with something that hadn't been there before." (For more information about Gallo Grants and ALAN, tune in to Episode 80 of the *Text Messages* podcast on ReadWriteThink.org, "An Invitation to the ALAN Workshop.")

Savvy and Strategic Matchmaking

As important as it is to guide individual readers to books that are right for them, matchmaking in YA pedagogy calls us to do more. Even as we provide students like

Gemma with carefully chosen books that say to them, *I see you. I am paying attention to your thoughts and feelings. I can help you use reading to figure out who you are, what you think, and what matters to you*, we must go further in our approach to matchmaking. We must consider multiple contexts and multiple dimensions of teaching in our matchmaking work.

We should begin by thinking broadly and strategically about the books we bring into the classroom. We need to ask ourselves, what kind of textured reading experience do I want students to have as YA readers in my class? Which stories do I want them to experience together? Which books are worthwhile for them to read but more appropriate to read on their own? Which books will stimulate discussions so spirited and passionate that students look around and say, "I want to read what *they're* reading"?

We also need to approach matchmaking with the real world of high-stakes tests, state and national standards, and politics in mind. As we choose books, we need to rehearse what we'll say when we're asked to speak about their value and why we've committed to teaching them. We need to select titles that will allow us to meet curricular goals, but we also need titles we're willing to stand behind for the artistry of their writing, the power of their storytelling, and the importance they may hold in the lives of teens.

To gain the knowledge and the confidence to do this work, the final part of matchmaking involves seeking support for ourselves. When we commit to teaching YA lit, we commit to a new phase of professional learning. As we enter into contexts that will help us to learn about the books, we enter into communities where we can forge connections with like-minded colleagues. When we share our YA reading with others, we can sharpen our vision and strengthen our teaching.

Along with classroom community, matchmaking stands as a critical element of YA pedagogy. When we conduct our matchmaking work within a classroom environment that cultivates reading community, we lay the foundation for students to construct complex reading experiences with YA lit. But students need more than a reading community and a knowledgeable teacher in order to grow and thrive as YA readers. They also need to be given meaningful things to do with YA texts. They need to engage in purposeful classroom tasks that connect them to real-world reading contexts and that call them to become agents of their own reading lives. As the third and final element of YA pedagogy, classroom tasks—tasks designed to promote complexity, agency, and autonomy—are the alchemy that will bring out the full potential of YA lit in the classroom.

Chapter Five

YA Pedagogy Element 3: Tasks That Promote Complexity, Agency, and Autonomy

Because she wants me to hear about YA literature from her students, Carrie Melnychenko has convened a focus group at Huron High School in New Boston, Michigan. On this half-day, students have just taken their last final exam of the second trimester, and almost everyone else has gone home. Out of loyalty to Carrie and, I think, as a way to pay tribute to the experience they had in her class, three former students have come to her room for a pizza lunch and conversation with me. Carrie's teaching partner, Leslie DesJardins, who helped Carrie design the YA lit course and still helps her teach it, is also here.

Our conversation begins, as these talks often do, with books the students have read and enjoyed. Brandon, a special ed student who worked closely with Leslie, started with Francisco X. Stork's *Marcelo in the Real World* and then made his way through most of Alex Flinn's novels. Leah, who reads voraciously and loves to analyze, connected with titles as different as *Wintergirls*, *Crank*, and *We Were Here*. Jacob, who came into Carrie's class as a nonreader and took time off from his job at Taco Bell to be here today, found his voice and a special kind of authority in discussions of *Saint Iggy*. For more than an hour, I listen to these students reflect on the conversations they had and the work they did in Carrie's class.

After they leave, Carrie talks with me about how students' tastes and preferences shift over the course of their trimester reading YA lit. As they gain experience and pick up momentum as readers, students come to realize that reading an entertaining book is not enough. Carrie explains how she sees this happen during literature circle time. "Although I might have kids who really dig that kind of [entertaining] reading, they're not going to get the same level of discussion [as the kids who are reading a more complex book]." The students who are reading simpler titles, such as *Bonechiller*, look around the room and listen in on the level of discussion in the other lit circles. "I'll hear [the *Bonechiller*] kids say, 'I want to read what *they're* reading!'"

Carrie was struck by her students' comment, and so am I. When kids look around the room and say, "I want to read what *they're* reading," they tell us something revealing about themselves, and they let us know something important about our work with YA lit in the classroom. Students want to read these books, but what they want from the books—and from the class—changes over time. Students notice that some books challenge their thinking more than others. They also discover that in and of themselves, the books aren't enough. It's what readers *do* with books that makes them meaningful. The books come to life, and they achieve greater power, when readers discuss them, debate them, and construct new understandings as a result of their interactions. Students *want* to engage in these forms of personal, social, and analytical meaning making. They want their experiences with YA literature to be complex.

Reinventing Traditional Classroom Tasks

As teachers we can show students how to find and make complexity as YA readers, and we can design classroom tasks to help students achieve this goal. As I mentioned in the last two chapters, YA pedagogy calls us to establish classroom reading communities that cultivate student engagement and to serve as matchmakers and guides, leading students to books that are right for them. But it's this third element—classroom tasks—that brings YA pedagogy to life. The power and effectiveness of the books and our teaching hinges on the tasks we design for students. Through these tasks, we provide students with tools and frameworks that enable them to make complexity as readers, which in turn helps them get more from their reading of YA texts. We also help them acquire the skills they need to be successful in English and in their lives beyond the classroom.

Experienced teachers know that the tasks we assign matter. However, as I discussed in Chapter 1, far too often our classroom tasks engage students in *either* personal work (such as journal entries focused on connections between their lives and the text) *or* analytical work (such as five-paragraph essays). Rarely do we invite students to blend these different dimensions of reading into one. Our use of these tasks keeps the pedagogical binary in place, and yet year after year we continue to rely on them. They are staples of the English language arts classroom, the vehicle through which we teach the curriculum. They allow us to achieve many important goals, and we hold on to them for a reason.

I want to suggest that as we seek to teach YA lit in new and creative ways, we don't have to abandon traditional tasks. Instead, we can reinvent them so that we pursue the same teaching goals while we work to break down the binary. We can call students to make their reading of YA lit both relevant and complex—all we have to do is shift our approach. We can recast familiar tasks by situating them in new literary, political, and social contexts. We can create a space in which students blend personal response with analysis of the text in a dynamic classroom community. At the same time, we can design opportunities for students to connect their work with YA literature to current happenings in the world outside the classroom. In this way, we still get students where they need to go in terms of the curriculum, but we honor the interests of teens in the current moment. We also legitimize YA as a literary field, and we help students see the complex relationship between YA lit and the larger world of writing and publishing.

So what would it look like to do this kind of teaching in the YA classroom? Which traditional tasks can we shift through YA pedagogy? The answer, of course, is all of them. Here, though, I focus on six tasks in particular that almost all of us include in our teaching at some point, regardless of grade level, course, or context. They are (1) literary analysis, (2) reader response, (3) thematic units, (4) genre study, (5) the study of literary periods and literary history, and (6) writing process/ writing craft (see Table 5.1). Drawing on the work of classroom teachers, teen services librarians, book critics, publishing representatives, and authors from around the country, I offer ideas on how we might recast and reinvent these tasks so that our teaching of YA lit will promote complexity, agency, and autonomy for teen readers.

For each task, I begin with an overview that summarizes the kind of work the task entails and the kinds of assignments that students do in traditional ELA classrooms. Then I offer a vision of what that same work could look like if we reinvent it with YA pedagogy. I provide teaching ideas and related resources that will help students and teachers alike put these tasks into practice while developing greater knowledge of YA literature as a field.

After my own list of possibilities for these tasks, I present snapshots of teachers who have created other versions of the same tasks in response to expectations and opportunities in their local contexts.

1. Literary Analysis

What Do Students Typically Do?

Through literary analysis, students learn the skills of close reading (Beers & Probst, 2013; Lehman & Roberts, 2014). Usually in the context of whole-class discussions led by the teacher, students use literary terms to analyze how a text is constructed, searching for literary devices such as symbols, figurative language, and literary allusions and looking for passages that embody and reveal a text's themes. They may apply one or more literary theories to read their text through a theoretical lens such as feminism or Marxism (Appleman, 2009). The product of this work is usually an analytical essay written for the teacher. Students develop an argument about the text, and they search for evidence to back up their claims.

How to Recast This as YA Pedagogy

Students can apply literary analysis skills to two forms of real-world work that involve reading and critically evaluating YA lit: writing book reviews and participating in mock award committees. Since YA books, just like adult books, are the topic of reviews, prizes, thoughtful discussion, and controversy, one way to shift the task of literary analysis in YA pedagogy is to immerse students in the world of YA criticism.

Students study the conventions of book reviews and the criteria for book awards such as the Newbery or the Printz. Then they look at actual reviews, along with blog posts on mock awards websites, to see how reviews and award committee

Table 5.1. Reinventing Classroom Tasks through YA Pedagogy

Kind of Work	What It Involves	Traditional Version	Recast in YA Pedagogy
1. Literary analysis	Close reading; applying literary terms to discussion of texts; searching for literary devices in texts (e.g., symbols, figurative language, literary allusions); looking for passages that embody and reveal a text's themes; studying how texts are put together; developing arguments about a text; searching for evidence to back up claims about a text	Traditional tasks and products: · Reading with sticky notes · Analyzing passages in the text · Applying literary theory lenses · Writing analytical essays	New tasks and products: · Writing book reviews · Participating in mock award committee meetings
2. Reader response	Reading with a focus on the transaction between the reader and the text; exploring how readers make meaning of written works based on the individual background knowledge, beliefs, and context they bring into the reading act (Rosenblatt, 1995)	Traditional tasks and products: · Writing letters or journal entries in reading notebooks · Meeting in literature circle groups · Presenting book talks or sharing creative projects with the class	New tasks and products: · Study of book marketing and author "branding" · Self-analysis of your "brand" as reader · Book previews designed to appeal to a particular audience
3. Thematic units	Reading a series of texts that explore the same concept or idea; examining how different texts provide different takes, perspectives, and insights on that concept; constructing more complex and nuanced understandings of the concept by examining how different authors have approached it	Traditional tasks and products: · Filling out comparison and contrast charts · Recording related bits of evidence across different texts · Writing analytical essays	New tasks and products: · Study of how different authors take up similar themes or story lines (e.g., school shooting books, LGBTQ books) · Literature circles or book bins organized by theme · Informational pamphlets
4. Genre study	Reading a series of texts that are written in the same genre; studying those texts to identify the defining characteristics of a genre, its common features and conventions, how genres are different from one another, and how authors blur genre boundaries and play with genre conventions	Traditional tasks and products: · Literature circles organized by genre · The Unfamiliar Genre Project (Fleischer & Andrew-Vaughan, 2009) · Multigenre papers	New tasks and products: · Study of YA books in a single genre to distinguish innovators from imitators · Study of the origins and evolution of new YA genres (e.g., verse novel, documentary novel) · Genre-based reading lists, or genre-based book reviews
5. Literary periods and literary history	Providing background information that helps students put a particular literary text in cultural and historical context (e.g., Puritans and Red Scare for *The Crucible*; Roaring Twenties for *The Great Gatsby*; Harlem Renaissance for Langston Hughes poems)	Traditional tasks and products: · Teacher lecture · Student research project in the form of a paper or presentation	New tasks and products: · Study of the history of and trends in YA lit · Study of conversations and debates in YA lit · Critical look at canons and how they are created · Students engage in a current YA lit debate · Students construct their own versions of personal and literary canons
6. Writing process/writing craft	Overview of process elements, often presented as a series of linear steps; language of writing process supports students as they develop their own piece of writing, usually in a teacher-assigned genre	Traditional tasks and products: · Study mentor texts in a genre such as memoir; participate in prewriting activities, drafting, and peer group meetings; plan revision; do further drafting and editing · Read novel or text set, fill in chart with textual evidence related to theme, develop thesis statement, complete worksheet or graphic organizer to create outline, draft analytical essay	New tasks and products: · Research the story behind a YA novel: how it was written and the process the author used to write it · Write "process portraits" of various authors, followed by commentary on what we learn about writing from studying their various approaches · Students use what they learn about an author's process to talk about their own process

members go about their work. They look for examples of how reviewers blend personal response and textual analysis, and they discuss how readers manage bias as they engage in award deliberations.

Teaching Ideas

- Study reviews across the big six YA review journals (*Booklist*, *Bulletin of the Center for Children's Books*, *Horn Book Magazine*, *Kirkus Reviews*, *Publishers Weekly*, *School Library Journal*). Examine what these reviews have in common and how they differ. Who are the leading YA reviewers and what stylistic traits distinguish their work? Compare professional reviews to those posted by everyday readers on Goodreads and Amazon. What are the similarities and differences?

- Find out what distinguishes a starred review from a regular review. How do different review journals decide to give a book a starred review? How do publishers and authors use starred reviews in their advertising and self-promotion? Start exploring answers to these questions with Roger Sutton's essay "Stars" in the September/October 2006 issue of *Horn Book Magazine*. Track starred reviews of YA titles each year by following Elizabeth Bluemle's updates in "The Stars So Far," a series of periodic posts on her blog, *ShelfTalker*, http://blogs.publishersweekly.com/blogs/shelftalker/.

- Study how leading YA authors talked about and critically evaluated top children's and YA titles in the most recent *School Library Journal* Battle of the Kids' Books, which is a March Madness–style bracket competition. An organizing committee selects sixteen of the previous year's best children's and YA titles and places them in brackets. A different author is invited to select a winner from each pair of titles. Authors write personal commentaries that explain the reasoning behind their decision. Students can read and discuss these commentaries, getting to know more about the kinds of reasoning involved in reviewing as well as the personalities of different authors. For more information, see http://blogs.slj.com/battleofthebooks/.

- Engage students in a Mock Printz experience just before the Youth Media Awards are announced at the midwinter meeting of the American Library Association in January. Study the Printz Award criteria shared on the *Someday My Printz Will Come* blog and use it to evaluate a set of nominated titles. Invite a local librarian who has served on an ALA award committee to visit class and talk about his or her experience. Use a formal voting process to come up with a winner. Compare results with those of other Mock Printz groups around the country. (For an example of a Mock Printz committee that meets through the Eva Perry Regional Library in Wake County, North Carolina, see https://evaperrymockprintz.wordpress.com.) Then watch the video webcast from the ALA Midwinter meeting to see the winners announced live. For access to the webcast link, visit the ALA Youth Media Awards News and Press Center at http://www.ala.org/news/mediapresscenter/presskits/youthmediaawards/alayouthmediaawards.

- Find out how to get involved in reading advance copies and nominating titles for the YALSA Teens' Top Ten list, a list of teens' favorite YA titles published each year. For more information, see http://www.ala.org/yalsa/teen-reading/teenstopten/yagalley.

- Look for places where teens write and publish book reviews, such as the Teenreads electronic newsletter. Evaluate the quality of teens' review writing. Have interested students apply to become Teenreads board members. Board members write reviews as well as blog posts. Applications are accepted each year during the summer. For more information, see http://www.teen-reads.com/teen-board-faq.

2. Reader Response

What Do Students Typically Do?

Reader response is an approach to reading that focuses on the transaction between the reader and the text. The emphasis is on the ways in which individual readers construct meaning based on the background knowledge, beliefs, and context they bring to the reading act (Rosenblatt, 1995). Reader-response activities usually take place within the context of a reading workshop where students write letter-essays or journal entries about their books in reading notebooks (Atwell, 2014; Rief, 2007; Kittle, 2013). They may also take on roles in literature circle groups that require them to pose questions, make connections, and interpret short passages (Daniels, 1994). Students often share the results of their reading in the form of book talks or creative projects presented to the class (Lesesne, 2006; Mitchell & Christenbury, 2000).

How to Recast This as YA Pedagogy

Students can use reader response as a lens to examine how publishers package and sell books. Students analyze how editorial assistants write copy for the inside cover flap and the back of the book to position it in relation to others of its kind. They study book cover art comparatively, looking for patterns in font, imagery, and overall design. They research the authors who have blurbed a certain book, and they speculate on what a blurb by a particular author might mean for sales. They examine the letters that school and library marketing directors, and sometimes authors or editors, write to accompany advance reading copies. They discuss how these marketing strategies are designed to construct a particular kind of reader response. Then students step back to look for patterns in their own YA lit tastes and preferences. They ask themselves questions like "Why do I read the books I do? What do they have in common? How have my own tastes been shaped by publishers and their marketing efforts?"

Teaching Ideas

- Choose a YA novel that has gone through multiple printings. How has the publisher changed the cover art over time, and what might the choice of cover art reveal about the publisher's target audience? For a good example, consider the case of Francesca Lia Block's *Weetzie Bat,* a book whose covers have featured both scrapbook-style collages with bubble gum pink accents and graffiti-style street art cast in darker, more masculine hues. Read the critical article by Cat Yampbell on the book's changing cover designs, published in the September 2005 issue of the literary journal *The Lion and the Unicorn*.

- Take a similar look at how a single author's body of work has been repackaged and "branded" over time. For example, compare the original covers of early Sarah Dessen novels published in the mid-1990s to the design of her covers today. What has changed? What might be the reasons for that change?

- Examine cover art more generally. Gather a set of YA novels that are similar in genre or story line. What patterns are visible across the covers? What do different publishing houses do to differentiate their books from the rest? What popular titles do publishers seem to be imitating or linking to in order to promote sales? For a guide to critical reading of book covers, see children's librarian Thom Barthelmess's essay "What Makes a Good Book Cover?" published in the March/April 2014 issue of *Horn Book Magazine*. Also look at teen services librarian Kelly Jensen's periodic book cover analyses on the blog *Stacked* (http://www.stackedbooks.org).

- Study the book selections and recommendations of an established YA librarian or critic. What does this person's choice of titles and style of comments reveal about his or her tastes and preferences in books? What seems to be his or her "brand" as a reader/reviewer? Two useful sources for analysis are the *Reading Rants!* blog, published by school librarian Jennifer Hubert Swan (http://www.readingrants.org), and Carte Blanche, a monthly column published in *Booklist* magazine by YA critic Michael Cart.

- After a critical analysis of book cover design, have students choose a book they think could benefit from repackaging. Drawing on what they have seen in the covers designed by professionals, have them design their own new cover and provide a rationale that explains who they were trying to target and how their intended audience guided their design choices.

- Study video marketing campaigns such as Scholastic's online previews (http://www.scholastic.com/onlinepreview/). How do authors and editors pitch their newest titles? Have students create their own video previews of the season's newest YA novels.

- Have a teen services librarian visit the classroom to discuss the concept of readers' advisory, or helping readers find the kinds of books they're looking for. How do librarians go about helping readers find books that fit their needs and tastes? Then have students create bookmarks that offer lists of readalikes (see Chapter 4). Have them use the tagline "If you liked [title X], you might also like [title Y]."

- Engage students in a self-analysis of their own "brand" as a reader. How is their taste in books shaped by their literary preferences, reading purposes, and/or the influence of marketing departments? Have students write critically about what they are finding—and not finding—in YA lit.

3. Thematic Units

What Do Students Typically Do?

Thematic units are designed to engage students in making connections across a series of texts that explore a common theme. Students examine how different texts provide different takes, perspectives, and insights on the same topic or different answers to the same question. By reading texts that are thematically related and examining how different authors have approached the same central idea, students construct more complex and nuanced understandings of topics and texts. (For examples of thematic units, see Daniels & Zemelman, 2014; Mitchell & Christenbury, 2000; Wilhelm, 2007.) Students typically fill out comparison and contrast charts as they work their way through various texts, and the product of their learning is often an analytical essay.

How to Recast This as YA Pedagogy

Thematic work looks similar in YA pedagogy, only here, teachers can make use of current publishing trends to ground students' work in a real-world context. They look at titles published over the past few years to identify topics that multiple authors have explored. They analyze how authors' treatment of these issues has differed from book to book or changed over time. Examples include books on teen pregnancy, LGBTQ books, and books that explore politics and war in the post-9/11 landscape. (I offer many of these topical and trend-based lists on *Text Messages*, a YA lit podcast I hosted for many years for ReadWriteThink [www.read writethink.org/textmessages].)

Teaching Ideas

- Consult *The Hub*, a YALSA blog that frequently features themed reading lists, for examples of patterns and trends in YA publishing. Also consult YALSA's annual themed lists of Popular Paperbacks for Young Adults. What topics and themes do teen services librarians choose for their themed reading lists, and what titles do they recommend?

- Have students come up with a list of books on the same topic. In a literature circle group, have students read as many of these books as they can. Then have them engage in a critical analysis of how authors' treatment of the same topic is similar or different. What variations do they notice in the questions authors are asking, the answers they are providing, and the themes they are exploring? What differences do they notice in writing craft and storytelling structure? Which books offer the most sophisticated, useful, or original treatment of this topic? For example, in light of the ongoing problem of gun violence in the United States, have students look at books such as Todd Strasser's *Give a Boy a Gun*, Walter Dean Myers's *Shooter*, Chris Crutcher's *Whale Talk*, Nancy Garden's *Endgame*, and Kathryn Erskine's *Mockingbird*. To extend the analysis, connect these books to the nonfiction title *Columbine* by Dave Cullen.

4. Genre Study

What Do Students Typically Do?

When students engage in genre study, they read a series of texts written in the same genre. They study text structures and features to identify the defining characteristics of a genre, its common conventions, how genres are different from one another, and how authors blur genre boundaries and play with genre conventions. (For examples of students working in unfamiliar genres, see Fleischer & Andrew-Vaughan, 2009; for examples of multigenre work, see Romano, 2000.)

How to Recast This as YA Pedagogy

Again, genre study looks similar in YA pedagogy, only here, teachers might focus on genres that are unique to YA lit, such as the verse novel (a novel written as a series of narrative poems) or the documentary novel (a novel that blends narrative text with scrapbook elements such as photographs, song lyrics, advertisements, and excerpts from speeches). Alternatively, students could study genres that have been prominent at some point in the field, such as dystopian or postapocalyptic novels, or genres that have experienced a creative and stylistic renaissance, such as YA nonfiction.

Rather than analyzing the ideas in these books, as they would in a thematic unit, in genre study, students study a text's structure, form, and style. Students can trace the origins and development of specific YA genres over time, and they can read comparatively to determine which texts are genre innovators and which are genre imitators.

Teaching Ideas

- Read several essays from the "What Makes a Good . . ." essay series in *Horn Book Magazine* to explore distinguishing characteristics across a range of YA genres (for example, "What Makes a Good YA Love Story?" [Hedeen & Smith, 2013] and "What Makes a Good YA Urban Novel?" [Ribay, 2013]). After reading several of these essays as a whole class, have students choose a single genre to explore. Read a number of titles in common and use the essay criteria to evaluate the strengths and weaknesses of each book.

- Invite students to choose a YA genre not covered in a *Horn Book* essay. Have students read in this genre and write their own essay modeled off the examples in *Horn Book*.

- Examine patterns in new and emerging YA genres. Have students research the history of these genres. What is the story behind their development and publication? Which titles were the originals? Who were the trailblazers writing in these forms? (For example, Mel Glenn and Virginia Euwer Wolff are known as founders of the YA verse novel with *Class Dismissed* and *Make Lemonade*, respectively; Deborah Wiles is known for introducing the documentary novel with *Countdown*.) Since the origins of these genres, which titles now stand out as exemplary? What distinguishes innovators from imitators?

- Examine innovations in more familiar genres such as nonfiction. For essays that narrate new developments in today's YA nonfiction, see Marc Aronson's "New Knowledge" and Elizabeth Partridge's "Narrative Nonfiction: Kicking Ass at Last," both published in the special nonfiction themed issue of *Horn Book* in March/April 2011. Also listen to YA author Candace Fleming talk about new developments in YA nonfiction on the ReadWriteThink podcast "A Conversation with Candace Fleming."

- Explore genre blurring or blending. How do authors play with genre as they write retellings of classics? What does a familiar genre, such as a memoir or Shakespeare play, look like when it's adapted into a different format, such as a graphic novel? For examples, look at Gareth Hinds's graphic novel versions of works such as *The Odyssey*, *Beowulf*, and *Macbeth*. Read the commentaries Hinds has written in his books and on his website for insights into the decisions and design choices he made as he created his adaptations. Similarly, read novelizations of Shakespeare plays such as *Hamlet* by John Marsden; *Exposure*, a retelling of *Othello* by Mal Peet; *Street Love*, a retelling of *Romeo and Juliet* by Walter Dean Myers; or *We Were Liars*, a retelling of *King Lear* by E. Lockhart. Discuss what is gained and lost by reinventing these plays in new genre formats.

- Practice critical reading by analyzing the ideological messages in a popular mainstream YA genre such as high society chick lit or vampire novels. For an example of this kind of critical reading, see Wendy Glenn's article on the Gossip Girl books in the September 2008 issue of the *Journal of Adolescent and Adult Literacy*.

- After extended study of a particular genre, have students create genre-based reading lists or genre-based reviews, organized by text features, publication date, or theme, that draw the line between genre innovators and imitators.

5. Literary Periods and Literary History

What Do Students Typically Do?

Usually in the context of a literature survey class, students learn background information that helps them place a particular literary text in its cultural and historical context. Through teacher lectures or independent research projects, students study the Puritans and the Red Scare when they read *The Crucible*. They explore the Roaring Twenties when they read *The Great Gatsby*. They find out more about the Harlem Renaissance when they read Langston Hughes's poems. Much of the time, students' work with literary history is fairly passive; they take in information that serves as a backdrop for more active work with the main literary text.

How to Recast This as YA Pedagogy

Students can study the history of YA as a literary field, from its origins in the New Realism of the late 1960s to the new golden age of YA lit in the early 2000s. Like any other field of literature, YA lit has evolved and changed over time.

Students can research major literary and commercial periods in the history of YA literature and major trends in YA publishing over the past four decades (e.g., the dominance of the problem novel in the 1970s, the rise of series books like Sweet Valley High and Fear Street in the 1980s, the glut of bleak books in the 1990s, and the emergence of the dystopian trend in the 2000s).

They can research authors whose books changed the direction of the field, such as Robert Cormier, whose dark depictions of human nature and abuse of power drew fire from critics but raised the stature of the YA novel as literary form. They can explore discussions and debates in the field on topics such as bleak books and the lack of diversity in YA publishing. Students can use their knowledge of YA literary history as context for examining the state of the field today.

Teaching Ideas

- Read books or articles on the history of YA literature. A few examples include Michael Cart's 2010 *Young Adult Literature: From Romance to Realism* (the definitive history of YA lit); Patty Campbell's 2010 *Campbell's Scoop: Reflections on Young Adult Literature* (essays spanning forty years of following the field); Roger Sutton's personal essay "Problems, Paperbacks, and the Printz: 40 Years of YA Books" (*Horn Book*, May/June 2007); and Jonathan Hunt's Borderlands essays: one on the first ten years of the Printz Award ("A Printz Retrospective," *Horn Book*, July/August 2009), the other on crossover novels ("Redefining the Young Adult Novel," *Horn Book*, March/April 2007). Create a timeline to mark major periods and events.

- In light of trends in YA lit and titles that rise above those trends, and in light of the longer history of YA lit and its groundbreaking books and turning points, students can debate which YA titles belong in a YA canon and why. Initiate a discussion about what distinguishes a "big book" of today—that is, a bestselling title—from a canonical title that has stood the test of time. Can the same book be both? More generally, who gets to decide these things, and how, and why?

- Have students explore the concept of a library archive (special library collections dedicated to the preservation of historical materials such as rare manuscripts, letters, and diaries) and seek out libraries with archives dedicated to YA literature. Explain that library archives give scholars access to primary sources (e.g., correspondence between authors and editors, draft manuscripts, galleys) that shed light on how individual books came to be written. In this way, library archives help tell the story and construct the history of YA lit.

  Students could investigate which YA authors have donated their materials to a library archive, and they could inquire into what sorts of materials different YA archives contain. They could explore questions such as: What do an author's private papers reveal about a novel's development and themes? How does it add to the stature of a book—or an author's career—when early drafts and correspondence around that book are housed in an archive? (For more information on one prominent YA archive, see Patty Campbell's essay on the Kerlan Collection at the University of Minnesota, published in the January/February 2007 issue of *Horn Book Magazine*, or visit the Kerlan website at www.lib.umn.edu/clrc/kerlan-collection. Through the Kerlan Collection Finding Aids link, available at www.lib.umn.edu/clrc/finding-aids, students can scroll through the list of hundreds of YA authors whose papers are held at the Kerlan and discover details about what each author's archive contains.)

- Read about arguments and debates in the field and trace their development over time. For example, a current issue in YA writing and publishing is lack of diversity, reflected in the #weneeddiversebooks campaign. Look for the roots of that campaign in historical articles by Nancy Larrick ("The All-White World of Children's Books," published in 1965) and Rudine Sims Bishop ("Mirrors, Windows, and Sliding Glass Doors," published in 1990) and more recent articles by Walter Dean Myers and Christopher Myers published in 2014 in the *New York Times* (along with Christopher Myers's 2015 Coretta Scott King Award speech published in the July/August 2015 *Horn Book*). Study statistics on diversity in children's and YA publishing compiled annually by K. T. Horning at the Cooperative Children's Book Center at the University of Wisconsin-Madison. Have students explore what has changed and what has stayed the same in the debate about diversity since the mid-1960s. What changes, if any, can we see in the publishing industry as a result of this debate? How might students contribute to the debate?

- Based on their timelines and historical research, have students construct their own YA canons of titles published since 1967 that stand the test of time. Or, alternatively, have students construct personal canons of books that changed something and/or stand the test of time in their own lives.

6. Writing Process/Writing Craft

What Do Students Typically Do?

Students are typically introduced to the concept of writing process in the early grades. They learn that writing involves a series of steps—prewriting, drafting, revising, editing, and publishing. Teachers use the language of writing process to support students as they develop and revise drafts across their years in English class. (For examples of students writing in the context of the workshop classroom, see Atwell, Graves, Kittle, Rief, and Romano.) The result of students' work might be a portfolio of original material written in a variety of student-selected genres; it might be a contribution to a class anthology or publication in a real-world context. Alternatively, student writing might be confined to a series of five-paragraph essays on teacher-assigned topics.

How to Recast This as YA Pedagogy

While students in a traditional process writing classroom explore their own writing processes, students in a classroom steeped in YA pedagogy might read stories, novels, or nonfiction works by a single YA author or a set of authors through a process lens, seeking to understand the writing processes of these authors. In addition to reading books, students read or watch interviews, listen to podcasts, and visit author websites and blogs to research how these books were written or, more generally, to learn about the process these authors follow as writers. They use the insights they glean about the writing processes of individual authors to think more deeply about their own writing process. They apply authors' ideas and routines to their own process, trying new approaches that may help them produce writing more easily and effectively.

Teaching Ideas

- Ask students to explore the writing life of a particular author. Find out as much as possible about where, when, and how much they write per day or week; what they do to create structures, routines, and overall discipline for writing; whether they write alone or with others; their preferred writing tools (e.g., writing by hand, on a typewriter, on a laptop); the struggles they've faced and how they've overcome them; and why they choose to write in the first place.

- Ask students to explore the story behind a particular book. What were the seeds for the story? Where, when, and how was it written? What stumbling blocks did the author face and how did she or he overcome them? What sorts of feedback did the author receive from an editor and/or peers? How did the author make use of that feedback? What was the timeline of this book, from origins to publication?

- For resources on authors and writing, students can consult individual author websites and blogs (A. S. King's "The Writer's Middle Finger" series, available on her blog, is a great example [http://www.as-king.info/2014/08/the-writers-middle-finger-how-to-grow.html]); YA author Sara Zarr's podcast *This Creative Life*, which features conversations between Sara and fellow authors about writing process and the writing life (http://www.sarazarr.com/archives/category/podcast); additional conversations with YA authors on *Text Messages*, a podcast available on ReadWriteThink.org (www.readwritethink.org/textmessages); the acknowledgments page or author's note in a book; annual author speeches (e.g., Printz Award) and lectures (e.g., May Hill Arbuthnot Lecture, Charlotte Zolotow Lecture, Zena Sutherland Lecture); feature articles about YA authors published in the *New Yorker* or the *New York Times*; and in-person author visits to bookstores or libraries in your town.

- After immersing themselves in an author's writing life, students write "process portraits" of various authors, followed by a takeaway: what we learn about writing process and craft from listening to them and studying their various approaches.

- Students use what they learn about an author's process to talk about their own process. They make connections between their writing challenges and ones they've heard authors talk about, and they propose changes to fix problems in their process based on the solutions they've heard authors come up with.

Examples from Teachers

Across the country, teachers are finding their own ways to recast and reinvent traditional classroom tasks through YA pedagogy. By creating contexts for reading that respect students' interests, invite collaborative meaning making, and connect students' learning to real-world contexts, these teachers are engaging teens as readers. They are calling students to make their reading of YA literature complex. At the same time, they're meeting the goals of the curriculum.

Renee Stites

In Wentzville, Missouri, seventh-grade teacher Renee Stites reinvented "Exploring Other Cultures," one of her district's required thematic units, by taking a local and teen-centered approach to text selection and writing assignments.

While most teachers at Renee's school used the cultures unit to study cultures from around the world, Renee chose to focus on cultures that her students engaged with and heard about on a daily basis. The goals of the unit, as outlined in the district's curriculum, were for students to understand that culture helps shape a

Middle Grade and YA Titles in "Exploring Other Cultures" Book Bins

By using book bins, Renee was able to incorporate many middle grade and YA titles into her unit. Here are just a few of them:

- *American Born Chinese* and *Boxers/Saints* by Gene Luen Yang; *The Rainbow People* by Laurence Yep

- *The Red Umbrella* by Christina Gonzalez; *Crossing the Wire* by Will Hobbs

- *Ask Me No Questions* by Marina Budhos; *Enemy Territory* by Sharon E. McKay

- *El Deafo* by Cece Bell; *Marcelo in the Real World* by Francisco X. Stork

- *Homecoming* by Cynthia Voigt; *One for the Murphys* by Lynda Mullaly Hunt

- *Chains* by Laurie Halse Anderson; *Nightjohn* by Gary Paulsen; *March: Book One* by John Lewis; *Feathers* by Jacqueline Woodson; *The Juvie Three* by Gordon Korman; *Black and White* by Paul Volponi; *When I Was the Greatest* by Jason Reynolds

person as an individual, and that considering differences across cultures helps us understand ourselves and the world. Renee and her colleagues also wanted students to think about why it's important to consider the perspectives of others and what we can gain by reading fiction and nonfiction texts on the same topic.

Renee organized her unit around text sets that focused on racial and ethnic groups such as Asian Americans, Latino/a Americans, and Arab Americans; social identities such as disability and homelessness; and, in the wake of protests nearby in Ferguson, Missouri, intersections between European Americans and African Americans over time. Each text set was housed in a book bin, and each bin contained at least a dozen YA titles, a few classics, and a handful of informational books and articles. Students were required to read at least three novels and four informational texts for the unit. Renee included YA lit in her bins by drawing on materials already available in the school library.

Renee knew it was important to include a social dimension in students' reading for the unit, but she wanted to try something different from traditional class discussion and literature circle meetings. She asked students to keep an independent reading journal and participate in peer and teacher conferences, but she added a third element that blended writing and talking: group journals. Each book bin contained a group notebook in which students wrote anonymously about the books and topics they were reading about. The same journals were used by students in each of her classes, which allowed students from first hour to communicate with students in second, fourth, and sixth hour.

Renee found that the act of writing in the group journals provoked mature and necessary conversations among her students about cultural stereotypes. Although students were not always reading the same texts, the issues across texts were similar enough to spark discussion. Renee saw the greatest learning of the unit occur in the group journals as students interacted with one another. Because students enjoyed the journals so much, Renee continued to use them throughout the rest of the year.

Renee also incorporated analytic work in the unit through mini-lessons focused on text structure, perspective, and the blending of fiction and nonfiction texts as a way of understanding a concept. For the final project, students created informational texts designed for seventh graders who would engage in the same unit the following year. Students produced guides for reading that conveyed some of their most enduring understandings—including the idea that social issues cross borders, cross cultural groups, and affect all of us.

Stepping back, we can see that Renee's approach to thematic units displays all the hallmarks of YA pedagogy. First, she set up a context for students' reading that was immediate and personal. Students chose their reading material from a mix of classic and contemporary literature, including a variety of YA novels and nonfiction texts. Rather than read to explore cultures far away, Renee asked students to connect their reading to the lives and experiences of people in their home community. Second, the work Renee asked students to do was simultaneously personal, analytical, and social. The anonymous group journals gave students a place to share and interact as readers of the books in a particular bin. Third, the informational texts students created for their final projects allowed them to blend what they had learned about text structures, perspective-taking, and cultural difference and share that with a real-world audience—next year's seventh graders. Developing a draft in the form of an informational text challenged them to write analytically, a useful complement to the reader-response writing they had done in the group journals.

Renee's approach illustrates just one of countless ways in which teachers are using YA

YA Lit and Censorship

Renee included several middle grade and YA novels about gay and transgender teens in her classroom library—titles such as *Five, Six, Seven, Nate!* by Tim Federle; *The Perks of Being a Wallflower* by Stephen Chbosky; *Winger* by Andrew Smith; *Aristotle and Dante Discover the Secrets of the Universe* by Benjamin Alire Sáenz; and *George* by Alex Gino. However, because she knew that stakeholders in her district would object if she assigned those books as required reading, she suggested them as supplemental texts during her cultures unit.

This raises the issue of YA lit and censorship. Whether it occurs publicly, in the form of a formal book challenge, or privately, in the quiet avoidance of titles that may stir controversy, censorship is something that all of us who teach YA literature need to think about. NCTE offers many resources to support teachers in anticensorship work. Through its Intellectual Freedom Center, you can access a Students' Right to Read statement, rationales for teaching challenged books, and guidelines designed to help districts implement a process of text adoption that is proactive. You can find these resources and many more at www.ncte.org/action/anti-censorship.

You can learn more about YA lit and censorship in Episode 30 of the ReadWriteThink *Text Messages* podcast, "Censorship and Your Freedom to Read" (www.read writethink.org/parent-afterschool-resources/podcast-episodes/censorship-your-freedom-read-30634.html) and in the September 2015 Twitter archive of #nctechat, "Say YA to Reading" (https://storify.com/NCTEStory/september-2015-nctechat-say-ya-to-reading). For a discussion of the dangers of gatekeeping and self-censorship, as well as the many book challenges each year that go unreported, see Teri Lesesne's essay "The Tip of the Iceberg" in the Fall 2014 issue of *The ALAN Review.*

lit and YA pedagogy to personalize required units while still achieving the goals of their district's curriculum. Renee used her knowledge of YA lit to meet the social and emotional needs of middle school students while challenging them academically. Reading YA texts in an interactive social environment gave students a deeper understanding of their own lives and the lives of others in their midst.

Kellee Moye

In Orlando, Florida, middle school teacher Kellee Moye has also used YA lit and YA pedagogy to reinvent thematic units. In contrast to Renee's book bins, Kellee leads students through a series of thematically related experiences anchored in Ginny Rorby's *Hurt Go Happy*, a Schneider Family Book Award–winning middle grade novel about a child who is deaf. While Renee's unit gives students new insights into diversity, Kellee's unit, which she has taught in grades 6, 7, and 8, invites students into political and ethical debates.

The foundation for all of Kellee's YA units is actually not a theme but rather a standard or a strategy. In the case of *Hurt Go Happy*, Kellee was searching for a way to teach middle school students the fiction elements of plot development and characterization. She wanted to teach those elements through whole-class reading of a book that was well written with complex characters and deep themes. While *Hurt Go Happy* met these criteria, its content allowed Kellee to build social and emotional goals into the unit as well.

With a story line that focuses on the experiences of a thirteen-year-old girl who's been deaf since the age of six but whose mother never allowed her to use sign language, *Hurt Go Happy* led Kellee to embed her teaching of literary elements in a larger exploration of empathy for people with disabilities. Because the novel's main character eventually does learn sign language from a scientist who uses signs to communicate with a baby chimpanzee, Kellee and her students participate in conversations that go beyond the single issue of disability. Class discussions touch on political and ethical topics such as research facilities, animal abuse, and wild animals as pets.

Following their reading of the novel, Kellee's students interview the author, Ginny Rorby. They generate questions, vote on which ones to ask, and then conduct a whole-class interview. The real-world connection they forge with Rorby is complemented by the real-world experience of visiting an animal sanctuary called the Center for Great Apes (CFGA) (www.centerforgreatapes.org), which is located just ninety minutes from Kellee's school. CFGA is the real-life model for a fictional animal sanctuary in the book, and it is home to three apes that are featured in Rorby's novel. Through their interview with Rorby and their field trip to CFGA, Kellee's students get a firsthand glimpse of how authors build novels that are based on real-world places and issues. Because Kellee connects students' reading of *Hurt Go Happy* with related texts such as Dr. Seuss's *The Lorax*, which focuses on caring for the earth; *Each Kindness* by Jacqueline Woodson, which focuses on caring for classmates who are different; and *The Dot* by Peter H. Reynolds, which focuses on open-mindedness, students engage in an extended exploration of the themes of caring and empathy.

Kellee notes that while students build classroom community through their shared experience of the text, they also practice analytical dimensions of reading such as asking questions, making connections, predicting, close reading, comparing and contrasting, and reflection. They study cause and effect, characterization, plot development, conflict, setting, voice, and the genre of contemporary realistic fiction. Even more than this literary knowledge, however, Kellee values the conversations that are sparked by this novel. As students learn about deafness, animal testing, and animal capture, their perspectives on the world change. Kellee sees this through the anticipation guide she administers at the start of the unit. She explains,

> Many [students] feel, when we begin the text, that being deaf wouldn't affect your life in any way except not being able to watch TV or listen to music, but by the end . . . [they understand that deafness leads to other challenges] such as having trouble communicating with loved ones and feeling isolated in social situations. Similarly, they grow in how they look at chimpanzees. By the end of the book, students begin to see the cruelty in using chimps in animal testing and capturing them as babies from their mothers, who are killed.

Like many other teachers who use YA novels as whole-class reads, Kellee felt nervous at first about bringing *Hurt Go Happy* into the classroom. "I was worried about talking with 11- to 14-year-old students about the tough topics in the book, specifically animal and child abuse. But I learned my worries were for naught. My middle school students have feelings and opinions about these topics and are very happy to discuss these and other tough subjects." Kellee adds that students' ability to navigate these conversations is increased by the skills they develop in working with the text. "Although my students do not always agree, their ability to use prior knowledge and the text to support their comments about these subjects without attacking each other shows real maturity."

For students who want to read other books that connect thematically to *Hurt Go Happy*, Kellee recommends YA novels such as *Endangered* by Eliot Schrefer; *Half Brother* by Kenneth Oppel; a middle grade book, *The One and Only Ivan* by Katherine Applegate, and a companion picture book, *Ivan: The Remarkable True Story of the Shopping Mall Gorilla*, also by Katherine Applegate; another picture book, *Me . . . Jane* by Patrick McDonnell; and two visual texts: *Wonderstruck* by Brian Selznick and the graphic novel *El Deafo* by Cece Bell. (For more information on Kellee's approach to teaching *Hurt Go Happy*, see her blog posts on *Unleashing Readers*, www.unleashingreaders.com, one posted on November 22, 2013, and another posted on July 18, 2014.)

Kellee's teaching of *Hurt Go Happy* offers another great example of YA pedagogy. Her students' reading of this novel challenges them to think deeply about themselves, other people, and larger ethical questions. Even as they participate in deep and powerful discussions, Kellee prompts them to work with the text analytically, calling on the shared vocabulary they have developed around reading processes and literary elements. Their reading is relevant because it is about the life of a teenager their age, but it becomes even more relevant when they meet the author and visit one of the settings in the book.

Kellee's approach to teaching *Hurt Go Happy* is one that keeps multiple dimensions of YA reading in play. Students' shared reading of *Hurt Go Happy* is clearly personal. We see evidence of this in the way Kellee testifies about the effect of reading the book on students' beliefs. It is also social: reading the book together gives students a chance to express their views and learn from one another, which enriches classroom culture. "*Hurt Go Happy* has become the number one community builder in my classroom," Kellee says. The analytical dimension is also prominent here, as Kellee identifies specific teaching practices she uses to engage students in close work with the text. Finally, Kellee keeps her students' larger reading lives in mind by offering readalike titles that both pull readers more deeply into *Hurt Go Happy* and provide them with further options for related reading.

Together, Renee's and Kellee's thematic units prove that there are many exciting possibilities for reading and teaching YA lit. With YA pedagogy, we make students' reading personal, complex, and, most of all, relevant in both school and their lives beyond the classroom.

Cultivating Complexity *and* Relevance

Through YA pedagogy, we recast traditional classroom tasks so that students' work with YA literature becomes relevant in real-world contexts. We engage students in tasks that teach them to find and make complexity as YA readers while we continue to teach traditional ELA skills. By adapting the ideas offered here and inventing new ones, we make students' classroom work with YA lit matter, and we promote agency and autonomy in teen readers.

Tasks in YA pedagogy are designed to make students aware that there are different dimensions of reading and that readers take different approaches to books in different contexts at different times. Reading is sometimes personal, sometimes social, and sometimes analytical. Most often, as the tasks I've outlined in this chapter show, it's a blend of all three. YA pedagogy acknowledges this, and it calls students to combine modes of reading they're often taught to keep separate in English class. That is, we ask students to couple their personal, emotional response to a book with some form of critical, analytical work that's done in the company of their peers. Teachers of YA lit welcome each of these modes of reading because we believe that reading becomes more powerful—and more complex—in the blending.

We can make these modes of reading more tangible for students, and we can help them see the value in each one, by linking each mode to a guiding question. For example, when we foreground the personal, we can ask, "What did I look for and find in this text?" When we foreground the social, we can ask, "What are other people saying about this text, and how does that change the way I think about it or what I see in it?" When we foreground the analytical, we can ask, "How might I shape the ways others view this text by writing and speaking about its style, substance, features, and themes?"

YA pedagogy calls teachers to create tasks that link these modes of reading to parallel kinds of relevance: *personal relevance*, in terms of students' interests and needs as individuals; *academic relevance*, in terms of students' current and future success in school; and *social relevance*, in terms of students' relationships with others and larger real-world contexts. By emphasizing relevance, we encourage students to cultivate the habit of applying literary concepts and literary ways of thinking to books they choose for themselves so that they'll read those books with increasing skill and insight. We encourage them to leave English class prepared to use their literary knowledge to read in ways that are purposeful and meaningful in their lives beyond the classroom.

The result of this approach is that students develop greater agency and autonomy as readers. They gain a stronger understanding of what the work they do in an ELA class can be good for, and that work takes on greater meaning because they see what it looks like in the real world. Students emerge as readers who are more equipped to read YA lit—and other texts—closely, actively, and thoughtfully.

We don't have to be experts in YA lit to teach in these ways. When we believe in the value of the books, and when we commit to doing all we can to engage students in relevant work with the books, we suddenly discover a host of exciting new possibilities for our teaching. Even if we're new to reading and teaching young adult literature, that lack of experience doesn't have to be an obstacle. A community of professionals committed to reading, writing about, and teaching YA lit is close at hand. All we need to do is tap into that community to begin imagining new possibilities for teen readers. With the help of our colleagues, and with a vision for teaching YA lit differently than we have in the past, we can change our classrooms—and students' reading lives—with YA pedagogy.

Chapter Six

New Approaches to Assessment in YA Pedagogy

At Riverside Academy in Dundee, Michigan, Daria Plumb has pulled aside a boy named Jalen to talk with me about his reading. He's one of two Latino/a students at her small alternative school. He arrived in the fall as a senior and a self-described nonreader, but when Daria introduced him to Matt de la Peña's books, that changed. Now he checks out three or four books at a time. He stays after school to read in the library. He's on fire as a reader: motivated, committed, and purposeful. Daria wonders if reading created a safe space for him at Riverside.

Because Jalen and I share a love of de la Peña's books, and because something transformative seems to have happened to Jalen through his reading experience with Daria, I'm eager to meet him. We sit at a table in the common area, and he begins by telling me that de la Peña is one of his favorite authors. Earlier this year, he worked his way through each of the author's five novels: *Ball Don't Lie, Mexican WhiteBoy, We Were Here, I Will Save You,* and *The Living.* (*The Hunted* hadn't yet been published.)

I ask Jalen what he gets from de la Peña's books that he doesn't get from other books he's read. He says that he can relate to the characters. Since I'm always trying to unpack the meaning of the word *relate* when students use it in this way, I ask what it is that he can relate to. "Just their personalities," he replies, "and their experiences." He mentions Miguel from *We Were Here*. "I've been through a lot of the things he's been through. I see through his eyes as I'm reading the book. He has his issues and I have mine as well. I can feel what he's feeling."

I ask what it was like when he finished this author's books and had to move on to try books by others. Jalen says it was hard at first. Daria guided him to other Latino authors such as Benjamin Alire Sáenz and Oscar Hijuelos. He says he liked the main character of Hijuelos's *Dark Dude*—liked that he is Latino. He likes a lot of books in which the main character is Latino. He can relate. And sometimes the author will use Latino/a slang, which he likes.

We talk about Benjamin Alire Sáenz. Jalen says he enjoyed the bond between the main characters in *Aristotle and Dante Discover the Secrets of the Universe*. Then he mentions Sáenz's novel *Last Night I Sang to the Monster*, a book about clinical depression. The main character is an older teen boy who's being hospitalized for this condition. I ask what about that story appealed to Jalen. "He's able to find himself in the book," he says. "He realizes a lot about life in the book. Helped me realize about life, too." I ask what he realized. "That life is important. He was going through hard times, but life is definitely worth it. It's not worth taking your life."

I ask Jalen if there are any other books he wants to talk about. He mentions his most recent read, Andrew Smith's *Grasshopper Jungle*, and I note that this book is nothing like any of the others we've talked about. It's set in Iowa, it's about three white teens, and an army of six-foot-tall praying mantises ends up destroying the world. I've read only the first five chapters, but I know the book is smart, strange, and irreverent. I ask Jalen what he's noticing and liking. "Everything," he says. "It's so different. I love everything." He says the book is weird—it's not something that would really happen, but the way the characters bond, the way they talk and inter- act, the way they think about things: it all appeals to him. It's also funny. I com- ment that this book seems to be stretching him in a new direction, and he agrees. He can't really say *how* it's stretching him, but he says he wishes there were more books like it.

Before our conversation wraps up, I want to ask Jalen a question that will help me understand what he's accomplishing through all this reading. I recall a question Daria told me she likes to pose as a journal prompt: Have you ever read a book that changed the way you thought about something? The question seems fit- ting for Jalen given how involved he's been in these different novels. Beyond liking the characters, I wonder how the books have made him *think*.

Jalen answers by coming back to Matt de la Peña. Instead of naming a specific title, he talks about de la Peña's books in general. I ask what they changed about his thinking. "Just how I feel at times." I ask him to tell me more. "I would say more of a positive self-image. I feel like I looked at myself worse than I really was. Matt's books just helped me. I really could feel myself in those books. I guess it was the way I—" He pauses. "I don't know. Like I thought of myself as a bad kid. I feel like his books helped me realize I *wasn't* a bad kid. I guess it's hard to explain."

What Can Jalen Teach Us about Assessment?

Talking books with Jalen is a pleasure. I love having the opportunity to listen to him reflect on his experiences as a reader. Our conversation leaves me thinking about the various things he's been able to do as a reader of YA lit and how personal his reading has been. He's developed a sense of kinship with a particular author. His choice of books has been intentional and deliberate. Guided by Daria, he's moved through de la Peña's entire body of work, and then he's gone on to read books in the same vein by other Latino/a YA authors. He can look across the titles he's read and identify patterns in what appeals to him. Reading has also affirmed his identity—both his racial identity and his social identity as a teen who's been through hard times and learned to see himself in a new light.

Beyond Jalen's personal story, our conversation leaves me thinking more generally about the gap between those personal dimensions of reading and what we typically focus on when we assess reading in school. The connections Jalen is forming with books right now, fueled by the experience of discovering books and authors to love, are key to his motivation and engagement as a reader. His personal investment in books serves as the foundation for his continued growth as a student in English class.

And yet it's this personal dimension of reading that our assessment is least likely to explore, or even consider. It's the great irony of teaching. We want students to love books as we do. Often we want them to love the same books that we love—books that are personally important to us. And yet if students *are* able to find and make their own personal connections, we don't give them much room to show it, especially not in our assessments.

When we rely on traditional assessments such as reading quizzes and multiple-choice tests, and when we assign writing assessments that center solely on argument and analysis, the message we send to students is that the personal doesn't count. Consequently, when students do connect personally to a text, they learn to keep that part separate from the work they do for class. It's no wonder they grow disengaged. We've all seen it—students who fail the test or choose not to write the paper after we've spent weeks studying a novel. Or, equally frustrating, students who turn in work that has no heart, life, or voice.

The fact is, our traditional forms of assessment capture only a fraction of who students are and what they can do as readers. Assessment ends up being one more place where we reinforce the binary paradigm and limit our opportunities for authentic teaching.

If we accept the core principles of YA pedagogy—that we must (1) give students chances to blend personal and academic dimensions of reading and (2) share their reading experiences with others while (3) engaging them in classroom tasks that foster complexity, agency, and autonomy (4) using literature that takes their concerns seriously in the present moment—shouldn't we also strive for an approach to assessment that explores and values the learning that results from this?

Reading is personal. Assessment, too, should be personal.

A New Approach to Assessment

We need an approach to assessment that honors the personal dimensions of reading and yet goes beyond simply listening to teens talk about their reading lives, as Jalen talked to me. We also need them to demonstrate the skills they've developed as students: their ability to comprehend, infer, analyze, connect, construct arguments, and work with textual evidence. We need to create assessment opportunities that allow them to do both personal *and* analytical work.

But we can go even further. What if we took a new approach to assessment, one that allows students to show us more, and allows us to see more, of what they are able to do as readers? What if our assessments were designed in a way that calls students to engage in continued learning and meaning making? What would it look like to invite them to do that work creatively, in the company of their peers, with real-world audiences in mind?

The ideas I offer in this chapter present assessment possibilities that allow for each of these things. No matter what approach we take to assessment, however, students' work still needs to be informed by close reading of the text. We must keep the analytical dimension alive in the assessment portion of YA pedagogy, just as we do in our class discussions and classroom tasks. Here as well as there, we set up opportunities for students to show their skills responding to and analyzing texts, but always in ways that collapse the binary by blending the analytical with the personal.

Most important, this approach to assessment gives students a chance to demonstrate the agency and autonomy they've developed as readers through YA pedagogy. We can call students to show us how they have learned to read for their own purposes—how they have become agents of their own reading lives who use tools they've acquired in the classroom to make personal and creative meaning, and how they have learned to share their reading with others.

Three Ideas for Personal, Creative, Blended Approaches to Assessment

Just as we saw in the chapter on classroom tasks, we don't need to invent entirely new forms of assessment to evaluate students' reading abilities. Instead, we can shift our traditional end-of-unit assignments and recast traditional assessment tasks in a new light. In contrast to the tasks I suggest in Chapter 5, which can be used to guide students' reading from day to day, the ideas I offer here for assessment call for more far-reaching forms of personal and analytical synthesis. Thus they are fitting to use to assess students' work at the end of a unit or at the end of a semester.

The three forms of assessment I introduce here—themed reading lists, the Brown Bag Exam, and Meeting of Minds performances—are linked to the blended dimensions of reading we seek to cultivate and value through YA pedagogy. They are personal in that they require students to construct their own understandings of a text; they are social in that they invite students to construct understanding in discussions with their peers; and they are analytical in that they expect students to make connections between books, across books, and in relation to larger ideas. They are also flexible in that they provide space for students to think creatively while linking their work to real-world contexts. They allow students to show what they know and are able to do as readers. At the same time, they give students the opportunity to interact creatively with books and their peers to make new meaning.

Characteristics of Assessment in YA Pedagogy

- Personal: constructing one's own understandings of a text

- Social: constructing understanding through interactions with peers

- Analytical: making connections between books, across books, and in relation to larger ideas

- Flexible: space for creative thinking and linking work to real-world contexts

Themed Reading Lists

When students have the opportunity to read YA lit independently, they do best when guided by a larger purpose. Themed reading lists ask students to focus their reading on a self-selected topic, theme, or idea. Students read as many books as they can on that topic, and then they share the best of what they find in the form of a print or digital resource that's composed for a real-world audience and presented in a relevant, real-world genre.

Getting started. Students need several kinds of help to plan and complete this project.

- *Audience help.* First, since students may not have had the opportunity to do work in school designed for real-world audiences, it's important to begin by talking about potential audiences for the project and how the audience they choose should make sense in the context of their personal goals for sharing YA lit with others. For example, if students want to see more YA titles taught in the classroom, they might make a list for teachers in other grade levels or departments. Or they could target specific teens in their lives, producing lists intended for younger siblings, neighbors, or youth they've met through volunteer work. A clear idea of audience guides students to do more targeted, strategic, and effective work with the books.

- *Genre help.* Similarly, since students probably aren't used to choosing their own genres for class assignments, it's important to talk about genre in relation to the project's purpose. What form should the book list take, based on the needs of the intended audience? Students will benefit from conversations about how audience and genre should shape what they say about the books. They will also benefit from studying lists created by others. We can guide them to look closely at the voice and style of the writing, as well as the information that is and isn't included, in light of the list's intended audience and genre. We can also guide them to explore real-world genres that are used for recommending and sharing books, such as reading guides, bookmarks, and blogs.

- *Book help.* Finally, students will most likely need help finding titles that fit their chosen topic. We can guide them to relevant books and to online resources such as the YALSA-BK listserv, described in Chapter 4, and YALSA's annual lists of Popular Paperbacks for Young Adults, described in Chapter 5. We can also encourage them to ask their classmates for help. In a room full of independent readers, students can draw on the book knowledge of their peers.

Reflective writing. To reinforce the idea that students should be making deliberate decisions throughout the development of their projects, they turn in a reflective essay on their process along with the final project. Those essays give students space to explain the principles that guided their project's development and the underlying logic for their project design.

Assessment criteria. Themed reading lists should demonstrate *focus*: a clear central organizing principle (specific theme, topic, genre, question, text structure, or stylistic feature that unites texts) and evidence that the list has been designed to meet the needs of a specific audience. *Text selection* should be informed and strategic. *Discussion of texts* should go beyond summary to provide critical commentary and analysis. Work with texts should be specific and detailed, invoking particular quotes, themes, or text features that are relevant to the organizing principle. Tone and voice should be tailored to audience. The *form* should be enticing and visually appealing; content should be effectively structured and organized, and the design should be appropriate to the project's purpose. Finally, lists should demonstrate *creativity and effort*: the work should be personal, interesting, and/or innovative.

Examples of student work. In my college classroom, students have created themed reading lists for their nieces and nephews, younger siblings, and young neighbors. They've devised lists for teens in library book clubs, health clinics, rehab facilities, and grief support groups. Students have used the themed reading list assignment to envision ways of including YA lit in their future careers as teachers, social workers, speech pathologists, and nurses. They've taken up the call to be YA lit advocates while synthesizing their learning about YA as a field.

One of the most memorable lists was Betty Gibson's on YA lit that pairs art and text. In the form of a handbook written for teachers, Betty organized her text set into three categories. The first category included books that feature actual visuals, such as original illustrations or reproductions of art (*Okay for Now, The Absolutely True Diary of a Part-Time Indian, A Monster Calls, The Real Boy, Why We Broke Up, The Book Thief*). The second category included books that have explicit references to art, either to particular paintings or to characters who are healed by creating art (*Speak, The Fault in Our Stars*). In the third category, the connection between text and image was slightly more abstract. For these books, Betty highlighted how art could be used as a lens to help readers understand the story in a deeper way (*Ask the Passengers*).

One of the most impressive elements of Betty's handbook was the systematic way she led teachers through possibilities for teaching YA lit through the lens of visual literacy. She began the handbook with an introduction and visual analysis protocol—a step-by-step guide for teaching students how to read an image. Then for each YA title, she included a sample quotation, a book blurb focused on the relevance of art to the story, and a series of discussion ideas. She concluded the handbook with a brief list of other possibilities for pairing art and text, such as pairing the Colosseum in Rome with *The Hunger Games*.

The background information and discussion ideas Betty provided for Daniel Handler's Printz Honor book, *Why We Broke Up*, illustrate how exploring the connections between art and YA lit can be simultaneously interpretive and literal, text-based and contextual, analytical and personal.

In her book blurb, Betty explained that the novel is written in the form of a letter composed by Min Green to Ed Slaterton explaining why they broke up. Accompanying the letter is a box that contains artifacts of their relationship. Each artifact is represented by a full-page color illustration drawn by artist Maira Kalman. Betty wrote,

In many ways the box of objects in *Why We Broke Up* is a museum of Min and Ed's relationship. Objects, whether ordinary or artistically rendered, tell a story. Imagine a history museum gallery. The objects plus the labels create a story. But in this case, we only get Min's interpretation of the objects. What would Ed's version be? The objects are hard evidence of the relationship and the letter interprets them for the reader from Min's perspective.

Discussion ideas:

- What do the images in *Why We Broke Up* represent?

- Can an object tell a story? How? What are examples of objects telling stories?

- What are your impressions of Min as a narrator? How do the objects reinforce or contradict her story?

- What object(s) can tell a story from your life?

- Based on *Why We Broke Up*, what is more ephemeral: relationships, objects, or stories?

In her reflection, Betty highlighted the analytical payoff of pairing art and YA lit. Her comments remind us of the continuing possibilities for guiding students to make complexity as readers and thinkers, no matter what the text:

Understanding art, like understanding literature, requires skills. The main skill is visual analysis. Unlike close reading, visual analysis is basically innate in young people because of the increasingly visual world we live in. Students understand advertisements, movies, and TV shows without thinking. Visual analysis just allows us to slow the comprehension down and break it into its parts. Then, it can be used to explain how to read literature. Furthermore, introducing art means introducing another genre—voilà genre study (something the Common Core is all about, by the way). Compare and contrast? Art can make that quick and fun. Like I said in the introduction, art can be adapted to fit many needs in an English classroom; it can add a layer of complexity, make something clearer, or increase student interest.

Other examples of themed reading lists created by students in my classroom:

- Abby Landes read YA novels set during the summer after high school and packaged her list in the form of a CD with liner notes. She chose a thematically related song to introduce each book, and she used liner notes to explain the book's story line and appeal. Abby designed the CD to be a gift for her boyfriend's younger sister, who was a high school senior at the time.

- Shannon McGuire created a poster on escapist reads to hang in a drug and alcohol rehab facility. Carrie Dvorak designed a brochure featuring books on eating disorders for use in a health clinic.

- Laura Plack created a reading guide on "damsel-free" YA lit for teens in a local library book group. Megan White created a reading guide for teachers on books featuring women in wartime.

- Other genres students have used to share their themed reading lists: websites, blogs, Tumblr pages, YouTube channels, podcasts, bookmarks, passports, Choose Your Own Adventure stories, video games, short movies.

Recasting traditional assessment tasks. The themed reading list has its roots in the most traditional reading assignment of all—the book report, in which students read books and engage in some form of summary and analysis. The themed reading list project demands more. Students are pitching books to particular kinds of readers and making connections across books that are somehow related. Themed reading lists allow students to put their knowledge of YA lit to use in service of a larger goal. Through their lists, students advocate for YA as a field and produce a resource designed to cultivate the reading lives of others.

Meeting the criteria for assessment in YA pedagogy. The themed reading list is guided by the four characteristics of assessment in YA pedagogy. Since students choose a central topic or theme for their list, their work is *personal*: they read books that they are interested and invested in. Their work is also *social*: the planning process invites them to seek out advice from their peers. They draw on the social context of the classroom to broaden their book knowledge and develop more strategic ways of sharing their books. The *analytical* dimension arises from the connections they must create across books and the decisions they must make about how to frame the set as whole. Identifying text features to highlight and constructing an argument about the books' value is also analytical work. Finally, the project provides space for creativity and real-world relevance. Students may choose to work in nontraditional genres that showcase their expertise in art or digital literacy, and they are challenged to make their work useful to an audience outside the classroom—even if it's just one teen reader.

Brown Bag Exam

The idea for this nontraditional test comes from Professor Denise Ousley-Exum, who presented the concept in cooperation with YA authors L. M. Elliot and Laurie Halse Anderson at the 2007 ALAN Workshop. In the social environment of the classroom, students pull artifacts that the teacher has strategically selected out of a brown paper lunch bag. Working alone and together, they connect the artifacts to specific moments and passages from a book they have read in common, and then they use those connections as a springboard for writing about the book's themes.

As Denise explained in an essay on the AdLit.org website, she designed the Brown Bag Exam to address the disconnect that she and her students were experiencing between instruction and assessment. Her instructional approach engaged students in reading and writing activities that connected literature to their lives, but she lacked assessments that matched the activities students had enjoyed. As Denise noted, "Tests showed what students *didn't* know, not what they had read, learned, or gained." Through found objects and images, the Brown Bag Exam invites students to express their understanding. Denise added that unlike traditional assessment, "The Brown Bag Exam is a joyful experience . . . filled with conversation, idea exchange, laughter, and learning." (For more information, see www.adlit.org/unlocking_the_past/brown_bag_exams/.)

The Brown Bag Exam typically comes at the end of a unit on a whole-class novel, but if students have read several whole-class novels over the course of the semester, the Brown Bag Exam can also serve as a midterm or final. The teacher creates one brown bag for each novel the class has studied. A representative from each literature circle group pulls an index card out of a hat; the card tells the group which book they'll be writing on. Each group writes about just one book from the larger menu of titles.

Getting started. Since the design of this exam is different from that of the tests students are used to, they need a clear idea of what to expect and how to prepare. They benefit from an opportunity to practice thinking in the associative, analytical, and metaphorical ways the exam calls for.

- *How students prepare.* As a way to familiarize students with the idea of writing about objects in connection to novels, have them brainstorm as many objects as they can think of for one of their whole-class novels. This helps them start thinking both literally and metaphorically about a book's events and ideas. They can prepare further by lining up quotes that connect to the objects they brainstormed.

- *Images instead of objects.* For teachers who feel overwhelmed by the prospect of gathering physical objects, a simpler approach is to gather color images from the Internet. Printing images makes it possible to include material objects (including ones that won't fit in a bag) as well as images that have conceptual relevance. When I designed a Brown Bag Exam for John Green's *The Fault in Our Stars*, for example, I included images to represent objects such as a cigarette, orange tulips, a hand grenade, a birthday cake, dinosaur bones, and a swing set. I also included images of conceptual items such as the symbol for infinity, a triangle graphic representing Maslow's hierarchy of needs, and a Venn diagram.

- *Exam template.* To guide students through the steps of the exam, it helps to provide a template organized as a series of blank boxes to write in. The boxes walk students through each step of the exam, showing them where to work independently, where to collaborate with their classmates, and where to make analytical connections with specific passages from the text.

What it looks like in practice. In the first few minutes, students open their bags and spread out the images. If they are sharing a single bag with members of their literature circle, this step involves discussion and negotiation as students work out who will write about which object. Students then write silently for several minutes, making connections on their own between the book and the image they've chosen. At this point, you can invite them to begin sharing ideas with their peers. After ten minutes or so, advise them to return to the process of writing on their own as they proceed through work with several more images and some kind of closing essay.

What will probably feel strangest to teachers and students alike is the idea of talking during the exam. And yet it's this social dimension that makes the exam experience so energizing. Glance around the room and you'll see students sitting in circles with books in hand, reminding one another of connections and helping each other track down quotes. The exam invites students to capitalize on relationships they've formed in their literature circles. As they talk and write, they simultaneously build on and draw from their previous conversations.

Grading the exam. In general, I prefer to avoid assigning points to student work, but allocating a set amount of points to each section of the Brown Bag Exam makes grading easier. When students brainstorm *connections* between an object and the book, I consider both the number of connections they are able to make and their ability to move from surface-level connections to deeper metaphorical meanings. I also look for connections across a range of literary elements, including plot, character, setting, and theme. When students write about *quotes*, I look for the relevance of the quote to the selected item and the level of insight in students' comments about it. When students write about *ideas they got from their peers*, I simply look for evidence that they shared with their group members and took something from the conversation, even if it was confirmation of what they were already thinking. I don't want to penalize a student if the group is unable to come up with new ideas beyond the ones they already have. On the *essay* portion of the exam, I often ask students to come up with their own brown bag item, and then I look to see how far they can go in explaining the item's significance in relation to the book's arguments and themes.

Examples of student work. In my college classroom, Anne Milne's work with Paolo Bacigalupi's *Ship Breaker* illustrated the power of the Brown Bag Exam to reveal students' ability to read a text personally, critically, and creatively.

In response to the image of a road winding through a forest, Anne made the following connections:

- Path to self-discovery
- Uncertainty seen in the foggy distance
- Change
- Cars drive on roads and use gas (fuel) like oil
- Having a car means certain wealth status

When asked to choose a relevant quote and explain its connection to the brown bag item, Anne chose the following:

> "Every time Tool spoke, his words were like a whip, lashing her. Nailer wasn't sure why, but he liked to see her embarrassed. Part of him sensed that she thought of him as something like an animal, a useful creature like a dog, but not actually a person. Then again, he wasn't too sure that she was a person either. Swanks were different. They came from a different place, lived different lives, wrecked whole clipper ships just so one girl could survive." (p. 210).
>
> Connections:
>
> - We all come from different places, having taken different roads to meet up with one another. Sometimes we travel on the same road.
>
> - At the time of this quotation, Nailer, Nita, and Tool are on the same literal journey of escape and survival. They are also on their own individual roads of self-discovery and [attempting to understand what it means to be] a person and [to honor] each person's worth/value.

In the space where she was asked to share a new idea she got from discussion with her fellow group members, Anne wrote, "The image of oil spilling out into the ocean water, contaminating its clarity and cleanliness. Similarly, the characters experience personal pollutants that muddy their clarity such as [how] Nailer's father dirties his journey toward the meaning of self, loyalty, and family."

When asked to invent a new item for the brown bag on *Ship Breaker*, Anne's fellow group member, Ashley Hopkins, chose the image of a hurricane. She wrote:

> The hurricanes in the book called City Killers were a consequence, a result of the warning theme of this novel, global warming. The hurricanes have increased so much that they have drowned cities and destroyed everything in their path. The hurricanes have worsened due to global warming which is due to pollution, which is due to industrial life. This book tries to accomplish a few things, but one is [to raise] awareness of global warming and the consequences of our current actions.

Using the Brown Bag Exam with high school students. At Cypress Creek High School in Orlando, Florida, literacy coach Beth Scanlon has used the Brown Bag Exam in several ways. When staff members decided to do a One Book/One Grade Level school-wide summer reading assignment in 2009, they chose the Brown Bag Exam as their common assessment for a number of reasons. As Beth explained:

- It allows students to engage in both independent and collaborative processing of story themes.
- It involves students in close reading and rereading of the text, and it asks them to show their skills citing textual evidence.

- It invites all students to contribute their ideas and expertise, including English language learners.
- It provides space for students who didn't read the book to join the conversation.
- It engages students in speaking, reading, writing, listening, and viewing—all the dimensions of English language arts.
- It encourages self-reflection.
- Its design makes administering makeup exams manageable.

The books that staff members at Beth's school chose for required reading included David Klass's *Firestorm* for ninth graders, Sherman Alexie's *The Absolutely True Diary of a Part-Time Indian* for tenth graders, Susan Beth Pfeffer's *Life as We Knew It* for eleventh graders (all of which are YA novels), and Mark Haddon's crossover novel (a book marketed to both teens and adults), *The Curious Incident of the Dog in the Night-Time*, for twelfth graders.

Because the Brown Bag Exam serves as a common assessment, teachers at each grade level chose the images for their book and wrote up answer keys. Even though teachers had a key to consult, students could provide different answers as long as they included evidence from the text to support their ideas. As the school literacy coach and exam coordinator, Beth put together a set of color images for each teacher and added two questions to Denise Ousley-Exum's original version of the exam: (1) What is one object that I didn't include but could have? Include specific evidence from the text to support your answer; and (2) What did you learn from the Brown Bag Exam process?

Teachers at Beth's school had many positive things to say about the Brown Bag Exam. First, students were more engaged in assessment because they were allowed to make choices. That helped them to feel they were more in control of the answers. The open-endedness of the design helped students feel more confident that they would be able to come up with answers. Teachers found the Brown Bag Exam to be a more useful way to informally assess students' skills than reading 150 poorly written essays. Teachers also liked the concept of blending images and text.

Students, too, appreciated that the Brown Bag Exam wasn't as pressure filled as normal exams and that it didn't start them off with a low grade during the first nine-week marking period.

In addition to the summer reading assessment, Beth has used the Brown Bag Exam in her own classroom. She's built more complexity into the experience by including quotations from other sources, along with individual words, in the bags. For example, in her exam on Sherman Alexie's *The Absolutely True Diary of a Part-Time Indian*, she included images such as fire, an old textbook, a kid with a black eye, a hurdle, lips, and white Converse high-tops. She also included the word *courage* and the following quotes:

- "Native Americans have a higher poverty and unemployment rate when compared with the national average, but the rates are comparable to those of blacks and Hispanics. About one in four American Indians and Alaska Natives were living in poverty in 2012. Among those who identify as American Indian or Alaska Native as their only race, the poverty rate was 29.1% in 2012." Pew Research Center, June 13, 2014. (Available at www.pewresearch.org/fact-tank/2014/06/13/1-in-4-native-americans-and-alaska-natives-are-living-in-poverty/.)
- "Don't live up to your stereotypes."—Sherman Alexie
- "Education is the most powerful weapon which you can use to change the world."—Nelson Mandela

Beth also put the Brown Bag Exam to work as an assessment for students' reading of nonfiction articles at the end of a nine-week marking period. To engage incoming ninth graders in conversations about motivation and focus, she put together a text set of articles on study habits, health, talking with parents, multitasking, and tips for school success. The Brown Bag Exam engaged students in both reviewing their reading and determining common threads across articles. Beth's exam covered the following list of articles:

- "You'll Never Learn! Students Can't Resist Multitasking, and It's Impairing Their Memory" by Annie Murphy Paul (available on Slate.com)
- "Motivation and the Power of Not Giving Up" by Steven Dowshen (available at TeenHeatlth.org)
- "A Little Deception Helps Push Athletes to the Limit" by Gina Kolata (published in the *New York Times*)
- "How Writing by Hand Makes Kids Smarter: Younger Americans Are Typing or Texting More and Writing Less, Even in School—and That's a Problem When It Comes to Brain Development" (published in *The Week*)
- "How to Make Homework Less Work" by Steven Downshen (available at TeenHeatlth.org)
- "Back to School: The Toughest Test of All Is 9th Grade: More Students Fail 9th Grade Than Any Other in Florida" by Dave Weber (published in the *Orlando Sentinel*)
- "Talking to Your Parents and Other Adults" by Neil Izenburg (available at TeenHeatlth.org)
- "Six Reading Habits to Develop in Your First Year at Harvard" by Susan Gilroy (a guide available through Lamont Library at Harvard College)
- "This Is Your Brain on Sugar: Study Shows High-Fructose Diet Sabotages Learning, Memory" (an article shared on the UCLA Newsroom website)

Beth explained that finding images to pair with nonfiction texts was no harder than finding images for fiction. In her text set on motivation, for example, Beth chose images such as a hurdle, a bear, and a Red Cross logo. Students were able to find connections between these seemingly disparate articles and the big ideas that linked them. Beth said that what she saw during the exam was students going back into the texts to find the connections. Their work was made easier because Beth had taught them a process of marking and writing about the texts. They didn't have to reread the articles during the exam; instead they could make good on the work they had already done by focusing on the big picture the articles had conveyed.

Recasting traditional assessment tasks. The Brown Bag Exam transforms the traditional essay test into a creative and social experience. Students are still writing about significant passages and themes in a novel, but by working with images and their peers, they have more latitude and more opportunity to be successful. As an open-book, open-note activity, the Brown Bag Exam invites students to immerse themselves once more in the pages of a text. The exam creates a space for them to see new things, arrive at new insights, and add another layer to their understanding. Unlike traditional exams that isolate students and set them up to compete against one another, the Brown Bag Exam fosters classroom community.

Meeting the criteria for assessment in YA pedagogy. Because the Brown Bag Exam involves choice, it has a *personal* dimension. If students choose their images wisely, they can write about aspects of the novel that hold personal meaning. The exam is *social*: students are held accountable for doing their own thinking, but their thinking is deepened by peer discussion and interaction. It is *analytical* in that students' creative ideas about a book must be anchored in specific textual evidence, and ideas about individual objects must connect to larger themes. Finally, it is *flexible*, providing space for students to make unexpected connections and insightful discoveries. Work on the Brown Bag Exam doesn't always extend to real-world contexts, but it does have resonance and meaning in the social world of the classroom.

Meeting of Minds

Meeting of Minds is a creative and performative assessment designed by Dudley Barlow, a retired English teacher from Canton High School in Canton, Michigan. Based on Steve Allen's 1970s PBS show, Meeting of Minds involves bringing together a group of notable figures and then engaging them in conversation on a common topic. While Barlow used Meeting of Minds as a final exam activity in his American Literature course, the assessment also works well in a YA lit class.

Meeting of Minds asks students to put characters, authors, YA experts, and teen readers in dialogue around a significant theme or idea from their learning during the semester. Conversations might focus on some aspect of young adult literature as a field, such as the publishing industry; the literary qualities of YA texts; authors' intentions and purposes; the contributions and influence of reviewers, critics, and award committees; or the challenge of censorship. Alternatively, conversations might focus on the reading lives of teenagers or the lives of authors and/or characters. Students work collaboratively to write a script, which they then perform in class on the last day of the unit or semester.

Getting started. Students need time in class to explore options, make decisions, and generate shared energy around their ideas.

- *Exploring options.* First, students need to establish a sense of possibility. Their thinking will be more generative if they understand the range of forms this work can take. Will their script be humorous, placing YA characters in a game show or some form of reality television? Will it be serious, bringing authors together to discuss a deep or controversial idea? Will it feature satirical impersonations of real people such as authors, guest speakers, or their teacher?

- *Making decisions.* Working in groups, students must decide on a cast, focus on a topic, and then write a script. As they develop their scripts, students must come up with an arc for the conversation: What questions will their guests explore? What will they seek to accomplish through their talk? They must also settle on a tone that is appropriate to their subject matter and a plan for how the host will facilitate conversation.

- *Working closely with texts.* To write a quality script, students need to ground their work in course materials. They may draw on notes from class discussions and literature circle meetings, visits with guest speakers, and assignments they've written. They should make a point of revisiting course books and articles. Whenever possible they should quote characters directly and/or strive to mimic characters' distinct voices. The script provides a space for students to take on the perspectives of others, engage in satire, and/or report factual information. Whichever direction students go, their work should reflect detailed knowledge of the books and the central themes of the course.

- *Performance expectations.* Since students perform their scripts in class, each performance should be between eight and ten minutes—long enough to present a complete conversation, or at least a significant chunk of one. Students don't need to memorize their parts, but they should have practiced enough so that their performance, while fully scripted, gives the appearance of spontaneous discussion. Although it's not required, they may wear costumes and bring props. If they choose, they can videotape their performance and play it in class. A video loses the qualities of immediacy and spontaneity, but it adds room for elements such as sound effects, music, lighting, and the use of real-world settings.

What it looks like in practice. On the day of performances, each group is responsible for writing feedback to students in one other group. Writing peer feedback adds a meta layer to the experience. Being asked to comment on another group's performance heightens students' awareness of how their design decisions were similar to or different from those of their peers.

After all the groups have performed, it's useful to debrief as a whole class. Students can reflect on what the performances reveal about YA lit as a field, their academic study of this literature, and their shared experience as a community of readers.

Reflective writing. In addition to a hard copy of their scripts, each group turns in a brief reflective essay on their group's process. Like the reflection they write for the themed reading list, the reflection for Meeting of Minds provides a space for students to explain how their group developed a vision for the script, made creative design decisions, and handled the steps involved in drafting the text.

Assessment criteria. The four most important qualities for Meeting of Minds scripts are substance, flow of conversation, authenticity, and originality. On the matter of *substance*, performers should engage in a discussion that is focused, thoughtful, and relevant to the central events, themes, and ideas of the course. As for *flow*, the discussion should feel natural, including points that build on previous points, characters who make individual arguments as they interact, and a host who does not have to ask too many questions after the characters become engaged with one another. Regarding *authenticity*, comments should be authentic to the characters; students should embody their roles and perform their parts believably. Finally, the script and the performance should be *original*, offering something new and going beyond summary or rehashing old story lines.

Examples of student work. In my college classroom, students have taken many creative approaches to Meeting of the Minds. Here are a few I've seen:

- A satire of the reality TV show *Survivor*, in which characters vote each other off the island.
- A radio call-in show where listeners pose questions and characters provide answers based on their life experience.
- A scene set in a bookstore in which a main character finds a book about herself and wonders why anyone would write about her life.
- A conversation between minor characters in which they reflect on the state of their lives a year later.

One of my favorite Meeting of Minds scripts took us backstage on an awards night where an audience had gathered to hear the announcement of Best Young Adult Novel Ever. Nominees for the award were the five novels we had read together as a class: *The Fault in Our Stars, Feed, We Were Here, Ask the Passengers*, and *We Were Liars*. Students chose their group's least favorite book, *Feed*, as the winning title. Then they let us listen in as Matt de la Peña, E. Lockhart, A. S. King, and John Green—the authors of the other four novels—stood around and debated why *Feed* won instead of their own book.

This scenario allowed group members to make us laugh at their clever impersonations of real authors, each of whom we had heard, seen, or talked to at some point during the semester. It also allowed them to do critical, analytical work at the end of the course. Through the authors' conversation, students were able to revisit many of the key ideas and questions that guided our shared reading, including the lack of cultural diversity in YA lit, layers of intertextuality in YA texts, the tension between literary merit and teen appeal in YA book awards, the wide range of story types we find in YA lit, where authors' stories come from, why authors write, the important issues that YA novels explore, and why we have book awards in the first place.

In their reflection, students wrote that they came up with their idea when they recalled the class discussion of *Feed* and remembered the questions their classmates raised about why this novel had received such critical acclaim. They explained how they went on to develop and focus their script:

> In the presentation, we reiterate many of the criticisms that our classmates had brought up, [and we linked them to] the point of view of the authors that we believed these opinions fit best with. We also included some discussion between the authors about the literary merit of *Feed*—including aspects of literariness that [we] learned throughout our course. Overall, our group wanted to create a script that included elements and opinions from previous class discussions . . . while bringing to light the literary aspects of each book. The script both defends and criticizes the novels that we read over the course of the semester, while ultimately approaching the topic in a humorous way.

Recasting traditional assessment tasks. Students in English class are sometimes asked to go beyond the story by writing a new ending or writing from the point of view of a main character. Meeting of Minds takes that type of creative work to the next level. Writing a script requires students to consider multiple perspectives at once. In creating a conversation about a relevant topic or idea, students must think beyond extending the plot. Instead they must evaluate the core issues in the course and synthesize their knowledge of factual information, characters, voices, and themes.

Meeting the criteria for assessment in YA pedagogy. Meeting of Minds scripts are *personal*, in that each group has the freedom to share their own understandings of what they have learned. Performances reflect students' individual personalities, interests, and humor. They also reflect inside jokes that make sense based on experiences students have shared over the course of the semester. The scripts are *social*, in that they capture the collective energy and creativity of each group as well as the meanings students construct collaboratively. Like academic essays, the scripts are *analytical*, in that they require students to work from course texts, quote lines of dialogue, and make thematic connections across books and ideas. Finally, they are *flexible*, allowing students the freedom to work in a mode that feels comfortable and to develop their ideas in relation to the dimensions of the course that feel most relevant to them.

Other Ideas for Assessment

The three assessment ideas discussed in this chapter are only the beginning of a much longer list of possibilities. Across the country, teachers are modifying and adapting these ideas, but they are also coming up with other approaches to assessment that give students space to reflect on their reading, personalize it, and make it useful to others.

At Rockville High School in Vernon-Rockville, Connecticut, early-career English teacher Ricki Ginsberg taught two YA lit elective classes. After three years teaching traditional English courses to tenth, eleventh, and twelfth graders, Ricki proposed and successfully defended a YA elective because she wanted to inspire students to read. Many of the students who took YA lit were already committed readers, but several enrolled because they wanted to rediscover their passion for reading. Though she taught YAL I for three years and YAL II for just one year before leaving her classroom to begin a doctoral program, Ricki gained a vivid understanding of what students are capable of when given the freedom to do meaningful work in reading assessment.

In her YAL II course, which Ricki designed to be completely student driven and independent, students worked on a final project over the course of an entire semester. Each student chose a project idea from a list of options that Ricki adapted from the YA lit class she had taken with Wendy Glenn during her undergraduate teacher education program at the University of Connecticut. On the assignment sheet, Ricki wrote, "As advanced students in the field of young adult literature, I respect your interests and knowledge [enough] to give you this college-level assignment. There is much freedom here, but please choose a project that you can work on for the entire semester. You should pick a project that will be fun and interesting to you." She added that students should not feel limited to items on the list. "Try to come up with a project idea that is unique from that of your peers and applicable to the real world."

Ricki's emphasis on projects that are both unique and applicable to the real world allowed students to be personal, creative, and purposeful in their work with YA lit. Each of her assignment options called students to put their knowledge of YA lit to use in service of a practical goal. Several options invited students to develop a piece of writing suited to their career ambitions. Those who aspired to become authors could write the first chapter of a young adult novel. Students considering careers as teachers could create a syllabus and a unit plan for a YA lit course. Students who wanted to take a scholarly approach to YA lit could write a manuscript with MLA citations to submit to a professional journal for publication.

Other options on Ricki's list called students to work as YA literature advocates and address their projects to local adult audiences. Students who wanted to raise awareness of YA lit among English teachers could create a pamphlet connecting classic novels to young adult literature texts or a fifteen-minute Prezi presentation to help teachers inspire students to like reading. Students who wanted to address district leaders could organize a presentation to give to the Board of Education about the power of reading and the value of the YA lit course at their school. Those who wanted to address the community could write a series of editorials about YA lit to submit to the local newspaper.

For students who wanted to share YA lit with their peers, Ricki offered a final set of advocacy-oriented options. They could organize book talks and present them to other classes throughout the year to recommend titles. They could seek permission from the principal and superintendent to organize a school-wide read-a-thon. They could get a group of peers to read a common book and then arrange a Skype session with the author.

At the end of the semester, Ricki used the final exam session as a space for students to share the results of their projects with their peers. Ricki asked students to address just two things in their oral presentations: (1) why they chose their project, and (2) what they learned from their project.

So what did students do when given the chance to create such personal, purposeful work in a high school YA lit class? "This project had fantastic results," Ricki told me. She listed some of her students' most memorable accomplishments:

- Several students created pamphlets or presentations for English teachers who might doubt the power of YA literature in the classroom.

- One student made it her mission to inspire her peers to read, but she found a way to do it secretly and anonymously. She printed QR codes on paper and posted them throughout the school—including the inside of bathroom stalls!—for the entire semester. When students scanned the QR codes with their phones, they were guided to the website of a high-interest, high-quality YA book.

- Five students did book talks around the school. Combined, they spoke to about thirty different English and non-English classes. In total, they book-talked about 150 books.

- Two students helped Ricki organize, run, and market a book fair. As a side benefit, the book fair generated funding that Ricki used to expand her classroom library.

- One student submitted three editorials to the local online newspaper. All were featured on the newspaper's website and Facebook page.

- One student organized a Skype session with YA author Julie Halpern. About forty students attended (and the event was held after school!).

Ricki's emphasis on student work that is fun, interesting, and applicable to the real world aligns perfectly with the principles that guide assessment in YA pedagogy. As with the themed reading lists described earlier in this chapter, the projects that students designed in Ricki's class were *personal*, in that they arose from students' individual interests and goals. Because Ricki conferenced with students about their projects eight times over the course of the semester, and because students developed projects in the company of their peers, the work was *social*. When students decided how to write about and share specific books in relation to their goals and the needs of their audience, their work became *analytical*. Finally, throughout the process, Ricki's project framework was *flexible*. Students had the latitude to think creatively and make real-world relevance a core element in their thinking and planning.

Making Room for the Personal in Assessment

When we recast traditional assessment tasks in a new light, students are able to make good on all they've learned through YA pedagogy. The ideas you've read about in this chapter highlight the importance of allowing for the personal in assessment. At the same time, they cultivate students' analytical skills. When given the freedom to put their knowledge to use in the service of real-world audiences, students develop agency and autonomy as readers. They read purposefully and deliberately toward their personal goals. They step back from the books to consider their value in the world and in the lives of other readers. In conversations with peers and in outreach to adults, students make new discoveries about what the books have to offer and what individuals can accomplish through reading.

Students like Jalen, whom you read about at the beginning of this chapter, and students like the ones Ricki taught are everywhere. As you have seen, when we provide them with books that are well matched to their interests and needs, these young people are ready and willing to read in personal, purposeful ways. When we invite them to show what they know and are able to do as readers, they rise to the challenge. They put their book knowledge to work, and they use it to make productive contributions in their classrooms, schools, and communities.

Teen readers want to feel a sense of connection to books, authors, and characters. They want to share their reading with others. They are enterprising, inventive, eager, and resourceful. Why don't we take advantage of the space that assessment provides and use it to find out what the teen readers in our own lives are capable of?

Being Proactive:
Helping Others
Understand YA Lit
and YA Pedagogy

Apart from questions about texts, tasks, and assessment, any teacher who's planning to teach young adult literature probably has one question that underscores all the others: how can we introduce YA titles, and frame the purpose of our work with them, if we teach in a context where YA lit is viewed as "less than"?

This question reveals a core vulnerability that many of us feel around the decision to teach YA lit. Historically, if YA texts have been included in the curriculum at all, they've occupied a position as a stepping stone to "better" literature. We may be frustrated by this hierarchy, but in the past, the strategy of connecting YA lit to the classics has been a practical way to get YA titles into classrooms (see, for example, Herz & Gallo, 2005; Kaywell, 1992–2000, 2010; Lesesne, 2010). As I have discussed throughout this book, however, such an approach still keeps us locked in the binary paradigm. It prioritizes the classics and therefore leaves the door open for too many people to continue to dismiss the quality of YA literature and the possibilities it offers teen readers.

These negative perspectives have pushed many of us into a defensive stance. We come to expect that parents, colleagues, and administrators will criticize us for our use of this literature. We brace ourselves for complaints, and we fall into the habit of voicing rebuttals to arguments framed by others rather than taking the lead in shaping a different conversation about books and reading.

When I faced this criticism during my own years of teaching YA lit in high school, my impulse was always to talk about the books. I thought that if I could just get other people to start reading YA titles, they would discover for themselves that the books are good, and they might then feel inspired to take the next step of bringing YA lit into the classroom. Looking back, I now see two problems with this approach. First, I led with an argument about the quality of the books instead of what we could do for teens by teaching them. Clearly, my strategy didn't work: only a handful of colleagues joined me in teaching YA lit, mostly by adding a unit of literature circles to the existing curriculum. Now I understand that no argument about the value of YA literature *as* literature is going to be strong enough to change the way people think about the place of these books in English class—especially in departments where the majority of teachers feel invested and secure in the work they're already doing with the classics.

The second problem with my approach was that I waited for colleagues to come to me with questions about YA lit rather than summoning the courage to initiate those conversations myself. As a result, the people I spent the most time talking with were those who were already inclined to give these books a chance, while those who viewed YA lit with skepticism became people I avoided. I didn't avoid those people out of dislike; it was more a matter of fear—fear of talking openly about our philosophical differences around reading and teaching, and fear that they looked down on me, intellectually and professionally, for teaching YA literature.

Based on these past experiences, I've come to believe that the way forward in conversations about YA lit is to offer a new vision for how we should be teaching reading and teens. Others have already done vital and important work in opening up that conversation (Atwell, 2007; Kittle, 2013; Lesesne, 2003; Miller, 2009, 2014). Here I want to extend the conversation by highlighting the unique role that YA lit can play in fostering teens' reading lives. While we must continually make the case for the inherent complexity and value of YA texts, we need to talk as well about what we want our students to be able to do as readers—and how YA lit, when taught with a dedicated YA pedagogy, will allow them to thrive. In this way, we shift the focus away from debates about the merits and drawbacks of specific books and toward the purposes and processes of reading. That shift in focus allows us to share with parents, colleagues, and administrators what students can do as readers of YA lit. If YA books invite students of all kinds to find personal meaning in reading, then YA pedagogy sets them up with tools they can use to read those books more complexly. When we explain the kind of work that's possible with YA literature within this paradigm, we create an opportunity to get others thinking in new ways about YA lit and how we might teach it. The framework of YA pedagogy gives us a way to change the conversation about texts, teens, and reading.

But to change the conversation, we have to be willing to be proactive. Rather than simply waiting for criticism of YA lit and responding from a defensive stance, we can look for ways to educate colleagues and parents about these books before criticism comes. We can engage in outreach that highlights what YA literature has to offer. We can be ready to explain why these books are so important in the lives of teens, and we can follow up with arguments about how a thoughtful YA pedagogy can help students break new ground as readers.

You may be thinking that since teaching YA lit already involves reading new books, learning about a new field, and adopting a new, shifted stance through YA pedagogy, doing outreach is just too much. Why take that on in addition to all of our other duties as English teachers? The answer lies in the positive energy we gain by getting other people on board with these books and this pedagogy. If we lead with outreach, we can turn the negative energy that comes from having to defend YA lit into positive energy that comes from sharing the good things that happen when teens read YA titles. Through outreach we discover new allies and new support for our work. We realize that we're not alone. Instead of feeling like we're fighting against the world by teaching YA lit, we feel like we're calling others to join us in cultivating new spaces of possibility for teen readers.

By educating parents and administrators about the work we're doing as teachers of young adult literature, we open the door for them to become our advocates rather than our adversaries. By sharing YA titles with colleagues, we open the door for new reading communities to form in our departments and school districts. When we find colleagues who want to partner with us in developing YA pedagogy, we have the chance to do exciting new things in our teaching with the help of others who can make us better at what we do. We invest in the work of outreach so that we can accomplish more with the teens in our classrooms.

Most of all, by doing outreach we empower ourselves as teacher leaders. We become more strategic in framing the issues and savvier at highlighting research that shows we're doing what's right for teens by teaching YA lit. We strengthen our voices in the educational debate, we grow as professionals, and we gain confidence as we work for change. (For more on the importance and power of outreach, see Fleischer, 2000.)

Ways of Doing Outreach

So what can YA lit outreach look like? What forms can it take and how can we make room for it in the midst of everything else we do as teachers?

The important thing to remember is that there are lots of different ways to do outreach. We can give ourselves permission to start small. We can try out different approaches and continue only the ones that feel manageable. Meanwhile, we can remind ourselves to stay focused on the big picture. The purpose of outreach is to get others thinking, talking, and reading YA lit in service of a larger goal, which is to support and deepen the reading lives of teens. We spread the word about YA lit in order to share a new vision for teaching reading and enlist support for that approach. We use the books and conversations about the books to build relationships outside the classroom that will make our work inside the classroom more effective.

With that in mind, there are two main ways to engage in outreach around YA lit. First, we can share information about the books. We can advertise the YA titles we're currently reading and alert colleagues when we come across useful YA resources. We can do this kind of outreach quietly, through signs on our classroom doors and posts to social media, or we can initiate in-person conversations with our colleagues. Those conversations can be quick and informal—the kind that arise spontaneously when we're standing in front of the copy machine—or, if time permits, they can happen in the more formal space of a department meeting or inservice workshop. In addition to educating others about the books, we can highlight what students are doing with the books as YA readers. Again, through something as simple as an offhand comment while we're walking to the parking lot after school, we can call our colleagues' attention to the things teens are saying, discovering, and accomplishing by reading YA lit.

We take the work of outreach to the next level when we organize opportunities for parents and colleagues to read YA books and then talk with one another about their reading. This form of outreach takes more effort, but it has more potential to be transformative. Just as we invest in the social dimension of reading as a core element of YA pedagogy, we create a social context for adult readers of YA lit because we know that their reading experience will be deeper if they share it with others. (And it's good to point this out to adult readers!) Furthermore, we expect that at some point, talk about specific YA texts will turn to talk of what we can accomplish by teaching these books. As discussion facilitators, we can prompt this talk by posing simple, open-ended questions such as: What do you think teens might do with a book like this? What might this book add to the menu of titles we're already teaching? Questions like these give us another way to start a conversation about YA literature. They can also change the direction of a conversation in progress. They allow us to talk with our colleagues about books and reading without feeling like we're merely proselytizing about YA lit or bragging about our students.

Investing in shared reading of YA lit with other adults makes good sense. In creating social spaces for adults to read young adult books, we're banking on the power of firsthand experience with them as something we can use to draw administrators, colleagues, and parents into deeper conversations about what our students need in order to become strong and committed readers. In the midst of those conversations, we ask others to think with us about what we can accomplish by teaching YA lit with YA pedagogy. We share the things we're already doing, and we ask our fellow teachers to help us dream up new ideas.

There are lots of possibilities for outreach along each of these lines. In the following section, I offer examples of things that I and other teachers have done to share information about YA literature and involve others in reading it. Some approaches are general: they cast a wide net that doesn't target any particular audience. The beauty of this approach is that we don't know who we're reaching. Through our efforts, we may attract the attention and support of people we weren't expecting to take an interest in these books or our ways of teaching them.

On the other hand, if we want to meet the needs of specific groups, we'll need to tailor our efforts. Since our fellow teachers may be unfamiliar with YA lit, and since our work will be more effective if they understand and value what we're doing—which may inspire them to try teaching YA titles themselves—it makes sense to invest particular effort in reaching out to our colleagues. Along the way, administrators may also join the conversation. As for parents, we can reach out to them using many of the same approaches we use to share YA literature with our colleagues. We simply modify the approach to address their specific interests and questions.

I provide possibilities for both general and targeted outreach in the following sections. Beginning with ways of sharing YA lit, I next offer ideas for inviting others to read these books. In each section, I start with approaches that don't require much effort and then move on to more elaborate possibilities.

Sharing Information about YA Lit

1. Starting small
   - *Share YA titles on your email signature line.* Add "Currently reading [title]" to your email signature line and update it regularly. This is the simplest way to show others that you are invested in building your knowledge of YA lit and getting the word out about new YA books. Teen services librarians do this regularly in messages they send to the YALSA-BK listserv and on posts they publish to *The Hub*, YALSA's YA lit blog.

Sharing Books through a "Currently Reading" Poster

At Wydown Middle School in Clayton, Missouri, eighth-grade English teacher **April Fulstone** uses a laminated 8.5" × 11" poster to share her reading. The poster is simple, consisting of the open-ended line "Mrs. Fulstone is currently reading . . ." followed by a space where she can write in the title and author. By laminating the poster, April can easily write on and wipe off her latest reading selection. She likes the way the poster puts book information out in public where anyone can see it and ask her about it. Because of the poster, she's been able to have informal conversations about books with both students and adults. People see what she's reading and they want to know more. Based on the success of the poster, April is in the process of imagining more ways to share books with her colleagues. "I'd like to start incorporating book talks into our department meetings because I do them for my students and my students do them for class," she says. "We keep a running list of books we've talked about in each class on giant Post-its. I've found that the consistent presence of book talks in my classroom has really enriched students' literate lives. They generate excitement about reading and give me great ideas for additions to the classroom library." April realizes that the same strategies she uses to share books in her classroom can easily be adapted for sharing books with other teachers—enriching their reading lives and the culture of reading throughout her school.

- *Display YA lit news on your classroom door*. Post "Currently reading [title]" on a sign outside your classroom door and update it regularly. Use the same approach to share what your students are currently reading by printing out copies of YA book covers and hanging them up. If you come across an article about YA lit in a magazine or newspaper, cut it out and hang that on your door as well.

- *Post lists of YA lit award winners in the teachers' lounge*. After the ALA Youth Media Awards in January, post lists of winning titles. Post the winners of YA literature awards given at other times of the year such as the Cybils Awards, given by the YA blogging community in February, and the National Book Award for Young People's Literature, announced in November. YALSA's annual list of Teens' Top Ten is useful to share when it's announced in August. You might also post YA-oriented lists that have strategic appeal to teachers, such as YALSA's Outstanding Books for the College Bound, which is updated every five years and organized around five disciplines: arts and humanities, history and cultures, literature and language arts, science and technology, and social sciences.

- *Initiate informal conversations about YA lit*. Talk with colleagues about YA books whenever the topic of reading comes up. Whether it's in the hallway during your planning period or in the office while you're checking your mailbox, be ready to share stories about YA titles your students are currently reading and why they might be of interest to others in your department. Use these conversations to spread the word about YA lit, but also to take the temperature, so to speak, of your colleagues' thinking. Have they heard of these books? Would they be interested in reading one? Who, among your fellow teachers, might be open to joining in a larger conversation about books, teens, and reading?

2. Getting bigger

- *Give YA book talks.* As April Fulstone imagined doing, stand up at a department meeting and give a YA book talk. Hold up a copy of a book you've recently read and say just enough about the plot to pique people's interest. Add a few words about what you noticed and appreciated in the writing, the characters, or the story line. If you see connections between topics in the book and themes your colleagues explore in their literature classes, make a note of these things. Then pass the book around so that others can get a look at the text itself. If your colleagues get a chance to page through the book first-hand, they might come away with a better sense of what it has to offer than if they just glimpsed the cover from across the room.

- *Share the YA books you're reading through social media.* It's easy to do this kind of sharing through Twitter: all you have to do is write something about the book in 140 characters or less. Include the title and a brief comment in the form of a sentence or descriptive phrase. If you tag the author (by typing their Twitter handle, preceded by the @ sign), he or she might respond to your tweet. If you want to make a statement that's longer than 140 characters, you can post a series of tweets about the book. Since many YA lit readers (and authors) are active on Twitter, you can also use this space as a resource for finding out about new titles that other YA lit fans are excited about. Finally, if you invite students, parents, and colleagues to follow you on Twitter, you're not only advertising your reading, but you're also creating a space where people in your local community can share information and talk about YA literature.

- *Blog about YA titles.* It takes more effort to design and launch a YA blog, but if you want to write about YA lit at greater length and in a more permanent space, a blog can be a valuable information-sharing tool. Through blog posts, you can delve more deeply into the complexity of YA texts and why they work well in your teaching. You can highlight qualities that make them teachable, or other texts they could be paired with, or the reasons why they might appeal to particular teen readers. If a colleague reads your blog, he or she might come to you wanting to find out more about a YA text you've recommended.

Sharing Books through a YA Blog

Teachers who blog about YA lit do so for a variety of reasons. Often they find that the process of sharing their book knowledge leads to professional connections and opportunities they never expected.

This was true for **Jennifer Walsh**, who blogs at *YApping about Books* (http://yappingaboutbooks.blogspot.com). Blogging gave Jennifer a sense of connection with a larger community of YA lit readers and a chance to network with publishers. Once she began blogging, Jennifer realized she could request advance reading copies (ARCs) of forthcoming titles to read and promote on the blog. Afterward, the ARCs were hers to share with students and colleagues. "Getting ARCs from Scholastic, Penguin, Bloomsbury, and others has opened a new door to me as a teacher. At school, I am known as the teacher who 'gets all the books early.' With other ARCs I get in the exhibit hall at NCTE [the annual convention], I've had the opportunity to actually give books away in the classroom. ARCs help me to plan what I might add to our library of novels for classrooms and units."

Jennifer's blog has been a solo effort, but sometimes teachers team up and blog together. After serving together on ALAN's Amelia Elizabeth Walden Award committee, **Ricki Ginsberg** and **Kellee Moye** launched a coauthored blog called *Unleashing Readers* (www.unleashingreaders.com). Ricki explains how the blog came about:

> We decided to start *Unleashing Readers* when we realized we both had a passion for connecting teachers and students to accessible, engaging texts. Our focus has always been finding great books and envision- ing creative ways to integrate them into classrooms. We wanted to be a resource for K–12 educators, so we decided we wouldn't limit ourselves to one age level. Our aim was for the website to feature a continual flow of teaching ideas, but we also wanted to review and promote quality texts. The majority of our readers are educators, but we do have regular readers who are book bloggers, bookstore workers, parents, and students.

Ricki and Kellee dedicate many of their blog posts to book reviews, and they take special care to make their posts useful to teachers. In addition to personal comments on a featured title, they share teachers' tools for navigation (which highlight teaching ideas), discussion questions, flagged passages, and other books that are similar to the featured title. At the bottom of each post, they make a recommendation for how they would use the text in the classroom: in literature circles/book groups, as a read-aloud, for close reading, and/or for the classroom library. They list teachable qualities about the text by category (e.g., mood, personification, point of view), and they tag each review with related topics or themes from the text (e.g., coming-of-age, death/dying, science). Teachers can specifically search these categories and tags to look for books by topic. Another resource they provide is a "Navi- gating Literary Elements" page, which provides book recommendations for teaching different literary elements, including characterization, conflict, language, setting, and voice.

Ricki and Kellee have been thrilled by the results of their outreach efforts. Like Jennifer, they've discovered that blogging about books has led to a sense of reading community and unexpected professional connections. For example, TeachingBooks.net links many of the teaching ideas and discussion questions on *Unleashing Readers* to their website, and they linked directly to the "Navigating Literary Elements" page to help educators find that resource. Ricki noted that their post about techniques for creating engaging classroom discussions was featured on NCTE's Facebook page and has been shared hundreds of times. Several thousand people have checked out their book recommendations post for struggling/reluctant middle grade readers.

- *Create a YA newsletter.* A newsletter provides another way to get the word out about the YA titles you're reading. Like a blog post, it's simple enough to write a short blurb about a few new YA books, pair each blurb with an image of the book's cover to add visual appeal, and bookend that material with an opening and/or closing to complete the newsletter. You can also use the newsletter to alert people when YA authors are coming to town as part of a book tour or library event. Alternatively, you could have students write copy for a YA lit newsletter that you send out to parents, sharing not just what students are reading, but what they're doing with their reading through YA pedagogy. If you send out the newsletter electronically through an email list, it's cost-free and relatively easy to produce and deliver.

3. Full-fledged

- *Give a YA presentation.* Offer to do a presentation on YA lit for colleagues—one that's designed to load them up with book recommendations. It could be formal, given in the context of a professional development day at your school, or it could be informal, offered after school for anyone who's interested. If you go the informal route, what I'm calling a presentation might not even take the form of a talk. Instead it could be a something as simple as a book open house where colleagues stop by the school library or your classroom to browse a collection of YA titles you've laid out on tables. Sharing books in this way could have a show-and-tell feel, or, if you've accumulated copies of books you no longer want or need, it could have the feel of a yard sale, except in this case the books are free.

- *Propose a YA literature course.* Design a YA lit elective course and pitch it to administration and the school board for approval.

Inviting Others to Read YA Lit

1. Starting small

- *Hand a YA title to a colleague.* Approach a colleague with book in hand and say, "I just read this. I thought it was really good, and I'd love to hear what you think!" Alternatively, slip a book into a colleague's mailbox with a note that conveys the same message. Then follow up later, asking if they had a chance to look at the book and telling them why you thought they might want to know about it.

Sharing Books through a YA Lit Course

Designing, proposing, and defending a YA literature course is one of the most ambitious outreach efforts a teacher can make. Most of us tend to approach such work with a mix of excitement and fear. That was true for **Carrie Melnychenko**, who explained,

> When I first asked my principal if he would support a YA class in our school, I was nervous that he would say no. He had told me in the past that he was hearing good things from the students about lit circles and that he was happy to see kids really reading, but still I was worried. I was teaching in a time when Laurie Halse Anderson's *Speak* was being challenged and it was making the news. My biggest fear was standing in front of the school board as some angry parent read a passage aloud from one of the novels from my class. I even sort of had a speech planned where I would defend the book and discuss its merits.

Carrie pushed past her fear and proposed the course anyway. She took a proactive approach, creating a permission slip so that parents understood the nature of the class as well as the fact that many of the books contained mature content. That strategy worked well for her—she wasn't challenged by any angry parents. Still, she faced other, unanticipated challenges, such as having to fundraise for books and needing to change the books more often than she expected.

Even though many things have gone right for Carrie, the need to defend the course has never entirely gone away:

> My current struggle is with the NCAA. According to them, my course is not rigorous enough to count as a core English course for incoming college athletes. The first time I submitted for course approval I was told that they needed more in-depth information regarding the skills that each unit addresses. I provided that information and was told that I needed to show rigor, so I submitted all of my assessments and project descriptions, including how the course was connected to the Common Core [State] Standards for English. I got a response that in my course, students had only two required novels and that wasn't sufficient. That is simply not true. Students are required to read five books (two of which the entire class reads, two that are literature circle choices, and one that's an independent read). NCAA provided me with the opportunity to defend the course one more time, and I submitted a two-page letter defending the course. I am currently waiting for a reply.

Carrie's struggle with the NCAA reminds us that alongside all the good, some aspects of this work are always going to be hard. When we teach YA lit, we have to be strong, determined, and resilient.

When **Ricki Ginsberg** proposed her YA lit course, she too was building on the positive momentum of teaching YA lit in a regular English class. After implementing a major yearlong independent reading unit with tenth graders, the following year those same students told Ricki they had stopped reading. They said there were too many reading requirements in their eleventh-grade course. Ricki started allowing students to hang out in her room to read during their study halls, which led to many conversations about books. One student told Ricki she wished she could get credit for the reading she was doing, and an idea was born.

Ricki's department head urged her to write a formal course proposal, so she did, citing scholarly research about in-school literacies versus out-of-school literacies and how the course might bridge the two. She also provided research showing the powerful impact of young adult literature in schools and on readers. "When I proposed my idea to the Board of Education, I was armed with statistics," she said. "I made a strong attempt to position myself as an expert. I spoke with confidence that this class could be a game changer. Our school was deemed one of the thirty lowest performing in the state. I believed (and still believe) that a course like this could impact reading scores in powerful ways."

The board's biggest concern was cost; they didn't want to spend money on books. Ricki explained that she already had a classroom library of hundreds of books, and she requested just $500 to purchase literature circle text sets. When board members worried that students wouldn't want to enroll in an elective reading class on top of their English course requirement, Ricki assured them that she had students who were interested. Because she wasn't asking that the course meet any of the graduation requirements, and because she wasn't asking for much money, there was little reason for the board to say no. They unanimously approved the course.

Despite Ricki's passion and the buy-in of many students, she still faced difficulty getting students to enroll in YA lit. "I knew so many students who loved young adult literature," she said, "but they admitted their worry that the course would be more work than the other elective options. Many worried that a reading elective would have the same page length requirements as their other English courses. I set out to spread the gospel that this course would be different." Every time she saw a student reading a book in the hallway, she asked if they'd heard about the course. She sought out former students to tell others about the course—and sometimes beg them to enroll. She created a flier and gave class sets to every English teacher, and she talked about the class on the morning announcements. Her efforts paid off, not just for students, but for her as a teacher. "Each day with them was fulfilling and exciting for me because we shared a passion," she said. "We loved reading and discussing books. Because it was an elective, there was no pressure to meet standardized test requirements."

- *Plant copies of YA books around your school.* Leave copies lying around school for others to pick up—in the teachers' lounge, on the counter in the office, at the coffee pot. (An organization called BookCrossing formalized this practice in 2001 with a website and a set of guidelines. Their idea was to give a book new life by leaving it in a public space such as a park, a train station, or a coffee shop for someone else to discover and enjoy. Through the BookCrossing website, www.bookcrossing.com, people who register the books they share can track where they go.)

2. Getting bigger
   - *Create a Little Free Library.* Set up a shelf or display in the school where others can borrow YA titles and contribute their own. You could also do this out in the community in a

space where parents of your students tend to gather, such as a church, recreation center, or bus stop. (Founded in 2009, Little Free Library is another organization you can read about online: visit their website at www.littlefreelibrary.org. In its simplest form, a Little Free Library is a box containing books that anyone can borrow. After you take a book, you bring back another book to share. Little Free Libraries serve as gathering places where neighbors can share books and connect as readers.)

Suggested YA Texts for a Teacher Book Group

It's important to think strategically about YA titles we might share in a teacher book group. They should be titles that have enough crossover appeal—that is, enough complexity and substance—to be engaging to adult readers in their own right. They should also be books that teachers could envision using in the classroom, so it's smart to look for titles that explore universal themes, refer to classic works of literature, link to current or historical events, expose readers to less familiar genres, and/or contain writing that's artful enough to be unpacked. Here are some titles that might work:

- *Code Name Verity* by Elizabeth Wein. Two young women: one a pilot, the other a spy. World War II setting. Memorable voices, two points of view, and a major plot twist. Not a love story. Feminist perspective. Thrilling page-turner.

- *The Astonishing Life of Octavian Nothing, Traitor to the Nation* by M. T. Anderson. A story of identity formation, trauma, loyalty, and the American Revolution. Breathtaking prose. Intertextual references to works of classical literature, music, and philosophy. Questions posed about the costs of our luxuries.

- *Far Far Away* by Tom McNeal. Narrated by the ghost of Jacob Grimm. A small town, a love interest, a bookstore, a game show, and a dark plot twist.

- *Beyond Magenta: Transgender Teens Speak Out* by Susan Kuklin. Nonfiction profiles and photographic portraits of transgender teens. Life stories, perspective taking, consciousness-raising.

- *Steve Jobs: The Man Who Thought Different* by Karen Blumenthal. Nonfiction biography. Narrative structure follows the arc of Jobs's Stanford University commencement speech. The complexities of public figures. The story of twenty-first-century technological change.

- *Graceling* by Kristin Cashore. Accessible feminist fantasy. Page-turning adventure and palace intrigue. A love story featuring a strong female character. An exploration of human gifts and liabilities.

- *The Knife of Never Letting Go* by Patrick Ness. First book in a literary dystopian trilogy. Original world building. A study of power, war, and human nature.

3. Full-fledged

- *Start a YA book group for teachers.* It's one thing to hand a YA title to a colleague; it's another to create an opportunity for teachers to read YA lit together. As with outreach efforts in general, a teacher book group is something you might commit to trying just once. Afterward you can reflect on how it went and evaluate whether it's worth doing again.

  Along with spreading the word about YA lit, a YA book group for teachers provides space to think with our colleagues about the concept of finding and making complexity. Through shared reading of a single text, we can discuss the forms of complexity we find in a book's style and substance, along with the complexity we make as readers. In a book group meeting, we can discuss questions such as: What connections did we create as we read this book—to our own lives, the lives of our students, issues the book raised, or other texts? What questions did we ask as we read, and what questions was the book asking us? What work was the book designed to do? In what ways was that work significant or ambitious, either in literary terms or in the potential payoff for teen readers? Who is likely to read this book, and who needs to read it? Given our answers to these questions, we can then discuss possibilities for teaching this book or others like it in our classrooms.

- *Start a YA book group for parents.* Similar to a book group for teachers, a YA book group for parents provides a space not only to introduce parents to YA titles but also to illustrate what YA pedagogy entails. You could invite parents to hear about YA texts students are reading as a whole class or in lit circles, and you could share what students have said and done with those texts. A book group is a way to get parents reading YA lit but also an opportunity to educate them about YA pedagogy and help them understand your goals for bringing YA literature into the classroom.

  You may find, however, that parents are less interested in the books as literary texts and more interested in what they offer in terms of the reading lives of teens. Parents will probably come to the group with questions such as: What books will interest my teen? What books will challenge my teen, or, alternately, feel accessible, relevant, and readable? They may also have practical questions such as: What books will help my teen improve his or her skills as a reader? What books will prepare my teen for AP classes or college? In addition to questions about academics, parents may also simply want to know what books are out there that will allow their teen to see himself or herself in the text. Where are the books that will help their teen feel seen, understood, and validated?

Given these questions, it makes sense to introduce parents to a wide variety of YA titles. A book pass would give them the chance to browse a large number of books in a short period of time. Then we can ask which books caught their attention and why. We can mitigate concerns they have about

Suggested YA Texts for a Parent Book Group

Just as we need to be thoughtful in selecting YA titles to share in a teacher book group, we need to be equally strategic in choosing YA titles for parents. We don't need to eliminate books with controversial content, but we should be judicious in our offerings. We should offer titles that reflect the depth of substance we can find in YA lit storytelling, but we also need to strive for titles that show parents a range of characters, story types, genres, and text structures. Possibilities include:

- *The Fault in Our Stars* by John Green. Bestseller read by thousands, maybe even millions. Worth including as a way to open up conversation about the current popularity of YA lit and reasons for its crossover appeal.

- *Wintergirls* by Laurie Halse Anderson. A novel about eating disorders. Directly relevant (and emotionally challenging) for some families. Intertextual references to the myth of Persephone. Good option for parents who want a follow-up to *Speak*.

- *How It Went Down* by Kekla Magoon. Fictional take on the Trayvon Martin shooting told from multiple and conflicting points of view. Ambiguity in the text invites debate about the "truth" of what happened as well as text complexity.

- *Seraphina* by Rachel Hartman. Popular and accessible fantasy. Main character's mixed-race identity—she's half-human and half-dragon in a world where dragons are reviled—functions allegorically as a story about LGBTQ teens who feel they must hide their sexual identity.

- *Hole in My Life* by Jack Gantos. Memoir about doing wrong and seeking redemption. Incarceration tale. References to Dostoevsky and longing for the writing life. Funny and honest take on the struggle to make up for past mistakes.

- *Marcelo in the Real World* by Francisco X. Stork. A soulful, intellectual main character asks questions about religion, music, and ethics while working in his father's law firm and coping with mental and emotional characteristics resembling Asperger's syndrome.

- *American Born Chinese* by Gene Luen Yang. Best-known YA graphic novel. Weaves together three related story lines: one about identity development, one about racist stereotypes, and one about Chinese folklore. Yang's appointment as 2016 National Ambassador for Young People's Literature may prompt conversation about YA authors as reading advocates.

the content of certain books by reminding them that no book is right for every reader. We can encourage them to preview books for appropriate content before passing them on to their teen.

You may want to think of outreach in a parent book group as happening in phases. First, introduce them to what YA lit has to offer, and provide them with the opportunity to take a book home and read it with their teen. Then you could follow up with a meeting at which you invite them to share what they—and, more important, their teen—thought about the book. Hearing their teen's response to YA lit might give them new insight into what the books have to offer and the different ways they resonate with teen readers. In this way, you invite parents to experience the social dimension of making complexity. Knowing what a YA title means to one's own teen might make a parent's reading of the same book more complex.

Preparing for Criticism with YA Lit Talking Points

Despite all our efforts to be proactive by educating parents, colleagues, and administrators about what young adult literature has to offer before criticism comes, we must acknowledge that at some point we're going to hear negative comments about our decision to teach YA lit. Criticism always hurts on some level, but being defensive about YA lit is never going to help our cause as teachers who are striving to make the case for this literature.

Being proactive by doing outreach is our first and best strategy for getting others on board with YA lit and YA pedagogy. But there is a second way for us to be proactive and that is to think in advance about positive ways to respond to the YA lit criticisms we know we'll face. As I said at the beginning of this chapter, we can use our arguments to change the conversation—and people's mindsets—about YA literature by focusing on the reading needs of teens and what we want them to be able to do as YA readers. Our strategy, once again, is to shift the discussion from the perceived negatives of YA lit to the positives of teaching it with YA pedagogy.

As a way to rehearse our responses to predictable critiques, we can rely on a list of YA lit talking points. With talking points in hand, we stand ready to put a positive spin on whatever negative perception of YA lit we happen to encounter. Since most people come to YA books with misperceptions, we rely on talking points to change people's minds about these texts. But we also strive to change their thinking about the kinds of experiences teens need in order to become better, stronger readers. That's where YA pedagogy comes in. We talk about what we do with these books in the classroom, not just the fact that we make the books available.

As YA lit advocates, each of us gradually comes up with our own way of talking about YA lit and explaining its value to others. Talking points help us get started. When we rehearse talking points ahead of time, we prepare ourselves to speak about YA literature with confidence. The more comfortable we become fielding criticism, the more effective we'll be when we're called to respond to our critics.

Here are five criticisms we often hear when we bring YA lit into the secondary classroom. Following each one, I offer arguments we can use to shift the focus of the conversation from the perceived limitations of YA books to the concrete possibilities of YA pedagogy. Then I provide specific talking points to flesh out each idea.

1. "They can read this stuff at home." We respond by saying, *Students need to read YA lit in school in order to experience the social dimensions of reading and benefit from our expertise as teachers.* We reframe the conversation by emphasizing the productive social context we create with YA pedagogy. We highlight the power of YA lit to engage students in a reading community, and we talk specifically about what students can accomplish with YA lit when we guide them to more complex ways of reading it. Specific talking points:

   - *Teens benefit from reading YA lit in a community.* YA pedagogy takes place in classrooms that are organized to foster social interactions around books. That's because talking with other readers helps us to make more complexity in our own reading. When students read books that challenge or disturb them, they often want to know what their peers think. Reading YA lit in school gives us the opportunity to capitalize on teens' desire to talk with one another about important issues. We can use that talk to enrich their reading.

     Reading in community with others can also motivate us to keep reading. In the real world, readers seek the company of other readers. Why do so many adults join Goodreads? Why do so many teachers share their reading on Twitter through #titletalk and #bookaday? When teens are struggling to stay engaged in a challenging YA text or to find the motivation to begin a new YA title, they can gain energy and inspiration from their classmates.

   - *Teens benefit from having a YA lit guide.* Students will make better choices as YA readers if they have a knowledgeable adult to guide them. Who better to recommend YA titles than an English teacher? Librarians know YA lit, but they might not know our students. Parents know their own kids, but they might not know YA lit. Recommending current and relevant YA titles to teens should be part of an English teacher's job description.

Also, when students read YA books in class, we can guide their thinking about reading through one-on-one and whole-class conversations. This too should be part of our job description. Through YA pedagogy, we create frameworks for reading and set up purposeful approaches to YA texts. We challenge students to take their reading and their thinking to the next level.

2. "The books are too dark." We respond by saying, *Look at the issues we can explore with young people when we invite them to read YA lit.* We reframe the conversation by shifting the focus to the potential of YA lit to get teens talking about difficult topics that they may want and need to know more about. We highlight the power of YA lit to depict the world honestly, raise teens' consciousness, and guide them in their living. Specific talking points:

- *YA lit gives teens honest stories.* Teens want to be told the truth, and YA lit is known for telling readers the truth about the world they live in. When YA titles give us honest stories, they set us up to have honest conversations with teen readers—conversations we might not have otherwise. YA pedagogy values the intersection between teens' personal responses to texts and their analytical take on how texts are crafted to elicit such a response.

- *YA lit can be used to spark teens' critical consciousness.* The best YA titles acknowledge that inequality exists and the world isn't fair. They challenge teens to step outside the limits of their individual experience to see their lives in a larger context. In YA pedagogy, we start with students' personal responses to texts and then challenge students to step back to explore the questions texts are asking and the answers they provide. In this way, YA lit gives us the opportunity to raise students' awareness of abuse of power, social movements, and the ability of individuals to work for change. Through YA lit and the conversations we invite through YA pedagogy, we can foster teens' development as citizens.

- *Discussions of YA lit can guide teens in their everyday living.* When students read YA lit that focuses on corruption or injustice, we can engage them in conversations about ethical and moral decision making. When characters in YA novels make bad choices or are coping with abuse, trauma, or self-destructive behavior, we can invite teens to consider what they would do in similar circumstances. Reading about other people's lives often leads us to reflect on our own. Through YA pedagogy, we communicate to students that there are many purposes for reading besides literary analysis. We invite students to view reading as a path to the development of self-knowledge, empathy for others, and a moral framework.

3. "The books are not complex." We respond by saying, *When we think differently about text complexity, we find many forms of complexity in YA lit.* We reframe the conversation by shifting the focus to the concept of complexity itself. We call for more complicated ways of thinking about complexity, highlighting the idea that finding and making complexity in our own reading of YA lit is the best way to begin discovering the kinds of complexity YA books have to offer. Specific talking points:

   - *YA lit contains many forms of complexity.* When we view complexity as something that we find and make as readers, we start to notice complexity in the style and substance of many YA titles, and we see how complexity deepens as readers respond to YA lit. YA pedagogy teaches students how to make complexity by engaging them in personal, social, and analytical work with YA texts. Through YA pedagogy, we guide students in an ongoing process of making complexity as they read these books with their peers and on their own.

   - *The complexity of YA lit becomes most visible when we read it ourselves.* The best way to discover the complexity in YA lit is to start reading it ourselves. Once we begin paying attention to the things we notice about the style and substance of YA texts, we can guide students to look for those same text features. YA pedagogy approaches reading as something that happens in a social context, which sets us up to share our processes of making complexity with students and learn from the complexity that they make.

4. "These are books nobody's heard of." We respond by saying, *Outside of school, many people are reading YA literature.* We reframe the conversation by shifting the focus from the perceived insignificance of YA lit to the significance of reading contexts and reading communities. We call for classroom environments that acknowledge the kinds of reading that go on in the real world. We highlight how YA pedagogy shows students how to do more and get more from everyday reading. Specific talking points:

   - *In the real world, many people are reading YA lit.* When detractors claim that YA titles are books nobody has heard of, that claim says more about the detractors than about young adult literature. All we have to do is look at book industry sales lists to find ample evidence that today's YA lit is drawing an enormous readership. Movies based on YA novels are also drawing large numbers of new readers to these books. YA pedagogy capitalizes on the popularity and currency of YA lit. As teachers we build on the energy and enthusiasm that the YA lit boom has produced. We also look for opportunities for parents and teens to share in reading YA crossover titles— that is, books that are marketed to teens but could have just as easily been marketed to adults due to their complexity and their crossover appeal.

- *Beyond the bestsellers, there are many more YA titles worth knowing about.* It's pretty certain that all of us have heard of a good number of YA bestsellers, including the Harry Potter books, the Twilight series, the Hunger Games trilogy, and *The Fault in Our Stars*. Through YA pedagogy, we draw attention to lesser-known YA titles, and we involve students in work designed to bring those books to the attention of more readers.

5. "Reading YA lit in school sets kids up to have a bad attitude about the classics." We respond by saying, *Reading YA lit in school sets kids up to have a good attitude about reading. It sets us up to talk with kids about what reading is for, and it gives us the chance to point out how often YA authors invoke the classics in their novels.* We reframe the conversation by shifting the focus to the purpose of reading and the kinds of texts that will help individual readers achieve their goals. We highlight the forms of personal, social, and analytical reading that YA pedagogy supports, and we emphasize that in the end, YA pedagogy invites students to apply those forms of reading to texts of all kinds, including the classics. Specific talking points:

- *Reading YA sets teens up to have a good attitude about reading.* Teens will have good attitudes toward reading when we give them books they are capable of reading and willing to read. We build on those good attitudes by continuing to hand teens books they feel excited to read. Then we give them titles that will stretch them as readers. Through YA pedagogy, we engage students in positive reading experiences by supporting them as individuals, affirming the worth of the reading they are able to do, and challenging them to take their reading to the next level.

- *Reading YA lit sets the stage for discussions of what reading is for.* YA pedagogy invites conversations about purposes for reading: that is, what texts have to offer, what we seek in texts, and how our stance toward a text shapes the complexity we make from it. The notion of stance applies to both YA titles and the classics. We don't demonize the classics; instead, we open a conversation about what we seek to accomplish as readers, both now and in the future, and then we discuss which books are best suited to our individual goals and needs.

- *Reading YA lit in school allows us to point out how often the classics are mentioned in contemporary literature.* Since many YA titles make intertextual references to the classics, rather than turn kids off to those books, reading YA lit may lead students to them. Intertextual references in YA books set up wonderful opportunities for discussions of intertextuality as a concept: what it adds to a text and why it matters. YA pedagogy encourages students to look for intertextual references as they go about finding complexity in YA lit. Through YA pedagogy, we can also open up conversations about the lasting impact of canonical texts, asking why the author chose to have a particular character encounter a particular text within the story and what that text might mean to the author herself or himself. YA pedagogy invites students to explore questions about why the classics still matter, to whom, and for what personal and cultural reasons.

A Final Kind of Outreach: Finding Fuel That Sustains Us as Teachers of YA Lit

Teaching YA lit is never going to be easy. We know that bringing these books into the classroom requires more effort than sticking with the status quo. Not only do we have to build personal knowledge of a new field of literature, but we also have to develop a plan for teaching it and an argument for its value in our local context. We have to throw ourselves into reading new books, imagining new ways of teaching, and speaking bravely about the choices we've made.

Despite the effort involved, the effect of doing this work is transformational. It changes the lives of students and it changes our lives as teachers. We commit to teaching YA literature and suddenly we're constructing new identities as readers, activists, and visionaries. The changes we experience in ourselves are fueled by the changes we see in our students and our classrooms. We offer students the chance to read YA lit and soon we discover they're not only completing the reading but they're asking for more. They're turning in assignments and producing work that demonstrates a new level of thoughtfulness and skill. The vibe in our classroom feels different. Students are talking about books and the talk matters to them. They come to class wanting to hear one another's ideas. They are fired up at the end of the hour, and the next day they're back, wanting more chances to find purpose and meaning through reading. English class becomes a space of energy, laughter, and joy.

The benefits of this work are easy to see in our individual classrooms, and we do our best to spread the word about the power of YA lit through outreach. But it's even more amazing when the benefits students experience in our classrooms start to change the cultures of our schools. The fact is, when students walk around the halls carrying the books they're reading, and when they choose to spend their time reading and talking about reading instead of playing games or texting on their phones, they are engaging in their own forms of outreach. In doing so, they make a final and irrefutable case for the value of YA lit. Once adults notice changes in students' attitudes and behaviors around reading, their view of YA lit begins to shift, sometimes without those adults ever having read a single YA book.

These changes don't happen overnight. We have to be patient and we may have to wait out early negative responses from our colleagues. This was true for Ricki Ginsberg when she began teaching her YA lit elective at Rockville High School. Ricki explained that her colleagues were generally supportive when she introduced her course, but not everyone approved of the idea. "All of them weren't crazy about YA lit," she said. "Some did not see it to be of equivalent merit to the classics." What Ricki learned, however, was that people's initial reactions can change. One of her colleagues who openly criticized the course changed her mind a year later when she discovered that the students who had taken it turned out to be much better writers than those who hadn't.

Often word of mouth about YA lit has to spread among students before a larger influence can be felt in a school. This too was the case for Ricki. The seeds for change lay in the books themselves. Students would hear about Ricki's classroom library from their friends, who said it was better than either the public or the school library. They would stop by to see it and end up taking her class. Gradually Ricki and her students started putting books in other school spaces. They sent YA titles down to the in-school suspension room, and they set up a book display in the seating area for students who'd been kicked out of class. Efforts like these affected the school as a whole. "One administrator told me that he felt I'd changed the environment of the school to be more positive toward reading," Ricki said. "This was the ultimate compliment for me. Obviously, everything wasn't perfect, but I hope I impacted the students."

I heard the same sentiment from Tom Walentowski, Daria Plumb's principal at Riverside Academy. During one of my visits, Tom made a point of coming over to talk with me after I finished an interview with a student. He handed me a spreadsheet that showed a significant increase in students' reading test scores over the five-year period since they instituted daily school-wide silent reading before lunch.

I thanked Tom and remarked that the scores were impressive. He agreed but said he didn't put too much stock in them. "Everybody nowadays wants to talk about data," he said. "I've been in this system too long to believe that numbers are that important. I guess we do what we have to do." Tom was far more interested in the changes he observed in students' attitudes and in the overall feel of the building. I asked what he'd seen.

"I think that some kids, they approach their free time differently," he said. "There are kids who are always carrying a book around with them. So in the last five minutes of class when technically they can wrap up and put stuff away, you might see a kid reading a novel that they started reading in the fourth hour class.

You see kids who never read anything before they came here, and now all of a sudden they can't get enough stuff to read."

When I asked Tom about the ingredients for that motivation and investment in reading throughout his school, he focused squarely on Daria. "I think that's more to do with Ms. Plumb," he said. "She works hard to convince them that there's got to be something they like out there. And she goes over and above. She's got a lot of books in her classroom, but if she doesn't have something that they like, she will go to the library and get it. She will do whatever she has to do to bring material they like into the classroom."

For every story like Ricki's or Daria's there's another one like it. Students are primed to become readers: all we have to do is give them books and experiences with books that they believe are worthwhile. Through our individual efforts—one book and one student at a time, guided by a bigger vision of what YA pedagogy makes possible—we can create a wave of change that will transform classrooms, schools, and lives. Every teaching story we hear, every student testimonial we read, offers another layer of evidence. Fuel for the cause is everywhere once we begin looking and listening.

"A Course You Take to Better Yourself in Life"

In one of my final school visits during the research for this book, I sat down with John, a senior in Carrie Melnychenko's class at Huron High School. John was one of the fieriest and most provocative participants in the discussion of Dana Reinhardt's *How to Build a House*. He was a student whom Carrie referred to as one of her "punky boys," and she told me that during class discussions, he made comments that were sometimes right on the edge of being inappropriate. He was also taking AP calculus, which intrigued me. What did an AP student with a strong aptitude for math get from his reading of YA lit?

On a Friday morning when school wasn't in session and all of his classmates were either sleeping in or getting ready for prom, John drove over to school to talk to me about YA lit. Over the course of a forty-minute conversation, we discussed what John experienced in Carrie's class and what he was taking away.

He began by praising the books. "All these books have overall meaning. They're very deep. . . . They're fictional, but they're based off of real things, actual events. They teach you that these things happen. Divorces happen all the time. Death happens all the time. They let us cope with it before it actually happens." John added that his reading about these topics was more than an intellectual exercise. For him it was personal—and visceral. "We are part of the book after we read it. We imagine ourselves in the book somehow. We see ourselves in it."

John noted that reading in this personal way didn't prevent him from picking up skills as a reader. "I've learned to read faster," he said. "I can skim read now. Before I was never able to do that, and now I can, but I don't do it that often. Also my comprehension level, even though it was already high, I think—um, way to be cocky—has grown." He also saw concrete applications of the reading he learned to do in YA lit to the reading he expects to do in college. "In college you're going to be reading intellectual things that you're going to need to be able to picture yourself in, whether or not they're about your age group. You're going to need to imagine yourself in those situations. In YA lit, you learn how to picture yourself touching down with the book. In college when you're reading a professor's essay or a professor's, I don't know, bio log, you're going to need to touch down with it. YA lit teaches you those skills—to be able to connect yourself to the reading, whatever book you're reading."

As we continued to talk, John had more to say—about class assignments that were both personal and intellectual, the importance of discussing "touchy subjects," finding metaphors in stories, and how reading YA lit sparked valuable conversations with his parents. He also praised Carrie, particularly for knowing him as an individual and knowing the books that would be right for him. He even expressed pride in the fact that I asked Carrie's permission to interview him. "When I heard Ms. Mel say, 'She might pick one of you to interview,' I thought, she's definitely going to pick Jesse, or one of the people that read so much, or are, like, smart. I'm smart, but I'm not English smart. I don't do grammar. I'm a math and science person. But the comprehension part is something I'm good at. That's the main reason why I liked these books. I was able to connect with them."

When I asked John what he was taking away from the YA lit class, he focused not on text elements or literary knowledge or skill development. What mattered most to him about reading YA literature was the insight the books gave him into other people's humanity. "I understand people's moments now," he said. "And their deepest faults. I've seen them in these books. You come out of this class, like, *knowing* more. And I'm not just talking about the school part. You come out of it with *life* skills. You learn things about people. As in, this could actually happen in real life. Maybe I should be more cautious about things. Or maybe our last moment with someone is tomorrow. Maybe I should not go and tell him I hate him. The books teach you something, and it's not just an English credit. It's an actual course you take to better yourself in life."

What more could we want for our teens? What more could we want for our work with teens in school? What are reading and learning really for if not to equip us with knowledge and tools that will help us live more thoughtful lives? John reminds us that the best reading—the most powerful reading—is always in some way personal, and that the notion of what personal means will be different for every reader.

When we teach young adult literature, we can do all the things that are expected of us in the English classroom. We can teach literary analysis and literary history; we can study genre and style; we can explore themes that give students deeper understandings of themselves and the world around them. When we teach YA lit with a YA pedagogy designed to blend students' personal experiences of books with analytical understandings of texts, when we offer students books that allow them to pursue their own interests and questions, and when we use our matchmaking skills to signal to students that we see them and value them, their lives will be changed. And so will ours. Young adult literature makes all of this possible, and more.

Annotated Bibliography

Teachers who choose to bring YA literature into the classroom benefit from resources that can connect them to YA titles, YA authors, YA as a field, YA reading communities, and sources that provide financial support for YA.

YA Titles

YALSA Book Awards and Book Lists

(www.ala.org/yalsa/bookawards/booklists/members)

The problem with recommended reading lists is how quickly they go out of date. YA book awards and booklists, presented annually by committees of librarians and book critics, provide one way for YA lit readers to stay current. My favorite source for these is YALSA, the Young Adult Library Services Association of the American Library Association. On their awards page, you can discover titles written by debut authors (the **William C. Morris YA Debut Award**) and titles honored for general literary excellence (the **Michael L. Printz Award,** the **Award for Excellence in Nonfiction**). You can find themed reading lists (**Popular Paperbacks for Young Adults**), books for dormant or struggling readers (**Quick Picks for Reluctant Young Adult Readers**), and novels recommended for their blend of literary merit and teen appeal (**Best Fiction for Young Adults**). YALSA also offers genre- and format-specific award lists (**Great Graphic Novels for Teens, Amazing Audiobooks for Young Adults**), books to prepare teens for college (**Outstanding Books for the College Bound**), and books voted as favorites by teens themselves (**Teens' Top Ten**).

Other Award Lists

No one organization can ever recognize all the quality YA titles published each year. To add more perspectives to the book awards conversation, you can refer to lists provided by the **National Book Foundation,** which established the **National Book Award for Young People's Literature** (www.nationalbook.org), the **Cybils Awards,** otherwise known as the Children's and Young Adult Bloggers' Literary Awards (www.cybils.com), the **Rainbow Book List** of titles with significant gay, lesbian, bisexual, transgender, or queer/questioning content (http://glbtrt.ala.org/rainbowbooks/), and the **Amelia Bloomer Project,** which recommends feminist literature for birth through age eighteen (https://ameliabloomer.wordpress.com).

YA Websites and Blogs

Blogs are another source for current YA titles. One of my long-time favorites is *Reading Rants!* (www.readingrants.org), published by Jennifer Hubert Swan, a school librarian at the Little Red School House & Elisabeth Irwin High School in New York. A blog I enjoy for its discussion of literary YA and annual award contenders is *Someday My Printz Will Come,* sponsored by *School Library Journal* (http://blogs.slj.com/printzblog/). For posts about current trends in YA lit, I always turn to *The Hub,* a blog run by YALSA (www.yalsa.ala.org/thehub/). Other blogs focus on issues of diversity in YA writing and publishing. *Reading While White* offers discussions of white privilege and racism in the children's and YA book industry (http://readingwhilewhite.blogspot.com), while the website **We Need Diverse Books** provides an array of resources, including a comprehensive list of blogs featuring diverse books across many categories (http://weneeddiversebooks.org/where-to-find-diverse-books/). For a list of soon-to-be-published YA titles and their release dates, visit the **YAlit** website (http://yalit.com).

YA Podcasts

For many years, I was the host of *Text Messages*, a monthly young adult literature podcast sponsored by ReadWriteThink.org, a partnership between the National Council of Teachers of English and the International Literacy Association (formerly the International Reading Association). Each podcast episode explored a topic, genre, or theme in YA lit and offered reading recommendations in relation to that theme. Themes ranged from fairy tale retellings, to international books for teens, to stories of teen resilience. Many episodes featured highlights from interviews I conducted with prominent YA authors. While the recommended reading lists are no longer current, they can still guide readers who are looking for titles of a certain kind, or who wish to explore the field more generally. All episodes are archived at readwritethink.org/textmessages.

Professional Review Journals

Before the Internet, I learned about quality new YA titles from *The Horn Book Magazine*. You pay to subscribe to the print version of *Horn Book*, but you can access some of its content for free online (www.hbook.com). I also receive their electronic newsletter, *Notes from the Horn Book,* in my email (www.hbook.com/notes-from-the-horn-book-newsletter/).

YA Authors

Author Websites and Blogs

Readers who want to learn more about YA authors now have an unprecedented level of access through individual authors' websites and blogs. There you can find out about authors' lives, their books, and scheduled events such as school visits, library appearances, and book tour dates. Authors often use their websites to provide links to newspaper and magazine articles about their work. Sometimes they also provide teaching guides for their novels.

Several authors have used blogs and podcasts to contribute to the conversation about writing and publishing. In July 2008, **Laurie Halse Anderson** launched her **15 Minutes a Day Writing Challenge**, which invited readers to commit to writing for fifteen minutes a day for the entire month (http://madwomanintheforest.com/wfmad). She continued the WFMAD challenge from 2009 to 2013. This site houses a wonderful archive of creative writing invitations, along with Anderson's thoughts on the book business. **A. S. King** also discusses the book business—specifically the struggle to write the books you want to write—in a seven-part blog series she called **The Writer's Middle Finger** (www.as-king.info/2014/08/the-writers-middle-finger-how-to-grow.html).

Author Podcasts

Podcasts offer readers the chance to hear YA authors talk, often to one another. Two of my favorites are *This Creative Life*, a podcast hosted by YA author **Sara Zarr** that explores writing process and careers in the arts (www.sarazarr.com/blog-podcasts), and *The Oral History Podcast,* a podcast hosted by YA authors **Carrie Mesrobian** and **Christa Desir** that explores writing about sex for teens (http://theoralhistorypodcast.com). While each of Zarr's podcasts features an interview with a fellow writer, artist, or publishing professional, Mesrobian and Desir use their podcast to talk to each other about their life experiences, their writing choices, and their current favorite YA titles dealing with sex and sexuality.

YA as a Field

Books

While there are many good books about using YA lit in the classroom, it's also important for teachers to build their knowledge of YA as a field through literary criticism. **Michael Cart** provides the definitive history of YA lit in *Young Adult Literature: From Romance to Realism* (2010).

Patty Campbell's essays, first published in *Wilson Library Bulletin* and later in *The Horn Book Magazine*, provide the definitive collection of critical writing on young adult literature. After Campbell gave up her career as a columnist, she published her favorite essays as a book called ***Campbell's Scoop: Reflections on Young Adult Literature*** (2010).

The other place to turn for book-length literary criticism is the **Scarecrow Studies in Young Adult Literature** series edited by Patty Campbell. With titles such as ***Exploding the Myths: The Truth about Teenagers and Reading*** by **Marc Aronson** (2001) and ***Sarah Dessen: From Burritos to Box Office*** by **Wendy Glenn** (2004), the Scarecrow series provides readers who wish to learn about the field from a critical perspective with a wonderful library of material.

Journals

For peer-reviewed articles on teaching and research in young adult literature, consult *The ALAN Review (TAR)* (www.alan-ya.org/publications/the-alan-review/). *TAR* publishes articles, columns, author interviews, and professional materials that support the learning and development of readers through YA lit. Since *TAR* is targeted to practitioners, it's a great source for teaching ideas as well as scholarship that backs the use of YA lit in the classroom.

Speeches and Lectures

Speeches and lectures offer another source for information about the history and critical significance of YA lit as a field. Annual speeches by winners of the **Printz Award**, **Morris Award**, **Nonfiction Award**, and **Margaret A. Edwards Award** (for lifetime contribution to the field) are archived by YALSA (www.ala.org/yalsa/2015-speeches).

Since 1970 the American Library Association has honored a single author, critic, librarian, historian, or teacher of children's or YA literature with the **May Hill Arbuthnot Award.** Each

Arbuthnot winner is expected to prepare a lecture considered to be a significant contribution to the field of children's literature. Several Arbuthnot lectures have been given by YA authors, including Walter Dean Myers, Philip Pullman, and Jacqueline Woodson. Past lectures are archived by the Association for Library Service to Children (www.ala.org/alsc/awardsgrants/bookmedia/arbuthnothonor/pastlecturers/pastlecturers).

The **Charlotte Zolotow Lecture** brings a distinguished children's or YA author or illustrator to the University of Wisconsin-Madison to deliver an annual free public address. Since the lecture series was launched in 1998, a number of YA authors have been featured, including Robert Lipsyte, Naomi Shihab Nye, Angela Johnson, Judy Blume, Gene Luen Yang, and Rita Williams-Garcia. Videos of many Zolotow lectures are archived by the Cooperative Children's Book Center at the University of Wisconsin-Madison (https://ccbc.education.wisc.edu/authors/lecture/czlecture.asp).

The **Zena Sutherland Lecture,** hosted at the University of Chicago since 1983, has also featured a number of YA authors. Some of these include John Green, Neil Gaiman, and Jack Gantos. The most recent Zena Sutherland lectures are archived on the *Horn Book* website (www.hbook.com/tag/zena-sutherland-lecture/) and reprinted in *The Horn Book Magazine*.

YA Reading Communities

Teachers who want to use YA lit in the classroom can find inspiration and support in professional communities dedicated to teens and reading. Some are virtual, such as the **YALSA-BK listserv** (http://lists.ala.org/sympa/info/yalsa-bk), an online forum for discussion of YA titles and topics related to teens and reading. Although YALSA-BK is hosted by teen services librarians, anyone can participate.

Twitter is another space where you can find a virtual YA reading community. You can follow authors, publishers, critics, bloggers, and fellow YA lit readers. You can also participate in monthly moderated conversations such as #title-talk, hosted by Donalyn Miller and Colby Sharp, where teachers come together to promote reading in today's classrooms and titles worth sharing with students. You can access the #titletalk archive at https://titletalkchat.wordpress.com.

Held each year on the Monday and Tuesday before Thanksgiving, the **ALAN Workshop** brings together YA teachers, librarians, critics, advocates, authors, and publishers for an in-person celebration of all things YA lit. Sponsored by the Assembly on Literature for Adolescents of NCTE (www.alan-ya.org), the workshop consists of panel discussions, breakout sessions, and keynote speeches by leading authors in our field. Attendees receive a free box of books as part of their registration, and authors are available to sign their books after each speech or panel session.

Financial Support for YA

Teachers of YA lit almost always need financial support, especially for building classroom libraries. Drawing on proceeds from *Book Love* (2013), Penny Kittle offers annual grants for teachers through the **Book Love Foundation**. Book Love grants are designed to fund starter classroom libraries of 500 books each. In its first three years, the Book Love Foundation gave away $100,000 in funding for classroom libraries. To find out more, visit http://booklovefoundation.org/.

Works Cited

Anderson, M. T. (2009). On the intelligence of teens. Retrieved from http://mt-anderson.com/blog/he-talks-talks-2/on-the-intelligence-of-teens/

Applebee, A. N. (1993). *Literature in the secondary school: Studies of curriculum and instruction in the United States*. Urbana, IL: National Council of Teachers of English.

Appleman, D. (2009). *Critical encounters in high school English* (2nd ed.). New York: Teachers College Press.

Aronson, M. (2011, March/April). New knowledge. *The Horn Book Magazine, 87*(2), 57–62.

Atwell, N. (1987). *In the middle: Writing, reading, and learning with adolescents*. Portsmouth, NH: Heinemann.

Atwell, N. (2007). *The reading zone: How to help kids become skilled, passionate, habitual, critical readers*. New York: Scholastic.

Atwell, N. (2014). *In the middle: A lifetime of learning about writing, reading, and adolescents* (3rd ed.). Portsmouth, NH: Heinemann.

Barthelmess, T. (2014, March/April). What makes a good book cover? *The Horn Book Magazine, 90*(2), 74–78.

Beers, K. (2003). *When kids can't read, what teachers can do*. Portsmouth, NH: Heinemann.

Beers, K., & Probst, R. E. (2013). *Notice and note: Strategies for close reading*. Portsmouth, NH: Heinemann.

Bishop, R. S. (1990). Mirrors, windows, and sliding glass doors. *Perspectives, 6*(3), ix–xi.

Bluemle, E. (2015, February 24). The stars so far. Retrieved from http://blogs.publishersweekly.com/blogs/shelftalker/?p=15151

Buehler, J. (2009). A conversation with John Green. Retrieved from http://www.readwritethink.org/parent-afterschool-resources/podcast-episodes/conversation-with-john-green-30333.html

Buehler, J. (2014). A conversation with Candace Fleming. Retrieved from http://www.readwritethink.org/parent-afterschool-resources/podcast-episodes/conversation-with-candace-fleming-31134.html

Buehler, J., Plumb, D., & Walsh, J. (2013). Young adult literature book awards: A guide for newcomers to the field. *The ALAN Review, 40*(3), 63–74.

Campbell, P. (2000, July/August). Middle muddle. *The Horn Book Magazine, 76*(4), 483–487.

Campbell, P. (2004, May/June). Our side of the fence. *The Horn Book Magazine, 80*(3), 359–362.

Campbell, P. (2007, January/February). Looking for YA lit in the Elysian Fields. *The Horn Book Magazine, 83*(1), 101–106.

Campbell, P. (2010). *Campbell's scoop: Reflections on young adult literature*. Lanham, MD: Scarecrow Press.

Carlsen, G. R. (1980). *Books and the teenage reader: A guide for teachers, librarians and parents* (2nd ed.). New York: Harper and Row.

Carlsen, G. R., & Sherrill, A. (1988). *Voices of readers: How we come to love books*. Urbana, IL: National Council of Teachers of English.

Cart, M. (2010). *Young adult literature: From romance to realism* (2nd ed.). Chicago: American Library Association.

Crowe, C. (1999). English teachers are from Mars, students are from Venus (But YA books can help with interplanetary understanding). *English Journal, 88*(4), 120–122.

Daniels, H. (1994). *Literature circles: Voice and choice in the student-centered classroom*. Portland, ME: Stenhouse.

Daniels, H., & Zemelman, S. (2014). *Subjects matter: Exceeding standards through powerful content-area reading* (2nd ed.). Portsmouth, NH: Heinemann.

Finders, M. J. (1998). Raging hormones: Stories of adolescence and implications for teacher preparation. *Journal of Adolescent and Adult Literacy, 42*(4), 252–263.

Fleischer, C. (2000). *Teachers organizing for change: Making literacy learning everybody's business*. Urbana, IL: National Council of Teachers of English.

Fleischer, C., & Andrew-Vaughan, S. (2009). *Writing outside your comfort zone: Helping students navigate unfamiliar genres*. Portsmouth, NH: Heinemann.

Gallo, D. R. (1992). Listening to readers: Attitudes toward the young adult novel. In V. R. Monseau & G. Salvner (Eds.), *Reading their world: The young adult novel in the classroom* (pp. 17–27). Portsmouth, NH: Boynton/Cook.

Gallo, D. R. (2001). How classics create an aliterate society. *English Journal, 90*(3), 33–39.

Glenn, W. (2008). Gossiping girls, insider boys, a-list achievement: Examining and exposing young adult novels consumed by conspicuous consumption. *Journal of Adolescent and Adult Literacy, 52*(1), 34–42.

Graham, R. (2014, June 5). Against YA. *The Slate Book Review*. Retrieved from http://www.slate.com/articles/arts/books/2014/06/against_ya_adults_should_be_embarrassed_to_read_children_s_books.html

Gurdon, M. C. (2011, June 4). Darkness too visible. *The Wall Street Journal*. Retrieved from http://www.wsj.com/articles/SB10001424052702303657404576357622592697038

Hedeen, K., & Smith, R. L. (2013, May/June). What makes a good YA love story? *The Horn Book Magazine, 89*(3), 48–54.

Herz. S. K., & Gallo, D. R. (2005). *From Hinton to Hamlet: Building bridges between young adult literature and the classics* (2nd ed.). Westport, CT: Greenwood Press.

Hipple, T. (1997). It's the THAT, teacher. *English Journal, 86*(3), 15–17.

Hunt, J. (2007, March/April). Redefining the young adult novel. *The Horn Book Magazine, 83*(2), 141–147.

Hunt, J. (2009, July/August). A Printz retrospective. *The Horn Book Magazine, 85*(4), 395–403.

Kaywell, J. F. (Ed.). (1992–2000). *Adolescent literature as a complement to the classics* (Vols. 1–4). Norwood, MA: Christopher Gordon.

Kaywell, J. F. (Ed.). (2007). *Dear author: Letters of hope: Top young adult authors respond to kids' toughest issues*. New York: Philomel Books.

Kaywell, J. F. (2010). *Adolescent literature as a complement to the classics: Addressing critical issues in today's classrooms*. Norwood, MA: Christopher Gordon.

King, A. S. (2015, July 2). How are you listening? Retrieved from http://hippodillycircus.com/2015/07/02/how-are-you-listening/

Kittle, P. (2013). Book love: Developing depth, stamina, and passion in adolescent readers. Portsmouth, NH: Heinemann.

Larrick, N. (1965, September 11). The all-white world of children's books. *Saturday Review, 48*(11), 63–65, 84–85.

Lehman, C., & Roberts, K. (2014). *Falling in love with close reading: Lessons for analyzing texts and life*. Portsmouth, NH: Heinemann.

Lesesne, T. S. (2003). *Making the match: The right book for the right reader at the right time, grades 4–12*. Portland, ME: Stenhouse.

Lesesne, T. S. (2006). *Naked reading: Uncovering what tweens need to become lifelong readers*. Portland, ME: Stenhouse.

Lesesne, T. S. (2010). *Reading ladders: Getting students from where they are to where we'd like them to be*. Portsmouth, NH: Heinemann.

Lesesne, T. S. (2014). The tip of the iceberg. *The ALAN Review, 42*(1), 77–81.

Miller, D. [Debbie], & Moss, B. (2013). *No more independent reading without support*. Portsmouth, NH: Heinemann.

Miller, D. [Donalyn] (2009). *The book whisperer: Awakening the inner reader in every child*. San Francisco: Jossey-Bass.

Miller, D. [Donalyn] (with Kelley, S.). (2014). *Reading in the wild: The book whisperer's keys to cultivating lifelong reading habits*. San Francisco: Jossey-Bass.

Mitchell, D., & Christenbury, L. (2000). *Both art and craft: Teaching ideas that spark learning*. Urbana, IL: National Council of Teachers of English.

Morrell, E. (2005). Critical English education. *English Education 37*(4), 312–321.

Mueller, P. N. (2001). *Lifers: Learning from at-risk adolescent readers*. Portsmouth, NH: Heinemann.

Myers, C. (2014, March 15). The apartheid of children's literature. *The New York Times*. Retrieved from http://www.nytimes.com/2014/03/16/opinion/sunday/the-apartheid-of-childrens-literature.html?_r=0

Myers, C. (2015, July/August). CSK Illustrator Award acceptance. *The Horn Book Magazine, 91*(4), 29–33.

Myers, W. D. (2014, March 15). Where are the people of color in children's books? *The New York Times*. Retrieved from http://www.nytimes.com/2014/03/16/opinion/sunday/where-are-the-people-of-color-in-childrens-books.html

National Council of Teachers of English, James R. Squire Office of Policy Research (2012). Reading instruction for *all* students. *Council Chronicle, 22*(1), 15–18.

Ousley-Exum, D. (n.d.). Brown bag exams: A creative way to assess learning. Retrieved from http://www.adlit.org/unlocking_the_past/brown_bag_exams/

Partridge, E. (2011, March/April). Narrative nonfiction: Kicking ass at last. *The Horn Book Magazine, 87*(2), 69–73.

Rabb, M. (2008, July 20). I'm Y.A., and I'm O.K. *The New York Times*. Retrieved from http://www.nytimes.com/2008/07/20/books/review/Rabb-t.html?_r=0

Ribay, R. (2013, November/December). What makes a good YA urban novel? *The Horn Book Magazine, 89*(6), 48–53.

Rief, L. (1991). *Seeking diversity: Language arts with adolescents*. Portsmouth, NH: Heinemann.

Rief, L. (2007). *Inside the writer's-reader's notebook: A workshop essential*. Portsmouth, NH: Heinemann.

Romano, T. (2000). *Blending genre, altering style: Writing multigenre papers*. Portsmouth, NH: Heinemann.

Rosenblatt, L. M. (1995). *Literature as exploration* (5th ed.). New York: Modern Language Association.

Salvner, G. M. (2000). Time and tradition: Transforming the secondary English classroom with young adult novels. In V. R. Monseau & G. Salvner (Eds.), *Reading their world: The young adult novel in the classroom* (2nd ed., pp. 85–99). Portsmouth, NH: Boynton/Cook.

Sarigianides, S. T., Lewis, M. A., & Petrone, R. (2015). How re-thinking adolescence helps re-imagine the teaching of English. *English Journal, 104*(3), 13–18.

Smith, M. W., & Wilhelm, J. D. (2002). *"Reading don't fix no Chevys": Literacy in the lives of young men*. Portsmouth, NH: Heinemann.

Sutton, R. (2006, September/October). Stars. *The Horn Book Magazine, 82*(5), 557–561.

Sutton, R. (2007, May/June). Problems, paperbacks, and the Printz: 40 years of YA books. *The Horn Book Magazine, 83*(3), 231–243.

Sutton, R. (2014, June 8). Why do we even call it YA anymore? *The Horn Book Magazine*. Retrieved from http://www.hbook.com/2014/06/blogs/read-roger/even-call-ya-anymore/

Wilhelm, J. D. (1997). *"You gotta BE the book": Teaching engaged and reflective reading with adolescents*. New York: Teachers College Press.

Wilhelm, J. D. (2007). *Engaging readers and writers with inquiry*. New York: Scholastic.

Yampbell, C. (2005). Judging a book by its cover: Publishing trends in young adult literature. *The Lion and the Unicorn, 29*(3), 348–372.

Children's, YA, Classic, and Popular Titles Mentioned in the Text

Alexie, S. *The Absolutely True Diary of a Part-Time Indian*.

Anderson, L. H. *Chains*.

Anderson, L. H. *The Impossible Knife of Memory*.

Anderson, L. H. *Speak*.

Anderson, L. H. *Wintergirls*.

Anderson, M. T. *The Astonishing Life of Octavian Nothing, Traitor to the Nation*.

Anderson, M. T. *Feed*.

Andrews, V. C. *Flowers in the Attic*.

Applegate, K. *Ivan: The Remarkable True Story of the Shopping Mall Gorilla*.

Applegate, K. *The One and Only Ivan*.

Asher, J. *Thirteen Reasons Why*.

Bacigalupi, P. *Ship Breaker*.

Bartoletti, S. C. *Hitler Youth: Growing Up in Hitler's Shadow*.

Bell, C. *El Deafo*.

Birnbach, L. *The Official Preppy Handbook*.

Block, F. L. *Weetzie Bat*.

Blume, J. *Forever*.

Blumenthal, K. *Steve Jobs: The Man Who Thought Different.*

Booth, C. *Tyrell.*

Bray, L. *Beauty Queens.*

Brontë, C. *Jane Eyre.*

Budhos, M. *Ask Me No Questions.*

Carter, R. *First Lady from Plains.*

Cashore, K. *Graceling.*

Chbosky, S. *The Perks of Being a Wallflower.*

Cisneros, S. *The House on Mango Street.*

Collins, S. The Hunger Games trilogy.

Condie, A. Matched trilogy.

Cormier, R. *The Chocolate War.*

Cormier, R. *The Rag and Bone Shop.*

Cross, C. R. *Heavier Than Heaven: A Biography of Kurt Cobain.*

Crutcher, C. *Whale Talk.*

Cullen, D. *Columbine.*

de la Peña, M. *Ball Don't Lie.*

de la Peña, M. *I Will Save You.*

de la Peña, M. *The Living.*

de la Peña, M. *Mexican WhiteBoy.*

de la Peña, M. *We Were Here.*

Dickens, C. *Great Expectations.*

Dickinson, E. "Dear March—Come In."

Doctorow, C. *Little Brother.*

Dostoyevsky, F. *Crime and Punishment.*

Dr. Seuss. *The Lorax.*

Erskine, K. *Mockingbird.*

Faulkner, W. *As I Lay Dying.*

Federle, T. *Five, Six, Seven, Nate!*

Fitzgerald, F. S. *The Great Gatsby.*

Flake, S. *Bang!*

Flaubert, G. *Madame Bovary.*

Gantos, J. *Hole in My Life.*

Garden, N. *Endgame.*

Gino, A. *George.*

Glenn, M. *Class Dismissed.*

Going, K. L. *Fat Kid Rules the World.*

Going, K. L. *Saint Iggy.*

Goldberg, N. *Writing Down the Bones.*

Golding, W. *Lord of the Flies.*

Gonzalez, C. *The Red Umbrella.*

Green, J. *The Fault in Our Stars.*

Green, J. *Paper Towns.*

Guinness World Records. *Guinness World Records 2015.*

Haddon, M. *The Curious Incident of the Dog in the Night-Time.*

Handler, D. *Why We Broke Up.*

Hartman, R. *Seraphina.*

Herriot, J. *All Creatures Great and Small.*

Hijuelos, O. *Dark Dude.*

Hinds, G. *Beowulf.*

Hinds, G. *Macbeth.*

Hinds, G. *The Odyssey.*

Hinton, S. E. *The Outsiders.*

Hitler, A. *Mein Kampf.*

Hobbs, W. *Crossing the Wire.*

Homer. *The Odyssey.*

Hopkins, E. *Crank.*

Hughes, L. "The Dream Keeper."

Hunt, L. M. *One for the Murphys.*

Hurston, Z. N. *Their Eyes Were Watching God.*

Katzen, M. *The Moosewood Cookbook.*

King, A. S. *Ask the Passengers.*

King, A. S. *Please Ignore Vera Dietz.*

King, A. S. *Reality Boy.*

Kinney, J. *Diary of a Wimpy Kid.*

Klass, D. *Firestorm.*

Korman, G. *The Juvie Three.*

Kuklin, S. *Beyond Magenta: Transgender Teens Speak Out.*

Landowne, Y., & Horton, A. *Pitch Black.*

Lee, H. *To Kill a Mockingbird.*

Levinson, C. *Watch Out for Flying Kids: How Two Circuses, Two Countries, and Nine Kids Confront Conflict and Build Community.*

Levinson, C. *We've Got a Job: The 1963 Birmingham Children's March.*

Lewis, C. S. *The Lion, the Witch, and the Wardrobe.*

Lewis, J. *March: Book One.*

Lipsyte, R. *The Contender.*

Lockhart, E. *The Disreputable History of Frankie Landau-Banks.*

Lockhart, E. *We Were Liars.*

Lowry, L. *The Giver.*

Lu, M. Legend trilogy.

Magoon, K. *How It Went Down.*

Marrin, A. *Black Gold: The Story of Oil in Our Lives.*

Marsden, J. *Hamlet.*

McDonnell, P. *Me . . . Jane.*

McKay, S. E. *Enemy Territory.*

McKay, S. E., & Lafrance, D. *War Brothers: The Graphic Novel.*

McNamee, G. *Bonechiller.*

McNeal, T. *Far Far Away.*

Mesrobian, C. *Perfectly Good White Boy.*

Mesrobian, C. *Sex and Violence.*

Meyer, S. *Twilight.*

Miller, A. *The Crucible.*

Myers, W. D. *Monster.*

Myers, W. D. *Shooter.*

Myers, W. D. *Street Love.*

Nelson, J. *I'll Give You the Sun.*

Ness, P. *The Knife of Never Letting Go.*

Ness, P. *A Monster Calls.*

Oliver, L. Delirium trilogy.

Oppel, K. *Half Brother.*

Palacio, R. J. *Wonder.*

Patterson, K. *Bridge to Terabithia.*

Paulsen, G. *Nightjohn.*

Peet, M. *Exposure.*

Perera, A. *Guantanamo Boy.*

Pfeffer, S. B. *Life as We Knew It.*

Plato. *Republic.*

Pullman, P. *The Golden Compass.*

Rabb, M. *Cures for Heartbreak.*

Reinhardt, D. *How to Build a House.*

Reynolds, J. *When I Was the Greatest.*

Reynolds, J., & Kiely, B. *All American Boys.*

Reynolds, P. H. *The Dot.*

Rorby, G. *Hurt Go Happy.*

Roth, V. Divergent trilogy.

Rowell, R. *Eleanor and Park.*

Rowling, J. K. Harry Potter series.

Ruby, L. *Bone Gap.*

Sáenz, B. A. *Aristotle and Dante Discover the Secrets of the Universe.*

Sáenz, B. A. *Last Night I Sang to the Monster.*

Sáenz, B. A. *Sammy and Juliana in Hollywood.*

Salinger, J. D. *The Catcher in the Rye.*

Schmidt, G. D. *Lizzie Bright and the Buckminster Boy.*

Schmidt, G. D. *Okay for Now.*

Schrefer, E. *Endangered.*

Selznick, B. *Wonderstruck.*

Shakespeare, W. *Romeo and Juliet.*

Sharenow, R. *The Berlin Boxing Club.*

Sheinkin, S. *Bomb: The Race to Build—and Steal—the World's Most Dangerous Weapon.*

Sheinkin, S. *Most Dangerous: Daniel Ellsberg and the Secret History of the Vietnam War.*

Shusterman, N. *Challenger Deep.*

Shusterman, N. *Unwind.*

Smith, A. *Grasshopper Jungle.*

Smith, A. *Winger.*

Steig, W. *Sylvester and the Magic Pebble.*

Steinbeck, J. *Of Mice and Men.*

Stork, F. X. *Marcelo in the Real World.*

Strasser, T. *Boot Camp.*

Strasser, T. *Give a Boy a Gun.*

Thoreau, H. D. *Walden.*

Trueman, T. *No Right Turn.*

Trueman, T. *Stuck in Neutral.*

Twain, M. *The Adventures of Huckleberry Finn.*

Ursu, A. *The Real Boy.*

Voigt, C. *Homecoming.*

Volponi, P. *Black and White.*

Walker, A. *The Color Purple.*

Walker, S. M. *Written in Bone: Buried Lives of Jamestown and Colonial Maryland.*

Watterson, B. *Calvin and Hobbes.*

Wein, E. *Code Name Verity.*

Wells, P. *Freaking Out: Real-Life Stories about Anxiety.*

Westerfeld, S. *Uglies.*

Wiles, D. *Countdown.*

Wolff, V. E. *Make Lemonade.*

Woodson, J. *Each Kindness.*

Woodson, J. *Feathers.*

Wright, R. *Native Son.*

Yang, G. L. *American Born Chinese.*

Yang, G. L. *Boxers/Saints.*

Yee, L. *Absolutely Maybe.*

Yep, L. *The Rainbow People.*

Zusak, M. *The Book Thief.*

Zusak, M. *I Am the Messenger.*

Index

Author

Jennifer Buehler taught young adult literature to high school students for ten years before earning her doctorate from the University of Michigan's Joint Program in English and Education in 2009. During that time, she also served as a teacher consultant for the Eastern Michigan Writing Project, a local site of the National Writing Project. Now an associate professor of English education at Saint Louis University, she teaches classes on young adult literature, writing pedagogy, secondary English methods, content literacy, urban education, and ethnography.

Buehler's research focuses on teaching and learning in urban schools, the experiences of marginalized students, and trends and innovations in young adult literature. She won the Dimond Dissertation Award at the University of Michigan in 2010 and the National Council of Teachers of English Promising Researcher Award in 2011 for her ethnographic work on urban school culture. Her articles and essays have appeared in *English Journal*; *English Education*; *The ALAN Review*; *Multicultural Perspectives*; *Race, Ethnicity and Education*; the *American Educational Research Journal*; and the *Journal of Teacher Education*.

She is formerly the host of *Text Messages*, a monthly young adult literature podcast sponsored by ReadWriteThink.org, and she served as president of ALAN, the Assembly on Literature for Adolescents of the National Council of Teachers of English, in 2016. She leads workshops for teachers on young adult literature, ways of incorporating it into middle and high school classrooms, and finding community with fellow YA readers. She can be found on Twitter at @ProfBuehler.

This book was typeset in Janson Text and BotonBQ by
Barbara Frazier.

Typefaces used on the cover include American Typewriter,
Frutiger Bold, Formata Light, and Formata Bold.

The book was printed on 60-lb. White Recycled Offset paper
by Versa Press, Inc.

30% Total Recycled Fiber